The Writings of

Venerable
Demetrius Augustin Gallitzin

Brother Francis Maluf, M.I.C.M.
Memorial Edition

Published by

Loreto Publications
P. O. Box 603
Fitzwilliam, NH 03447
www.loretopubs.org

ISBN 978 1-930278-90-x

Printed and bound in Canada

Dedication and Acknowledgements

We dedicate this book to our dear
friend, mentor, and teacher, Br. Francis, who taught us to love and appreciate the beauty and depth of Holy Scripture. We will be forever grateful to him for his guidance and example, and for showing us that

> ....Catholic truth is not a sad story for which we need to apologize; it is a proclamation of the greatest good news that could ever be told.

— Arnie and Theresa Filipi

A special thanks to: Joseph Filipi for searching and finding Gallitzin's works, Ramona Acosta for her cover art, and Sister Anna Maria Maluf and Miriam Maluf for clarifying points regarding Brother Francis (including spelling).

A special thanks to: The Saint Benedict Center in Richmond, New Hampshire, for permission to publish *Sentimental Theology* from their website catholicism.org

Monetary assistance for the publication of this book has been generously provided by: Elias and Rachell Filipi, Darrick and Rebecca Baab, Paul and Heidi Schmitt, Jonathan and Mary Germain, Patrick and Michelle Filipi, Peter and Majella Lynch, and Arnie and Theresa Filipi.

Contents

Foreword vii

Editor's Notes xi

Sentimental Theology 1

A Defense of Catholic Principles 15

    Article One: A Summary of Catholic Doctrine 23
    Article Two: Confession. 46
    Article Three: The Eucharist, or Lord's Supper. 53
    Article Four: The Sacrifice of the Mass. 72
    Article Five: Communion Under One Kind or Form. . . 78
    Article Six: Purgatory and Prayers for the Dead. 82
    Article Seven: Honoring the Saints
            and Applyng to their Intercession. 92
    Article Eight: Images, Pictures, and Relics. 103
    Article Nine: The Pope. 110
    Article Ten: Toleration. 123
    Conclusion. 131

An Appeal to the Protestant Public 141

A Letter to a Protestant Friend
on The Holy Scriptures 153

    Prince Demetrius Augustin Gallitzin. 155
    Preface. 159
    Letter. 169
    Six Final Points. 238
    Postscript. 251

Biographical Sketches 267

    Brother Francis Maluf, M.I.C.M. 267
    Prince Demetrius Augustin Gallitzin. 271

Prayer for the Conversion of America. 275

Foreword

When we stood before Br. Francis' grave on September 10th, 2009, we realized how much more we might have done during his lifetime to express, in a tangible way, our deep gratitude to him for all that he had done for us. On that very day, we determined that on the first anniversary of his death there would be some work in print that would pay tribute to this truly great man. Those who have had the grace and the privilege to be personally present at his lectures know what a daunting challenge lay before us.

After much consideration, we elected to reprint a work by Fr. Demetrius Augustin Gallitzin, a 19th century Russian prince who converted to the Catholic Faith, was ordained a priest, and became a pioneer missionary in the United States. We recalled the many times Br. Francis lamented that so few good Catholic books were in print and therefore unavailable to a modern world starved for wholesome literature. So, from his eternal resting place, we are convinced that Br. Francis is pleased with our choice. Fr. Gallitzin was a staunch defender of the Faith, and Rome has recognized him as a holy man. On June 6th, 2005 he was pronounced a 'Servant of God' by the church, and he is therefore entitled to have his name prefaced with the term 'Venerable.'

But what, some may ask, does a priest who died in 1840 have in common with a religious brother who died in 2009? Remarkably, their lives and apostolates paralleled each other in many significant ways.

Both men had their roots in Eastern Rite Christianity but, sadly, neither of them was well formed in the Faith in their early years. Demetrius converted to Roman Catholicism from the Russian Orthodox church when he was seventeen years old, while Fakhri Maluf (Br. Francis) embraced the Catholic Faith at the age of twenty-nine and remained a Melkite Catholic (the rite of his ancestors) all his life. Both were men of deep and strong feelings, and had experienced the keen sorrow of having fathers who died outside of the church—at least as far as the very limited mind of men can know. Perhaps God, in his infinite mercy, granted these family members deathbed conversions due to the prayers offered daily for this intention by these two faithful sons.

Another similarity is that both men were sons of prominent families. The Gallitzins were a family of Russian and Lithuanian ancestry whose lineage can be traced back for centuries. So highly were they placed in Russian society that Catherine the Great was Demetrius' godmother. And Maluf was no mean name in Lebanon, where their ancestral roots are traced to the famous Ghassani tribe, who were among those families who resisted submission to Islam by retreating to the mountains of Lebanon where they lost their worldly power but kept their precious Faith. The list of illustrious family members includes statesmen, poets, and bishops among them.

America became the adopted home of these two men. In both instances, one of the instruments God used to bring about their displacement was war. Millions in Europe anxiously watched the events unfolding in France—would the hellish Masonic Revolt (the French Revolution) engulf the entire continent? Demetrius' parents, having agreed that Europe was not perhaps the best place for the young man to be at the time, decided to send him to the New World. He arrived in the United States of America on August 18ᵗʰ, 1792 and he never returned to Europe to live. In the case of Fakhri, he got 'stuck' in America when World War II broke out. He was in the United States on a fellowship and travel restrictions did not allow him to return to his native Lebanon. He too, lived the rest of his life here.

But the most striking similarity is the loving vehemence with which each man 'took' to the Faith. It was not a casual decision for either of them; indeed, both were consumed with a burning desire that all men join, and learn to love and serve, the church that Christ had founded. Their entire lives were given over to this missionary endeavor. Fr. Gallitzin's efforts were spent not only in caring for his tiny flock, greatly out-numbered by various protestant sects, but also in evangelizing the often anti-Catholic majority that surrounded his little Catholic community. Undaunted, he writes, "Protestants! As long as I live I shall consider it *my duty* (emphasis added) to undeceive you." He would go to great lengths to bring a soul into the church, and there is a tradition that in October, 1795, he traveled 130 arduous miles through wild and dangerous country to bring a dying woman into the Catholic church.

Br. Francis tramped through a wilderness of a different sort, but no less real. While Fr. Gallitzin was challenged many times by a physical wilderness, Br. Francis faced a spiritual and academic desert, a world where the hearts of men had grown cold, a world not only indifferent to truth but also often openly hostile to it. Br. Francis realized in the 1940s that it was not only the protestants, pagans, Jews, etc. who needed conversion, but also people who called themselves Catholic. Catholics, including many members of the hierarchy, had effectively ceased to believe the most fundamental truths of the Faith, even if some still professed it with their lips.

Fr. Gallitzin, in *A Letter to a Protestant Friend*, and Br. Francis, in *Sentimental Theology*, both pleaded with their readers to think deeply and clearly about matters that would determine their eternal destiny. They knew, with St. Paul, that "our wrestling is not against flesh and blood; but against principalities and powers, against the rulers of the world of this darkness, against the spirits of wickedness in the high places" (Eph. 6:12). They understood also that these "spirits of wickedness" devise a myriad assortment of deceptions to ensnare the unsuspecting and unaware. Fr. Gallitzin and Br. Francis accepted the challenges they were confronted with and hurled back, with reason and faith, the church's responses to these false prophets. They were warriors engaged in the ultimate battle for the salvation of souls, ever ready and willing to pay any price that almighty God might ask of them.

Both men had a deep and reverential love for Holy Scripture. In their respective apostolates (Fr. Gallitzin's to convert protestants and Br. Francis' to convert Catholics) these two extraordinary missionaries often used the same "tool" one ancient, but ever new, Holy Scripture. Fr. Gallitzin has left for posterity several works wherein he quotes Holy Scripture in order to defend the church and to bring back souls to the bosom and unity of their Holy Mother. Br. Francis, with the same intention, year after year throughout his life, gave weekly lectures on Holy Scripture to anyone willing to listen. He favored the Gospels, which he memorized. He could recite Matthew, Luke, and John in Latin and. Mark in Greek.

So, what did Fr. Gallitzin and Br. Francis have in common? Everything that matters in eternity! America is a richer and more blessed land for being graced with the presence and labors of these two Catholic giants. May they never forget their poor, adopted country. May they pray, from their eternal resting place, for it's conversion.

— *Arnie and Theresa Filipi*

Editor's Notes

It might be thought odd to publish a book as a memorial edition in honor of one man consisting primarily of the works of another, so we thought it appropriate to supply a few words of explanation to the curious reader.

We originally considered issuing another of Br. Francis' works, but, being constrained by circumstances outside our control from publishing the next volume of his philosophy series, we considered that one of the defining moments of his life, indeed of the life of the church in the 20th century, was the publication of his article *Sentimental Theology* in the September 1947 issue of *From the Housetops* magazine. In this article Br. Francis decried the lack of zeal for truth and absence of true charity for those outside the church, evinced by the unmanly manner in which the Faith was being proclaimed in mid-20th century America, and that he had called for men who would teach the Faith in a strong and virile fashion and not "with the subdued and hesitant voice of sentimental theology".

We do not know whether or not Br. Francis had Demetrius Gallitzin in mind when he wrote that challenging article in 1947, but what we do know is that the church, on June 6th, 2005, declared Venerable, a man who spoke to and taught his fellow Americans in the manner that Br. Francis thought proper and admirable. The fact that Fr. Gallitzin had a strong enough devotion to the Holy House to give the name of Loretto to the town in Pennsylvania that he founded has not escaped the notice of those of us who are among the founders of an organization named in honor of the very same relic.[1] In fact, Br. Francis was the inspiration behind the founding of Loreto Publications. So therefore, it seemed appropriate to us to make more widely known to our countrymen, Catholic and protestant alike, the writings of this great Catholic and American hero, Ven. Fr. Demetrius Augustin Gallitzin, and to do so in tribute to Br. Francis Maluf, M.I.C.M.

The three articles by Fr. Gallitzin included here were originally published in sequence over a period of several years. The first, *A Defense of Catholic Principles*, was published in response to a public sermon of a protestant clergyman who used the occasion to attack the church. The second, *An Appeal to the Protestant Public*, was published after the clergyman responded with a public *Vindication* of his remarks and accusations, which utterly failed to address Gallitzin's *Defense*. One of the results of this exchange was that a friendship developed between Gallitzin and another protestant minister who eventually converted. It was made clear to Gallitzin that any attempt to convince protestants of the truths of the faith must depend for its effectiveness, not upon appeals to authority or tradition, but rather to scripture. This he did in his *Letter to a Protestant Friend on the Holy Scriptures*. All three articles are masterful, manly, and effective.

---

1. The name of our publishing apostolate, Loreto Publications, follows the Italian spelling.

Many protestants converted. We are pleased to make these writings available to a new generation of Catholic evangelists.

The three articles have been typeset and updated with some changes to the original text. The alterations are as follows:

We have changed the spelling of many words to match modern American spelling rules. Some examples are: neighbor for neighbour, show for shew, labor for labour, favor for favour, etc..

We have made use of more modern punctuation and capitalization rubrics.

We have made uniform the notations of scripture references in the currently accepted fashion. For example, we use Mt. 24: 6-9 instead of Matt. 24: 6, 7, 8, 9,

Unlike some modern editions of Gallitzin's work, we have not altered any of his words or deleted any of the more strongly worded phrases or paragraphs. These are exact copies of his original works.

Among the last thoughts that Br. Francis uttered before his death was an ardent plea that those of us who knew him would remember to pray for his soul. We pass on to you that plea, and we hope that you too will heed his last request.

In the hearts of Jesus, Mary, and Joseph,

The Editor
Loreto Publications

Sentimental Theology

Sentiment is a human thing, and nothing human is either scorned or despised by a Christian. In Christianity there is a place for the exercise of every impulse that God put in human nature. A Christian is not a Stoic who shuns his emotions, nor a Quaker who lets them simmer under the surface of a placid face. He does not pretend to deny the reality of human sufferings like a Christian Scientist, nor does he glut in them like a Jansenist. A Christian finds time for weeping and time for laughter, for gaiety as well as solemnity, for emotion as well as sentiment. Our Lord was not ashamed to show emotion when He wept as He heard of the death of His friend, nor did He hesitate to explode with anger when He saw the wicked and the avaricious desecrate the house of God. He manifested sublime sentiment when He inspired and guided the discovery of the real Cross and made it an object of veneration in His Church. And so, what I am about to condemn in this article is not sentiment, but sentimentality.

1

Sentimentality is not only a sentiment out of place; it is a sentiment without object. It is like falling in love with love, hoping for hope, or making a sincere effort at being sincere. It is good sentiment to guard the gifts of those you love; it is sentimentality to crowd the house with all kinds of things you throw away. Sentimentality is not even an act; it is just a state of the mind. It is an atmosphere which softens the character, suffocates the mind, and inflicts the will with paralysis. A sentimental mother would let her child die rather than allow a surgical operation to wound his body. In the same way, a sentimental Christian would let his friend miss the opportunity of salvation and go to hell rather than hurt his feelings. Sentimentality is inimical both to charity and to truth. Am I intelligent as a Christian if I allow those who are dear and close to me to incur the slightest danger of losing the friendship of God for all eternity by giving them in return my friendship in this short life? And would I not be endangering my own soul were I to drive this bargain?

I know I am not wasting punches at a straw man. Sentimental thinking about religious matters is very much with us today. A great deal of what is being said by Catholics today sounds in very sharp contrast with the accent of the authentic voice of the Church, teaching, warning, and defining. The sharp weapons of Christ are being blunted, and the strong, virile doctrines of the Church are being put aside in a conspiracy of silence.

While talking to a Catholic group recently, I was shocked to a realization of what is happening to the Faith under the rising wave of liberalism. I happened to mention casually the Catholic dogma, "There is no salvation outside the Church." Some acted as if I were uttering an innovation they had never heard of before, and others had the doctrine so completely covered with reservations and vicious distinctions as to ruin its meaning and destroy the effect of its challenge. In a few minutes, the room was swarming with the slogans of liberalism and sentimentalism, utterances which are beginning to have the force of defined dogma. Taken in their totality and in the manner in which they were used and understood by their utterers, these slogans constituted an outlook incompatible with the Catholic Faith and with the traditions of the Church. "Salvation by sincerity." "Membership in the soul of the Church." "Don't judge." "Don't disturb the good faith of unbelievers." "It is not charitable to talk about hell or to suggest that anybody may go there." "Isn't faith a gift?" And "How about the baptism of desire?" and so on, and so forth. I am not concerned with these phrases as they might occur in a theological treatise with sufficient explanations and with only proportionate emphasis.[1] I am rather concerned with a practical attitude of mind which seeks and selects precisely these phrases and builds them into a closed system of thought, ready to justify every act of cowardice, disloyalty to the Church, or encouragement to infidels and heretics who have set themselves up as teachers of religion.

For example, the statement: "Faith is a gift" is only half a truth. Faith is also a response. It is very evident, from the way Our Lord sought this response and blamed and reprimanded those who failed to give it, that faith is also a response. Our Lord did not say: "I feel sorry for the poor Pharisees because, although they see the evidence of My divinity, yet they are not given the gift of faith." And yet this is what we are asked to say of our modern Pharisees who, by their own testimony, cannot be ignorant of the divine authority of the Catholic Church, but would

---

1. Today, as in 1947, our primary concern in this regard remains the same. After intense studies during the intervening years, however, we have developed increasingly greater concern over theological abuses of some of those phrases.

not submit. To take another example, Franz Werfel[2] is supposed to have had the baptism of desire during a long period of time when the sacrament of baptism with water was clearly available.

Are we saved by mere sincerity? If this were the good news Jesus brought into the world, this would be the way to proclaim it: "You shall be sincere, and sincerity will bring you to heaven; your own devices may be your way to the Father." Or at least, "There are two ways to God: I am one and your personal integrity is another." But, on the contrary, this is the way Our Lord speaks: "You shall know the truth, and the truth will make you free"; "I am the way, the truth, and the life"; "He that believeth not shall be condemned." And when He proclaimed, saying: "Amen, amen, I say unto you: except you eat the flesh of the Son of man and drink His blood, you shall not have life in you," He did not stop to apologize, or to explain, or to add so many reservations which can mean nothing to an unbeliever, and which can only add to the weakness and hesitancy of those who believe.

Some Catholic liberals and sentimentalists, who think that it is not very nice to talk about hell, give you the impression, by what they say and do, that humanity divides into two neat classes: those who belong to the body of the Church, and those who belong to its soul. You almost wonder at times whether it isn't nobler and more magnanimous, and perhaps even safer, to belong only to the latter. As a matter of fact, when you seek a responsible theologian on this doctrine, and after he has finished

---

2. Franz Werfel, who was Jewish, first gained international attention with his novel *Forty Days of Musa Dagh* (1933), which told of an Armenian village's heroic struggle against invading Turkish Moslems. His biography of St. Bernadette of Lourdes entitled *Song of Bernadette* — on which the award-winning movie of the same title was based — made him popular in Catholic circles.

explaining and interpreting and adding reservations, you wonder whether the doctrine was worth announcing to the public at all, and whether it has any real practical application for us. You certainly begin not to wonder at the fact that Our Lord has left these minor and secondary truths to be discovered by the theologians and restricted Himself exclusively to the proclamation of the Christian challenge in unhesitating terms.

Let us consult *An Explanation of the Baltimore Catechism of Christian Doctrine*, by Rev. Thomas L. Kinkead, on the subject of salvation outside the Church:

> Q. Are all bound to belong to the Church?
>
> A. All are bound to belong to the Church, and he who knows the Church to be the true Church and remains out of it, cannot be saved.
>
> Anyone who knows the Catholic religion to be the true religion, and will not embrace it, cannot enter into heaven. If one not a Catholic doubts whether the Church to which he belongs is the true Church, he must settle his doubt, seek the true Church, and enter it; for if he continues to live in doubt, he becomes like the one who knows the true Church and is deterred by worldly considerations from entering it.
>
> In like manner one who, doubting, fears to examine the religion he professes lest he should discover its falsity and be convinced of the truth of the Catholic Faith, cannot be saved.
>
> Suppose, however, that there is a non-Catholic who firmly believes that the Church to which he belongs is the true Church, and who has never — even in the past — had the slightest doubt of that fact — what will become of him?
>
> If he was validly baptized and never committed a mortal sin, he will be saved; because, believing

himself a member of the true Church, he was doing all he could to serve God according to his knowledge and the dictates of his conscience … that person would be saved; because, being baptized, he is a member of the Church, and being free from mortal sin he is a friend of God and could not in justice be condemned to hell. Such a person belongs to what we call the soul of the Church. He would belong to the body of the Church — that is, he would attend Mass and receive the sacraments — if he knew the Catholic Church to be the only true Church.

I am giving you an example, however, that is rarely found, except in the case of infants or very small children baptized in Protestant sects.

Suppose you went to a doctor and inquired whether a man with double pneumonia should be placed on the danger list, and suppose the doctor's reply was: "Well, a man with double pneumonia is not necessarily in danger of death, for if this man had a thorough immunity against all diseases, and if he had never been in serious illness before, and if all his organs are in absolutely perfect condition, and if no further complications arise, and perfect medical attention is given to him, this man might pull through." Wouldn't the doctor be of greater practical service to you if he had said, "Yes, a man with double pneumonia is in grave danger"? The same is true of men in any way severed from the unity of the Church and without the divinely established and infallible guidance of the Holy Father; they are in a grave and permanent state of danger as far as their eternal salvation is concerned. If some of them are saved, it would not be because of their heresy, but rather in spite of it,[3]

_____

3. The author in no way here intends to imply that persons holding heretical opinions are saved, but that God, Who is not outdone in generosity, would give them the grace to see their error clearly

and on account of the sufferings of Christ, Who continues to suffer for the salvation of the world in His Mystical Body, the Catholic Church.

I can speak at least for myself with absolute certainty. The qualifications given by Father Kinkead for belonging to the soul of the Church never applied to me as a heretic after I had reached the age of reason.[4] Not only one of these qualification failed, which would have been enough, but every single one of them. And yet I met in my life hundreds of Catholics who kept me in the hell of unbelief precisely because they pretended to think that I was sincere and therefore secure. These Catholics did not act with respect to me with supernatural Catholic charity, but with sentimental sociable charitableness. Regarding all my non-Catholic acquaintances, there is not a single person to whom Father Kinkead's qualifications apply with any show of probability. On the contrary, the evidence is very much on the opposite side.

I know that the next slogan to be shouted by the liberals and the sentimentalists is: "You are judging people, and Our Lord said 'Don't judge.'" To take the transcendent utterances of Our Lord and to apply them in such a ridiculous fashion is really the limit in misinterpretation. Is it possible that Our Lord could have intended to de-humanize us so thoroughly as to prohibit us from using our highest power, the power of judgment, in any way or manner? And if that were the intent of Our Lord's injunction, how is it possible that the Church has so completely misunderstood Him, because this interpretation is certainly not compatible with the history of the Church, its practices and traditions, with its

---

so that they might repent of it. For no one can enter heaven in schism or heresy.

4. The author was raised as a Presbyterian and joined Freemasonry in early adulthood. He converted to the Catholic Faith in 1940.

militancy for the preservation and defense of truth, with its glorious inquisitions and crusades,[5] with its resounding anathemas and excommunications, and with the teachings and polemics of its saints and doctors. Our Lord also said: "By their fruits ye shall know them," If he intends us never to judge, why should he give us the criteria by which to judge? He also said: "Beware of the leaven of the Pharisees, which is hypocrisy." He obviously, therefore, intended that we should judge hypocrisy, for how can we beware of hypocrisy if we can never judge that we have a case of it at hand! "And whosoever shall not receive you, nor hear your words; going forth out of that house or city shake off the dust from your feet. Amen I say to you, it shall be more tolerable for the land of Sodom and Gomorrah in the day of judgment than for that city. Behold I send you as sheep in the midst of wolves. Be ye therefore wise as serpents and simple as doves. But beware of men." (Mt. 10:14-17.) Clearly therefore, any interpretation of Our Lord's saying, "Judge not, that you may not be judged," must also take into consideration all these other sayings too.[6] Indeed, there is a judgment which we must leave to God, but what kind of judgment?

---

5. Anti-Catholic "historians", having monopolized the field of history since the Protestant Revolution, have so distorted the actual character and history of both the crusades and the inquisitions that virtually all Catholics today share some sort of collective guilt complex in their regard. This is especially so where the inquisitions are concerned. Reading a true historical account, such as William Thomas Walsh's *Characters of the Inquisition*, would show the propriety of the term "glorious" in referring to these frequently misunderstood episodes in Catholic annals.

6. Besides, it is a law of the Church that we "admonish the sinner." Clearly this law necessitates that a judgment first be made of a sinful act or matter before the sinner can be admonished.

The person who chose to quote Our Lord's saying "Judge not" was himself judging that a man can get to heaven by sincerity, and also that the heretics he knew were on the whole sincere. Of these two judgments, the first is one which no man could or should make. When I say that there is one way to heaven, and that this way is the Catholic Church, established by Christ and led by His vicar on earth, I am not making a judgment. I am simply submitting to a divine judgment. With my natural mind I could never have reasoned to the beatific vision as man's destiny, and consequently, neither could I have figured out the way to the beatific vision. This is a judgment which I leave entirely to God, and which I accept entirely on His authority. But my antagonist on this issue is the one judging on the authority of human reason that a man's sincerity can earn him the beatific vision. On the other hand, judging that a particular man with whom I am dealing is, or is not sincere, is a human judgment and may be made in the light of ordinary human evidence. This is the kind of judgment I am making when I assert that all the non-Catholics I know, with the exception of irresponsible idiots, are and could only be insincere on the subject of religion. Knowing that, I can pray for them, and when they die, I can hope that they repented their insincerity in the last split second of their life. And then, of course, when I can do nothing more for them, I leave them to the mercy of God. But my antagonist is making a judgment even on this issue, although his judgment is hypocritically and — at best — from sentimental motives, flying in the face of the evidence.

When a man dies, we leave him to the mercy of God. This is the kind of ultimate judgment no mortal can take into his own hands. But the public teachings of that man are things we must judge, and if we fail to judge, we are opening the door for future heresy and sowing the seeds of future schism. If I were asked whether Franz Werfel is in heaven or in hell, now that he is dead, I would certainly reply: "I do not know. I can hope that in the last seconds of his life, when he was no more a public issue but a sheer person, he did something opposite to what is known publicly about him, and contrary to the spirit of all his vicious doctrines which are still doing their harm in the world." Franz Werfel wrote: "I am a Jew by religion and have never been baptized. On the other hand, I wish to profess here, before you and the world, that, as is evident from the major part of my work, I have been decisively influenced and molded by the spiritual forces of Christianity and the Catholic Church. I see in the holy Catholic Church the purest power and emanation sent by God to this earth to fight the evils of materialism and atheism, and bring revelation to the poor souls of mankind. That is why, although standing *extra muros*, I have made it my purpose to support with my modest and humble abilities the struggle which the Catholic Church fights against those evils and for the divine truth." (Franz Werfel in a letter to the Archbishop of New Orleans.)

When Werfel wrote this paragraph, he was clearly on the way to hell and not on the way to heaven. These are the words of a proud messiah to whom evil is something in the world outside. They are not the words of a contrite sinner seeking salvation. There is not even any evidence of "baptism of desire." Baptism of desire is a desire for the baptism of water and not a wish for the baptism of desire.[7] Only a man who does not know about baptism,

---

7. As has been shown in other writings from St. Benedict Center, all allusions by the popes, the councils and learned doctors of the Church to this subject matter agree, that only an explicit desire for the actual Sacrament of Baptism can effect justification. What is disputed is whether such desire is sufficient for salvation. We hold, with many of the saints, the same literal meaning of Our Lord's words: "He that believeth and is baptized shall be saved; he that believeth not shall be condemned." (Mk. 16:15)

and who has not rejected it explicitly, can be supposed in any sense to have an equivalent or virtual desire for it. If Franz Werfel is not in hell, it must be because he has since reversed his direction. If he is now in heaven, it could only be because he has since regretted the pride he paraded through life, and heartily desired the baptism of water, which he evaded when it was available, and belonged to the spirit of the Church by doing all that was possible to him to be incorporated in its body. As far as we are concerned, there is evidence only to the contrary, and to his obstinacy to the very end.[8]

If for any sentimental considerations we are going to fail to utter these truths, then our Catholic children are going to think that it is all right for them to read the books of Franz Werfel, C.S. Lewis, Mortimer Adler, John Wild, Charles Malik, P.A. Sorokin, Lloyd C. Douglas, Evelyn Underhill, Robert Maynard Hutchins, Nikolai Berdiaev and Russell Janney. And if our Catholic children continue to read these proud, deliberate and unrepentant heretics,

---

8. To many, Werfel's sentiments as quoted in this article may seem, at worst, only a trifle misguided if not entirely benign. Thus, the author's appraisal of those sentiments and the man may seem strongly worded. Indeed, perhaps he would express himself differently were he discussing the same subject today. But saints have used much harsher terms to unmask and chastise such subtle and, yes, damnable pride posturing as humility and virtue before others. It is self-evident that God had given this man sufficient grace to know and embrace the true Faith, and yet Werfel continued to stand "*extra muros*," (outside the walls) *extra ecclesiam*.

Nevertheless, both Father Feeney and the author always insisted that God surely does reward authentic good will in non-Catholics, though never by means of an end-run around His own Ordinances. Evidently, Franz Werfel finally proved himself truly a man of good will; we have learned on good authority, in more recent times, that he was baptized a Catholic before his death in 1944.

they will lose their faith. The writings of these men, when they give occasionally a convincing semblance of orthodoxy, are the closest human approximation to that diabolic trick whereby Lucifer is said to make himself an angel of light. This semblance of orthodoxy cannot be an overflow from the abundance of the heart; it cannot be the fruit of a living faith, which these individuals do not possess. It can only be the artful effect of intellectual trickery. This matter can be judged *a priori*, that is, from cause to effect, from person to writings. A Catholic has no need to study the works of these individuals in order to reach this conclusion. How can anybody be edified by an argument, which sounds convincing when it did not convince even its utterer?

But, says the sentimentalist, is it not possible that these men will be converted? Of course it is possible; but why not wait until it happens before we take them into our Catholic schools and into our Catholic homes? When these men have retracted their obstinacy, and when God has changed His mind with regard to them, I will change my mind too. The Church does not send its fattened calf to the strange country, but waits for the prodigal son to come home, and waits at home. If and when these men are really converted, you will see that they themselves will be telling you at least as much as I have said about their pre-conversion period. From the days of St. Paul, this is what every real convert has done. St. Augustine did not come into the Church to chant the eulogies, nor even the apologies, of his sinful days outside. To the end of his life, St. Augustine was still confessing and retracting the hangovers of heresy, which continued to cloud the brilliance of his thoughts even after he had become the great saint and doctor of the Church. The world will never forget his resounding, exclamation: "Too late have I come to know thee, O my God!"

But wouldn't our profession of faith in such uncompromising terms make non–Catholics unhappy?

Would it not disturb them to know that we think they are not on the way to heaven? Well, it could disturb them only the moment they begin to believe the Christian story, and then they need not remain worried. The Catholic Church does not proclaim the exclusive salvation of one race or one class of people, but invites every man to the great joy of being united with Christ in the communion of saints.

The Catholic truth is not a sad story for which we need to apologize; it is a proclamation of the greatest good news that could ever be told. No matter how sternly its message is phrased, it is still the one and only hope in the world. Only love and security can afford to be severe. When we say that outside the Church there is no salvation, we are also and at the same time announcing that inside the Church there is salvation. The world already knows the sad part of our story, because the world finds no salvation in the world. The Church does not have to tell the unbelievers that they are in sin and in despair; they know that in the depth of their hearts. What is new to the world in the Christian story is that, through Mary, the gates of heaven are opened, and that we are invited to become brothers of Jesus in the Eternal Kingdom of God. This is not a story which can be told with the subdued and hesitant voice of sentimental theology.

The Church Teaches:

EX CATHEDRA: "There is but one universal church of the faithful, outside of which no one at all can be saved."
— Pope Innocent III, Fourth Lateran Council, 1215.

EX CATHEDRA: "We declare say, define, and pronounce that it is absolutely necessary for the salvation of every human creature to be subject to the Roman Pontiff."
— Pope Boniface VIII, the Bull *Unam Sanctam*, 1302.

EX CATHEDRA: "[The Holy Roman church] firmly believes, professes and teaches that none of those who are not within the Catholic church, not only Pagans, but Jews, heretics and schismatics can ever be partakers of eternal life, but are to go into the eternal fire 'Prepared for the devil, and his angels' (Mt. 24:41), unless before the close of their lives they shall have entered into that church; also that the unity of the Ecclesiastical body is such that the church's Sacraments avail only those abiding in that church, and that fasts, almsdeeds, and other works of piety which play their part in the Christian combat are in her alone productive of eternal rewards; moreover; that no one, no matter what alms he may have given, not even if he were to shed his blood for Christ's sake, can be saved unless he abide in the bosom and unity of the Catholic church."
Mansi, Concilia. 31, 1739.
Pope Eugene IV, the Bull *Cantate Domino*, 1441.

St. John 15:1-7   St. Matthew 16:18-19, 18:17-18; Ephesians 1:22-23; 5:23, 30, 32;   2 St. John 1:9-11

14

A Defense of
Catholic Principles

Preface

A sermon preached by a protestant minister, on a day appointed by the government for humiliation and prayer, in order to avert from our beloved country the calamity of war, has been the occasion of the present letter.

The professed subject of his sermon on such a day was, or should have been, to excite his hearers to humility and contrition, and to a perfect union of hearts and exertions during the impending storm: but he, very likely alarmed at a much greater danger, of which nobody else but himself dreamed: alarmed I mean, and trembling for the ark of Israel likely to be carried off by those Philistines called the Roman Catholics; or alarmed, perhaps, at the very probable danger of an intended invasion from the pope, who would, to be sure, avail himself of the confused state of the country to assist his English friends in the conquest of it, that he might by that means extend his jurisdiction; or in fine, alarmed perhaps lest our treacherous Catholics would take advantage of the times, and by forming a new gunpowder plot, would blow up the congress hall, state

17

houses, and all the protestant meeting houses of the United States: alarmed, at least, by something or another, he suddenly forgets his subject, and putting on a grave countenance, enters the most solemn caveat against popish and heathen neighbors; cautions his hearers against their superstitions, and gives them plainly enough to understand that such popish neighbors are not to be considered their fellow citizens.

It is no small source of astonishment to see in a country so liberal, polished, and enlightened as the United States of America, a continuation of violent attacks, unjust prejudices, and foul calumnies against the Roman Catholic church. As attacks of that kind are so very common, and generally proceed too evidently from ignorance or impotent rancor, to merit attention, I have always treated them hitherto with silent contempt. The present one I thought necessary to notice, both as it proceeded from a respectable quarter, and as I judged that silence, if invariably observed, would be construed by many into an admission of the charges against us. I expected, at first, that a few respectful lines, which I published in a gazette, would have been sufficient to draw from the gentleman an apology for his uncharitable expressions. I found myself deceived in my expectation. After having waited in vain from September until some time in the winter, I made up my mind to send the gentleman the following *Defense of Catholic Principles.*

Dear Sir,

After your unprovoked attack upon the whole body of Roman Catholics, it was expected that an apology for the same would have been considered by you as due to them. To exhibit above one hundred and fifty millions of Catholics,[1] who undoubtedly constitute the most numerous and imposing Christian society in existence, as standing upon a level with heathens, to represent the whole of them as a superstitious set, wandering in the paths of darkness, and finally, to exclude the Catholics of the United States from their rank of citizens, cannot be considered by you

---

1. The number of one hundred and fifty millions* will not appear exaggerated to anyone who considers that Italy contains nearly twenty millions of Catholics; France, upwards of thirty millions; that Spain, Portugal, Austria, Bohemia, Hungary, Belgium, Ireland, Poland, South America, and some parts of North America, *viz*: Cuba, Mexico, Lower Canada, etc., are inhabited almost exclusively by Catholics; that they are numerous in the United States, and still more so in the protestant kingdoms of Europe, for instance, five millions in the dominions of the King of Prussia; that there are flourishing churches and missions in Turkey, throughout the vast continents of Asia and Africa, in the islands of the Pacific and the southern ocean; that the Philippine Islands contain two millions, and the Diocese of Goa alone, nearly half a million of Catholics. From these and other facts, we are inclined to believe that the total number above mentioned, instead of being overrated, might, on the contrary, be raised to one hundred and seventy, or perhaps, one hundred and eighty millions.

*This was written nearly fifty [now, in 2010, nearly 175] years ago.

as a trifling insult. Now, Sir, as a gentleman, you cannot be ignorant of the common principles of civility. As a Christian, and especially as a teacher of the Christian religion, you cannot be ignorant of that great precept of Christian charity, which our blessed savior declares to be the very soul of religion on which depend the whole law and the prophets (Mt. 22:40). Wishing to act under the influence of those principles, I shall, according to the direction of our common savior (Mt. 5:44), return you good for evil, and pray God to bless you, whilst you are persecuting and calumniating us. And, though your alleged charges, it is true, destroy themselves, and their falsehood must be evident to anyone who is even slightly acquainted with Catholic doctrines; nay, every reflecting mind should thence infer the weakness of that cause which stands in need of such aid for its support;[2] yet, as you refuse us (what we think we are justly entitled to)

---

2. "It is an observation," says Count de Maistre, "which I recommend to the attention of all those who think and reason: truth, when it combats error, is never angry. Amidst the immense number of our controversial works, it requires a microscopic eye to discover one single effusion of anger, which might escape from human weakness. Such men as Bellarmine, Bossuet, Borgier, etc., were able to dispute all their life, without suffering themselves to use, I do not say the slightest insult, but even the slightest personality. This character the protestant writers possess in common with the Catholic, when-ever they combat incredulity. The reason of it is, because, in this case, it is the Christian that is combating the deist, the materialist, and the atheist; and therefore, it is still truth refuting error. But, now, let these men only turn their arms against the church of Rome, behold, everything at once is altered; they insult her with the gross-est violence. And why? Because error is never calm, when it combats against truth. This two-fold characteristic is visible everywhere, as also it is everywhere decisive. There are few demonstrations which conscience sees more clearly."

an apology, and as such charges continue to be repeated, I have deemed it expedient to give you and the public an explanation of our tenets, in order to convince every candid mind that we are not guilty of superstition.

With respect to the personal insult reflected on us from the odious colors in which we and our doctrines are exhibited, it excites in us rather compassion than anger. Our only wish is that our separated brethren may be enabled by the light of God to know the truth, and having known it, by his special assistance to embrace and follow it.

If, instead of accusing us in a general manner, you had been pleased to state distinctly in what particular points we are guilty of superstition, a great deal of time would have been saved, as my defense would be confined to those particular points of attack; but now, not knowing those against which the attack is intended, I must be ready at all points.

In order to ascertain whether we are or not guilty of superstition, it will be necessary, in the first place, to give a distinct definition of the word superstition. Many disputes originate altogether in the misunderstanding of words, and might be entirely avoided, by first agreeing about the meaning of those words.

Such as have treated of superstition, give the following definition of it, which everyone will readily grant to be correct: Superstition is an inordinate worship of the true, or of a false divinity.

To accuse us of superstition, then, is to say, that we either worship the true God in an inordinate manner, or that we worship false gods, or that we are guilty of both.

To which of the tenets of the Catholic church does any of these three modes of superstition apply?

I reply boldly, to none; and in order to convince you and your hearers that I am justified in saying so, I shall give you a short sketch of our Catholic principles; but do not expect to find, maintained by them, those pretended

Catholic principles which ignorance, prejudice, and, I am apprehensive, sometimes malice and ill-will, falsely attribute to Catholics. Thus I shall say nothing of the pope's power to grant licenses to commit sin, or dispensations from the oath of allegiance, about the worship of saints, and many other articles falsely attributed to Roman Catholics, and which (I have too much reason to believe) are industriously propagated to answer certain selfish and iniquitous purposes.

May the great God give me grace to display before your eyes and those of the public, the beauties and perfections of the Catholic church, that in her you may behold the true and immaculate spouse of Jesus Christ (Eph. 5:31, 32); ever subject and ever faithful to him (24); ever loved and cherished by him (25); that in her you may behold the kingdom of which Jesus Christ is the king, (Lk. 1:32); the sheepfold of which Jesus Christ is the shepherd (Jn. 10:16); the house of the living God (1Tim. 3:15); the pillar and ground of the truth *(ibid)*; always one (Jn. 10:16; Eph. 4:4–5); always visible (Mt. 5:14); unconquerable by the united efforts of hell and earth (Mt. 16:18); that none may fall under the sentence pronounced by St. Peter (2Pet.2:12), these men, blaspheming what they know not, shall perish; and by St. Jude (Jude 10), these men blaspheme what they know not. Woe to them, etc. On the contrary, that all may feel themselves compelled to exclaim with Balaam, How beautiful are thy tabernacles, O Jacob; and thy tents, O Israel (Num. 24:5).

Article One:

A Summary of the Catholic Doctrine

We believe, dear Sir, that almighty God is perfect in himself, and perfect in all his works. After creating the world and all that it contains, God saw all the things that he had made, and they were very good (Gen. 1:31). By the help of natural philosophy, anatomy, astronomy and other sciences, many of the beauties and perfections of nature, have been discovered, which give us the most exalted idea of the power and wisdom of their creator; many more, however, are, and will remain wrapped up in mystery, and are thereby the better calculated to give us some — though faint — idea of the immensity of God. From the discoveries which have been made, we are struck with astonishment at the wonderful harmony displayed in the whole system of nature and in every part of it. The progressive development of our faculties, the gradual — though slow — advancement of knowledge, has enabled us to penetrate into a few of the secrets of nature. Every discovery has paved the way to new ones, and were the world to last millions of years, we should still discover more, and yet be obliged to own that we have scarcely obtained one drop out of an ocean. This world, Sir, which we so much admire, will pass away, notwithstanding all its beauties and perfections. It was created, we believe, for the use of man during his mortal life, to afford him a comfortable and happy existence. But, Sir, man is not created for this visible world alone; his body was formed of clay, and his soul, his immortal soul, is the image of God — the breath of the most high: And the Lord God breathed into his face the breath of life, and man became a living soul (Gen. 2:7). We believe that the soul of man was created for everlasting happiness, and that created in the image of God, we are to rest forever in the bosom of God. With St. Augustine we exclaim, "Thou hast made us for thyself, O Lord, and our hearts are restless until they repose in thee."

We believe that, although created to the image of God, we may defile in ourselves that image, and thus remove ourselves from our original destination. We believe we shall attain the objects of our destination, only if we try to preserve in ourselves that image undefiled or, in other words, if we try to be and to become more and more similar to our creator; be perfect (says our savior) as also your heavenly Father is perfect (Mt. 5:48). We believe then, that in order to become ripe for heaven, we must try to keep ourselves pure and undefiled, show the most perfect obedience to our creator, the most perfect submission of our hearts and understandings, practice humility, chastity, justice, and above all, the most perfect charity; that is, we must love God above all things, and our neighbor as ourselves. The will of God must always be the only rule of our conduct, we must love what he loves, hate what he hates, and with due proportion, do as he does. Consequently, we must consider sin as the greatest of all evils, and be willing to sacrifice even life itself, rather than offend our creator, by a willful transgression of his commandments. As almighty God is infinitely just, infinitely good to all men, even to the worst of men, so must we be strictly just and charitable to all men, even to our enemies, without distinction of believer or unbeliever Christian, Jew, Mahometan, or heathen, etc. In short, Sir, we believe that, in order to become saints in heaven, we must lead a holy life upon earth, and that all the external acts of religion, which we practice, can never afford a substitute for a holy and virtuous life. We hear taught from all the Catholic pulpits in the world, and believe, that confidence in external acts of religion, unsupported and unaccompanied by the practice of virtue, is a most abominable presumption and real superstition.

To convince you, Sir, that such is the real belief of Catholics, I refer you to all Catholic catechisms, prayer

books, meditations, sermons, in short, to all the spiritual
books of any kind that ever were published in any part
of the Catholic world. Being provided with books of that
kind from almost every Catholic country in Europe, I
readily offer them to the inspection of any person curious
to ascertain the doctrine of Catholics on so important a
subject, on which misrepresentation has created so many
prejudices. What is more common, indeed, than to hear it
said that a Catholic — or if you choose, a papist — puts so
much confidence in his priest, that it matters little to him
whether he commits sin or not; for after having broken all
the commandments of God, he thinks he has nothing to do
but to confess his sins to the priest, and behold, from the
gulf of perdition, he leaps at once into paradise!

Catholics, then, among whom there are thousands and
thousands of men eminent for their genius and learning,
men of the most transcendent talents, celebrated in all
the different branches of literature, and, what is much
better, famed for the most genuine, the most heroic virtue;
Catholics then, I say, are believed, or at least represented,
to be most brutally stupid! But let us proceed.

We believe that man, originally created to the
image of God, has in a great measure denied that sacred
image, by tasting the forbidden fruit. We believe that, in
consequence of that sin which we call original sin, man
fell under the curse of God, was not only driven out of
the earthly paradise, but what is infinitely worse, forfeited
his right and title to the happiness of heaven; and we
believe that it was not in the power of man to offer to
the irritated justice of God a satisfaction adequate to the
offence. As the malice and iniquity of an offence must in
a great measure be determined by the degree of dignity
and elevation of the being to whom the offence is given —
God being infinite in power, dignity, and perfection — the
offence must be in some measure infinite in its malice. Man,
on the other hand, being limited, can have nothing to offer

by way of reparation or satisfaction, but what is limited in its value, and of course, not adequate as a satisfaction. The wrath and the justice of God demanded a victim; all mankind must be sacrificed, must suffer, and their sufferings must be infinite, which they cannot be, unless they last forever, or a being equal to the offended creator, must step forward and pay the ransom. As every act of an infinite being is of infinite value, one word, one sigh, from such a being, would be an adequate satisfaction. Here then, is the pivot upon which turns the whole Christian religion, with all its profound mysteries. Mankind being doomed to eternal torments, and not being able to satisfy God's infinite justice, within any limited period, Jesus Christ, the Son of God, equal to his Father, burning with zeal for his glory, and with love for man, offers himself as the victim of God's infinite justice. The ransom is accepted, and a new chance of heaven is offered to man.

The main point to be explained now is in what manner we believe that Jesus Christ has accomplished the redemption of man. This will, of course, exhibit all that Catholics believe of the church of Christ, of the Christian religion, and of all its mysteries.

We believe that Jesus Christ, in order to become a victim of propitiation for our sins, assumed human nature, which being united to his divine nature, formed one person. As God he could not suffer; but by becoming a real man, assuming a real human soul, and a real human body, he made himself liable to sufferings, and by being God, his sufferings became of infinite value, and of course, adequate as a satisfaction.

We believe that Jesus Christ was conceived in the womb of the spotless Virgin Mary, by the power and operation of the Holy Ghost (Lk. 1:35). We believe that Jesus Christ, immolating himself for our sins, acted in the capacity of a priest, a priest being the minister of a sacrifice; we believe that he is both high priest and victim (Heb 5:7-10).

Mankind having fallen by original sin into a wonderful state of depravity, the light of their reason being almost extinguished, their understanding perverted (witness the many ridiculous and abominable systems taught by their wise men and philosophers), their hearts corrupted and given up a prey to all the passions, Jesus Christ came not only to satisfy for our sins, and by that means to open for us the gates of heaven, but he also came to show both by word and example, what means we must take in order to obtain heaven.

We believe that in Jesus Christ we have a perfect example and pattern of a holy life, and an infallible teacher of salvation.

We believe that in the gospels is recorded a part, though a very small part, of what Christ did and preached during his visible existence on earth (Jn. 21:25).

We believe the authors of these gospels to have been inspired by the Holy Ghost, and therefore, we believe every word contained in them as proceeding from the fountain of truth.

As we believe the gospel of Christ to be a divine book, so we believe that none but a divine authority can expound it. We shudder at the idea of bringing that divine book before the tribunal of limited and corrupted reason, and we candidly confess that although we were provided with a greater share of wisdom and knowledge than Solomon possessed, we should still be unequal of ourselves to the task of understanding and explaining the gospel, or other parts of holy writ. In this we are confirmed by St. Peter, who says that "no prophecy of the scripture is made by private interpretation" (2Pet. 1:20).

As we believe that holy scripture is the word of God, so we believe that holy scripture misinterpreted is not the word of God, but the word of corrupted man; and that scripture is often misinterpreted, we are obliged to believe from the assertion of St. Peter, who tells us that the unlearned and unstable wrest the scriptures to their own perdition (2Pet. 3:16); and likewise from our own observations: for as common sense tells us that the Holy Ghost cannot be the author of contradictory doctrines, so it tells us of course, that numbers of doctrines preached pretendedly from scripture, must be false, as they stand in contradiction to other doctrines drawn from the same scripture.

We believe that true faith is indispensably necessary to salvation. He that believeth not, shall be condemned (Mk. 16:16); and, without faith, it is impossible to please God (Heb. 11:6).

We believe that Jesus Christ, requiring faith as necessary to salvation, must have provided us with adequate means to obtain faith — that is, to believe without doubting all those things, which he has taught and instituted as necessary for salvation. If Jesus Christ has not provided us with such means, he must be a tyrant indeed, as he would require of us what we could not otherwise possibly perform.

We believe that Jesus Christ has established the holy Catholic church for the above purpose, namely, as the supreme tribunal to regulate our faith, or in other words, to keep the precious deposit of revelation unaltered, to explain to us (without any possibility of error) the meaning of every part of holy writ necessary to salvation and likewise to preserve and transmit to posterity, undefiled, all that part of Christ's divine doctrine, which was delivered only by word of mouth, either by Christ or by his Apostles, according to these words of St. Paul, "Therefore, brethren, stand firm, and hold the traditions which you have learned, whether by word, or by our epistle" (2Thess. 2:14). We believe that the unwritten word of God, transmitted to us by tradition, is entitled to the very same respect as the written word.

We think it absurd to assert, that Jesus Christ has taught or preached nothing essential, but what is written in the few pages of the gospel. We do not find in the gospel the instructions which Jesus Christ gave his Apostles, during the forty days that he appeared to them after his resurrection; and yet it is beyond all doubt, that Jesus Christ during these forty days, the last days he spent with his Apostles, instructed them particularly in the mysteries of his kingdom, or of his church (Acts 1:3).

These last instructions which Jesus Christ gave his Apostles, before parting, and when they were about to enter into the arduous duties of the ministry, these last instructions I say, are not lost, although not recorded in the gospel. They form a part of that precious deposit entrusted to the church, and have, by an uninterrupted succession of pastors, been transmitted undefiled to our present days, and will be thus transmitted to the most remote generations, even to the consummation of time.

We believe, then, that the holy Catholic church is the supreme judge, in matters of faith, both to determine the true sense of scripture, and to settle our belief with regard to that part of Christ's doctrine, delivered by word of mouth.

Whenever the church has pronounced, the controversy is settled, doubts vanish, and we are as certain as if Jesus Christ himself had spoken.

This unerring authority of the church we discover first in the positive and most unequivocal promises of Jesus Christ; second, in the dictates of common sense; third, in the positive promises of Jesus Christ: "Upon this rock I will build my church, and the gates of hell shall not prevail against it" (Mt. 26:18).

If the church could possibly teach damnable errors, then the gates of hell could prevail against her, contrary to the above promise. "Go ye therefore, and teach all nations; baptizing them in the name of the Father, and of the Son, and of the Holy Ghost, teaching them to observe all things whatsoever I have commanded you; and behold I

am with you all days, even to the consummation of the
world" (Mt. 28:19-20).[1] Christ addressing his twelve
Apostles on the present occasion, evidently speaks to all
his ministers, successors of the Apostles, to the end of
time, which, I think, needs no proof. Now, Sir, upon that
subject, I form the following argument, which sound logic
will find correct. Christ promises that he himself will
be with his Apostles, baptizing, preaching, and teaching
all nations, until the consummation of time: now Christ
cannot tell a lie; therefore, Christ has fulfilled his promise,
and consequently, during these 1,815 years past, Christ
has always been with his ministers, the pastors of the holy
Catholic church, and he will continue to be with them to
the end of time, and will accompany and guide them, when
they preach his word and administer his sacraments. "And I
will ask the Father, and he shall give you another Paraclete,
that he may abide with you forever, the spirit of truth"
(Jn. 14:16, 17). [2] It appears that Christ asked his heavenly

1. The passage taken from Matthew 28:19-20 is very forcible, and one
   of those which will forever silence every artifice and subterfuge of
   error. In fact, those words of almighty God, "I am with you", are
   used in a hundred places of the sacred Scriptures to designate a
   certain and infallible protection (see Ps. 22:4; Jud. 6:12; Isa. 8:10).
   Our Lord making use of the same, wishes them to signify a similar
   protection with regard to his Apostles and their successors. But,
   how can he be said to assist the pastors of his church in so special
   a manner, if he permit them to deviate from the truth? How can he
   be said to remain with them all days to the end of the world, as he
   positively promises so to do, if it can ever happen to them to teach
   error and superstition?

2. The same observation that was applied to the above text of St. Matthew may be applied to this of St. John (14:16-17). Some, perhaps,
   may object to it, that the prayers of our Lord have not always been
   efficacious, for example, that which he addressed to his heavenly

Father to bless his ministers, the pastors of his church, with the spirit of truth forever; pray, Sir, did Christ offer up any prayer in vain? And if his prayer was heard, how could the pastors of the church ever preach false doctrine?

"But when he, the Spirit of Truth, shall come, he will teach you all truth" (Jn. 16:13). "The church of the living God, the pillar and ground of the truth" (1 Tim. 3:15). If the church itself, as it comes out of the hands of God, is the very ground and pillar of truth, it will never want the reforming hand of corrupted man to put it right; it will always teach the truth, the whole truth, and nothing but the truth: and instead of attempting to reform this most perfect of all the works and institutions of God, you and I must be reformed by it. To quote all the texts that prove the holy church of Jesus Christ to be infallible, or invested by Christ with a supreme and unerring authority in matters of faith, would be endless. I said that we discover this unerring authority even in the dictates of common sense. Yes, Sir, common sense tells us, that the works of God are perfect in their kind. Now the church being most emphatically the work of God, it most assuredly must be perfect; the church, however, must be very imperfect indeed, if it wants the main perfection, which is our guide and director to heaven, it therefore must have that of always teaching truth, that of always supplying the wants of our limited and corrupted reason, that of always carrying before our eyes the bright and divine light of revelation.

Father in the garden of Olives (Mt. 26:39), "My Father, if it be possible let this chalice pass from me." But, that this was a prayer merely conditional, it is easy to discover from the words which immediately follow: "Nevertheless, not as I will, but as thou wilt." On the contrary, that the success of his prayers made without restriction and condition, as the one referred to (Jn. 14:16-17), is infallible, he himself assures us in John (11:41-42), "Father, I give thee thanks because thou hast heard me; and I know thou hearest me always."

Show us a church that is not infallible, which owns itself fallible, wanting, of course, the main perfection which the church of Christ must have, and you show us a church of corrupted man, not the church of Christ. Common sense tells us that, without an infallible tribunal, unanimity in faith is a thing impossible. Without a center of unity, a fixed standard, an absolute and infallible tribunal, a living oracle to determine the mind, it is absolutely impossible, that men, framed as they are, should ever come to one and the same way of thinking. Whoever renounces this infallible authority of the church, has no longer any sure means to secure him against uncertainties, and to settle his doubts; he is in a sad and perplexed situation, tossed to and fro by every wind of doctrine.

We are confirmed in the above suggestions of common sense, by our observations. Unity in faith, we find nowhere but in the Catholic church; above a hundred and fifty millions of Catholics, scattered over the face of the earth, are perfectly one in matters of faith. We meet from the distant parts of the globe, ignorant of one another's language, manners, customs, etc., yet our thoughts and principles about religion and its mysteries are exactly alike. Pray, Sir, is that unity to be found among those, who have shaken off the authority of the church?[3] Since they have presumed to reform (as they call it) the Catholic church, what do we see but one reformation upon another, hundreds and hundreds of different churches, one rising on the ruins of another, all widely different from one another, each

_____

3. Our articles and liturgy, says Dr. Tomline, bishop of Lincoln, in his charge to his clergy, 1803, do not correspond with the sentiments of any of the reformers upon the continent, or with the creeds of any of the protestant churches that are there established. Our church is not Lutheran, it is not Calvinistic, it is not Arminian, it is scriptural. Query; which did his Lordship believe the others to be, scriptural or unscriptural?

styling herself the church of Christ, each appealing to the
gospel for the orthodoxy of her doctrine, each calling her
ministers, ministers of Christ, each calling the sermons of
her ministers, the word of God, etc. [4]

Common sense tells us, that the gospel, the written
word, could not have been intended as the supreme judge,

4. Very striking is the conduct of protestants with respect to the necessity of the authority of the church to settle disputes concerning faith.
They have been compelled, through want of other efficacious means,
to establish among themselves that authority, or rather its shadow.
This was particularly the case at the famous Synod of Dort. There
indeed, the greater number of Calvin's followers, *viz.* the Gomarists,
strove to crush their opponents, the Arminians, by the weight of Syn-
odal, and even civil authority: thus arrogating to themselves a power
which they refused to acknowledge in the church, notwithstanding
her incontestable claims; admitting in practice, what they denied in
theory; and contradicting their principles in the face of the whole
world. See Bossuet's *Exposition and History of Variations*, Book 14. Nor
is this, however, peculiar to the Synod of Dort. The same has taken
place in the reformed churches of France, in the established church
of England, and, generally, in all protestant societies. All of them,
after reviling the exercise of authority in matters of faith, as an act of
tyranny, have nevertheless been reduced to resort to it themselves. In
all of them, the leaders exercise over their flocks the most arbitrary
despotism, and arrogate to themselves the privileges of infallibility,
by requiring implicit submission of their deluded followers. A gross
inconsistency, it is true; a full contradiction to the principles of protestantism; but which shows, after all, how necessary is a living authority
to settle all differences concerning matters of faith. Now, which of the
two is to be preferred: the authority of a few men, who have received
from God no mission whatever, and do not so much as agree amongst
themselves; or the authority of the Catholic church, who derives,
through a regular succession, her claims from the Apostles, and has no
other origin than that of Christianity itself. See Bossuet's *Exposition,
and Fletcher's Controversial Sermons* (Note K to Sermon 2).

to fix our belief in matters of faith. First, because it may be misunderstood.

The many contradictory doctrines, drawn from scripture, prove that it is often misunderstood, and even in matters which Christ declares it indispensably necessary for salvation. Witness the following: "Except a man be born again, of water and the Holy Ghost, he cannot enter into the kingdom of God" (Jn. 3:5). "Unless you eat the flesh of the Son of man, and drink his blood, you shall not have life in you" (Jn. 6:54). "Without faith it is impossible to please God" (Heb. 6:6).

You will readily acknowledge that these several texts, although directing us to do certain things as indispensably necessary for salvation, are interpreted in contradictory ways, and of course misunderstood.

Some find in the gospel the necessity of Baptism for salvation; others find in it, salvation without Baptism.

Some find in it the necessity of receiving the flesh and blood of Christ; others find, that Christ gave us nothing but bread and wine, as memorials of his death.

Some find in the gospel that faith alone will save; others find in the gospel, the insufficiency of faith alone.

Some find in the gospel absolute and unconditional predestination; others reject it as impious and blasphemous.

Now, Sir, are all these right? Or, will it be said, that it is immaterial which of these contradictory opinions we embrace? No, Sir, common sense tells us that holy writ was not given us to be misunderstood, that when misunderstood, it leads us astray, whereas it was intended to guard us against the misfortune of being led astray. Common sense tells us then, that scripture being a dead letter, a dumb book, which cannot explain itself, Christ must have provided some visible and living authority, some supreme and unerring tribunal, to explain scripture, and that this is and can be none other than the church.

Otherwise, Jesus Christ, the uncreated wisdom, would have acted less wisely than human legislators, who indeed do not establish laws, without establishing tribunals to explain them. So much the less wisely, as the holy scriptures are in several parts full of obscurity: witness St. Peter, who says of the epistles of St. Paul: "in which are some things hard to be understood, which the unlearned and unstable wrest, as also the other scriptures, to their own destruction" (2Pet. 3:16). Witness also the difference, and even contrariety of expositions, given by protestants themselves, on points of the greatest importance.

A second reason why scripture cannot be our supreme judge in matters of faith is because there are many that cannot read.

A third reason is the gospels and epistles were not written for many years after the church of Christ was established and spread among many nations. For many hundred years after that, the art of printing not having been discovered, the holy scripture could not have been in the hands of many persons; and yet during that time the precious deposit of faith was as well kept as it has been since holy writ is in the hands of everybody. Yes, Sir, and better; everybody cannot read, but everybody, learned or unlearned, can submit to the church, transmitting to both, by the assistance of the Holy Ghost, the doctrine of Christ uncorrupted and in its primitive purity. Here, Sir, is a mode of instruction adapted to everybody's capacity.

A fourth reason is if I must take up my creed by reading scripture, I must be convinced that the book which is put into my hands, and called the holy scripture, is really the genuine scripture, as written by the Apostles; I, a poor illiterate man, not having enjoyed the benefit of a liberal education, hardly acquainted with my own language, how shall I know whether the English bible which you put into my hands is a faithful translation of the original Hebrew and Greek or not. I shall have to take your word for it!

If I do, my faith then is pinned to your sleeve. But no, Sir, I cannot submit to do so, because I find material differences in different translations of the scriptures; of course, I am kept in suspense, if I know of none but a barely human authority in support of each of the different translations.

A fifth reason is that the bible alone affords no security as to faith. For, it is not only concerning the fidelity of the translations, and the true sense of the scriptures, that protestants should entertain the most perplexing doubt; but, they should do the same concerning the very authenticity and inspiration of that sacred volume — Catholics, indeed, have not yet received a satisfactory answer, nor will such an answer, consistently with the principles of protestantism, ever be given to the following questions: how do you know that the different books of the Bible are authentic; how do you know that all of them, and no other books, are to be received as sacred; why do you admit neither more nor less than four gospels, etc.?

Here protestants cannot appeal to the scriptures themselves, because this would be to beg the question, and, moreover, the scriptures are silent on these points.

Neither can they appeal to the testimony of past ages; because they reject the authority of tradition with that of the church, and, in their opinion, the testimony of any body of men is fallible.

Nor to the contents of the sacred books, *viz:* prophecies and divine revelations; because most of these books are merely historical or moral. Moreover, this would suppose as proved, the very fact which is to be proved, *viz:* the authenticity of the scriptures.

Nor to the holy doctrine which they contain, nor to the wonderful effects produced by them; for, *The Spiritual Combat, The Following of Christ, The Sinner's Guide*, etc., contain a most pious doctrine, and have produced most happy effects in innumerable souls; nevertheless, they are, by no means, considered as divine and sacred nor, in fine,

to a certain interior light, or illustration of the Holy
Ghost. The obscurity or simplicity of several books of
the Old and New Testament, the difference of opinions
among protestants on the canonicity of some others;
in a word, both good sense and experience show that
this last reason is to be rejected as quite unfounded,
as a mere illusion.

Thus it is that protestants who cease not to appeal to the
bible, cannot according to their principles, be confident of its
divinity, and find themselves stopped at the very outset. Still
they admit the bible: but why, and on what grounds? Is it
sufficient of itself without the four great characteristics of
the church, *viz:* unity, holiness, catholicity, and apostolicity;
and is it conformable to the great maxim of protestantism,
according to which every body of men is liable to error?

A sixth reason is that on examining the conduct of
protestants, I find it quite at variance with their principles.
A protestant, to be consistent, must neither believe
nor disbelieve anything which he has not previously
discussed. Hence, I would reasonably suppose, that he
has compared his religion with all others that differ from
it, and consequently, is convinced that his own religion
is divine, and all others merely human institutions. But
on the contrary, I find that with very few exceptions,
the protestant believes as he does, because accident has
placed him in the society of protestants. For after having
rejected the tradition of the universal church, he, with
strange inconsistency, implicitly submits to the yoke
of the particular tradition of the society to which he
happens to belong. This, properly speaking, is the only
guide of all, or nearly all, [5] of the reformed sects, with

5. As for those amongst the protestants, who, like the Methodists,
   Quakers, etc., have adopted for their rule of faith immediate and
   private inspiration, they do nothing but wander still farther from
   the right path. For, is it not evident, that such a system is mere fanaticism; quite contrary to every idea which we ought to entertain

regard to every part of their doctrine. In fact, before reading the holy scriptures, in order to form his faith, a protestant, whether he be a Calvinist, an Episcopalian, or a Lutheran, has his belief already formed by the catechism which he learned from his childhood, as well as by the discourses with which his ears have constantly been greeted at home, at school, and in church. When he opens the sacred volume for the first time, he cannot fail to find in every text, the sense commonly affixed to it in his society. The opinions that he has already imbibed, are for him the dictates of the Holy Ghost. If he chanced to understand the scriptures in any other sense, and dared maintain his private interpretation, he would be excommunicated, proscribed, and treated as a heretic.

Such has ever been the conduct of heretics since the first ages. "Those who advise us to examine," says Tertullian, "wish to draw us after them. As soon as we have become their followers, they establish as dogmas, and prescribe with haughtiness, what they had before feigned to submit to our examination" (*de Praescript*, cap. 8). Would not one imagine that Tertullian intended to portray the reformers thirteen hundred years before their birth?

Another proof that the belief of protestants is founded upon their particular tradition is that they repeat, even in our days, the arguments, the impostures, and the calumnies of the first pretended reformers, although a thousand times refuted, and they believe them as the word of God himself.

These are sufficient reasons to induce us to believe that holy writ (although certainly God's word) was not

---

of the wisdom of God, and of his providence with respect to his church; capable of producing as many sects as it has professors, and of leading men into every error and superstition? The experience of all ages, from the time of Montanists down to our own days, evidently confirms what we here assert.

intended to be our supreme judge in matters of faith; and to convince us that Christ has provided us with a living, visible, and supreme authority, to settle all our doubts with regard to the true translation of the scripture, the true sense of it, and likewise with regard to many other essential matters not to be found in holy writ, but delivered by tradition. We believe then, that the Catholic church is this living, visible, and supreme authority; and if we are asked where we believe this authority resides, we answer, in the body of Christ's ministers, the pastors of the Catholic church, united with their head, the Roman pontiff, and the lawful successors of those pastors, whom Jesus Christ appointed, and invested with full authority to discharge the functions of his ministry. To that body of pastors we look for heavenly instructions, in them we see the legates of Jesus Christ, invested by him with the same authority that he himself had received from his heavenly Father, "As the Father hath sent me, I also send you" (Jn. 20:21).

In them we behold the organs of the Holy Ghost, "He that heareth you, heareth me" (Lk. 10:16). "And I will ask the Father, and he shall give you another Paraclete, that he may abide with you forever, the spirit of truth" (Jn. 14:16-17). "But when he, the spirit of truth, shall come, he will teach you all truth" (Jn. 16:13).

Dear Sir, are we then guilty of superstition in putting full confidence in these assertions and promises of Christ, and in thus believing that the spirit of truth never has departed, and never will depart from the pastors of Christ's church? In our pastors we behold men invested with the keys of the kingdom of heaven; that is, with the power of administering absolution or the forgiveness of our sins (Mt. 16:19, 18:18; Jn. 20:23). To them we apply, and from their hands we receive our heavenly and spiritual food, the sacred flesh and blood of Jesus Christ, which he enjoins us to receive (Jn. 6:48, 59); and which he empowers his ministers to procure for us (Lk. 22:19).

Can it be superstition, dear Sir, to believe that our pastors are really in possession of the power, which Christ himself asserts he gave them, and which he promises shall remain with them forever? Since Jesus Christ has pledged his sacred veracity for the existence of those several powers in the pastors of his church, and since he has likewise promised, that the very fountain of truth, the Holy Ghost, shall be, and shall remain with those pastors forever; we should think ourselves guilty of a great sin, if we refused the submission of either our understanding or will, to their decisions and their precepts, and of a most daring presumption, and diabolical pride, if we would, even for one moment, permit our limited reason to sit in judgment over the decisions and precepts of those, whom Jesus Christ thus declares to be guided by the Holy Ghost forever. Seeing then that the pastors of the church of Christ, have always been secured by the infinite power of God, against the danger of being themselves led astray, and of leading those under their care astray into false and erroneous doctrines, we rest secure under their guidance, and knowing that the understanding of the most transcending genius can never penetrate into the mysteries of the most high, we, both learned and unlearned, take the easy and only safe way of submission, that path in which holy writ assures us, that the very fools cannot enter (Isa. 35:8).

It is perhaps necessary to observe, that we do not believe this unerring authority to reside in any individual pastor. No, the pope himself, the successor of St. Peter and the supreme pastor of the Catholic church, is not by any article of Catholic communion believed to be infallible.*6

This unerring authority is by all Catholics believed to reside in the body of the pastors, united with their head.

---

*6. EDITOR'S NOTE: The infallability of the pope was not *precisely* defined until Vatican I, in 1870.

If it does not reside there, it resides nowhere on earth; and the plain promises of Christ are made void, and we left to be tossed to and fro by every wind of doctrine, which Christ meant to prevent by the establishment of pastors (Eph. 4:11, 12, 13, 14).

If we are asked how a body of sinful and fallible men, can give infallible decisions?, we answer, by the power of God. How can there be life in a lump of clay? We find the answer in Genesis "And the Lord God breathed into his face the breath of life, and man became a living soul" (Gen. 2:7).

How can there be infallibility in the decisions of a body of fallible men? We find the answer in John 20:22. He (Jesus Christ) breathed on them, and he said to them, "receive ye the Holy Ghost", etc.

"The weak things of the world hath God chosen, that he may confound the strong" (1Cor. 1:27).

We readily grant that men, even the most learned, are fallible and subject to errors, whilst depending upon their reason, and their learning alone; and for this reason we believe, that not even the most extraordinary talents, improved by the most liberal education that can be obtained upon earth, will ever alone qualify a man for a minister of Christ, a pastor of souls, a spiritual guide to heaven; to pilot us surely and securely through the raging billows of a tempestuous sea, into the harbor of eternal peace. No, dear Sir, this would be for the blind to lead the blind: for, if after nearly six thousand years of unrelenting exertions, human wisdom and philosophy have not been able to penetrate into one of the millions of secrets of this material world, which in a short time will be destroyed by fire: how much less can the limited understandings of even the most elevated geniuses penetrate into the dark recesses of God's sanctuary, where all is mystery? How much less, I say, can they comprehend and explain the profound mysteries of this spiritual world, the church, created for the soul of man, which is to last forever and ever, so long as God shall be God.

Here, then, God in his mercy interposes his infinite power. Wishing to give us sure guides to lead us safely into the harbor of eternal life, Jesus Christ, God-man, by infusing his Holy Spirit of truth into those fallible men, whom he appoints his successors in the ministry, and promising never to take that spirit from them again, supplies at once the want of that knowledge which no genius, no talents, no education, ever will be able to give.

The body of pastors then, being guided by the Holy Ghost, every individual pastor draws his knowledge from that body, from the whole church. The most learned among them is willing to say with Jeremiah the prophet, "Ah, ah, ah, Lord God, behold, I cannot speak, for I am a child" (Jer. 1:6). He is willing to acknowledge the depth of those mysterious truths of religion, in the investigation of which he must stumble at every step, unless directed by an unerring guide. Thus he applies to the decisions of the church, for the true sense of holy writ, for the true doctrine of Christ delivered by tradition, for the knowledge of all those tenets of religion necessary to be known for salvation. Thus, the pastor himself is led, and he is fit to be a pastor only because he is led by an infallible guide, and instead of consulting his limited and fallible reason in the interpretation of scripture, instead of delivering from the pulpit his opinions of the sense of scripture, and calling such fallible opinions the word of God, he gives no instruction to his flock, but what he derives from the decisions of the church, guided by the Holy Spirit of truth. Thus thousands and hundreds of thousands of pastors, scattered over the whole globe, of different nations and tongues, deliver to their respective flocks one and the same doctrine, on all the different parts and mysteries of religion, and this doctrine they deliver not as opinions, but as a matter of certainty; as certain as that God is God. Is it not a pity that things on which our salvation essentially depends should be only matters of opinion? It is my opinion, says one, that children may be saved without Baptism; it is my opinion, says another, that God is too merciful to damn souls forever; I think, says another, that it is immaterial what a person believes, or what religious creed he adopts, so he leads a good life. It is your opinion! And you think! Pray, are you certain? And if you are not certain in matters of such weight, how can you be happy? Good God! Will you leave it to the day of judgment to disclose whether you are right or wrong? Or, will you not rather renounce that fallible guide, your limited and corrupted reason, which never can give certainty in matters of revelation, and apply for spiritual knowledge to the fountain of eternal truth, the holy Catholic church, guided by the Holy Ghost, that you may no longer feed on opinions and uncertainties, but repose in the bosom of certainty.

The true minister of Christ, dear Sir, speaking in the name of his divine master, must speak with authority, with certainty, without any hesitation, on all the different mysteries of religion, on which he is obliged to instruct his flock. Woe to the wretch who shall deliver his private opinions, his own uncertain notions as the word of God; and thus often give poison for wholesome food, the productions of weak and corrupted reason for divine revelations.

The idea which we have of a minister of Christ, you will perceive, is precisely the same that the first Christians must have had. Surely, dear Sir, the church in 1815 must be the same as it was in the beginning: the same kind of pastors, provided with the same powers, administering the same Baptism, the same Eucharist or Lord's supper, in short, all the same sacraments, and preaching the same doctrine. For the words of God are unchangeable (Mk. 13:31); his promises, infallible (2Cor. 1:20); his gifts, without repentance (Rom. 11:29). Jesus Christ intended not to establish different churches, but only one, which being once founded, should last with the same faith, the same prerogatives, the same government, until the end of the world.

The Apostles of Christ, scattered over the globe, preached one and the same doctrine, because Christ was with them (Mt. 28:19-20). The ministers of Christ in 1815, scattered over the globe, preach likewise one and the same doctrine, because Christ is still with them. "I am with you all days, even to the consummation of the world" (Mt. 28:19, 20). The Apostles of Christ received the confessions of the faithful. And many of those who believed, came confessing and declaring their deeds (Acts 19:18). They had received from Jesus Christ the power of forgiving and retaining sins (Jn. 20:22, 23). The ministers of Christ in 1815 likewise hear the confessions of the faithful, because they have no idea that Christ ever deprived them of that power.

Apostles of Jesus Christ proposed as infallible the decisions of the whole church because they knew the church to be guided by the Holy Ghost; witness the first council held at Jerusalem, which settled the question about circumcision, to the decisions of which all submitted. "It has seemed good to the Holy Ghost and to us, to lay no further burden upon you than these necessary things. He (Paul) went through Syria and Cilicia, confirming the churches: commanding them to keep the precepts of the Apostles and the ancients" (Acts 15:28, 41). And again, "As they passed through the cities, they delivered unto them the decrees for to keep, that were decreed by the Apostles and ancients who were at Jerusalem" (Acts 16:4).

The ministers of Christ in 1815 likewise submit to the decisions of the general councils of the church, because they know that the Holy Ghost is as much with the church in 1815, as he was immediately after her institution. "I will ask the Father, and he shall give you another Paraclete, that he may abide with you forever" (Jn. 14:16). In short, Sir, we do not conceive why less spiritual powers should be attributed to the ministry of Christ in 1815, than in the year 100 or 300, etc., for at all times, and in all ages, the ministry is, most assuredly, intended for the same functions, as is evident in Matthew 28:19, 20.

A minister of Christ in 1815 is a preacher of the truth, as well as in the year 100, and the truth, in 1815, is certainly the same as in the year 100. Some, indeed, he gave to be apostles, and some prophets, and others evangelists, and others pastors and teachers, for the perfecting of the saints, for the work of the ministry, for the edifying of the body of Christ: until we all meet in the unity of faith, etc. (Eph. 4:11-13).

A minister of Christ in 1815 is a minister of reconciliation, as well as in the year 100. You will readily allow that men in 1815 are sinners as well as in former years, and therefore stand as much in need as in former years of those heavenly means and remedies, which our blessed Lord sent his Apostles to administer. "Go ye, therefore, and teach all nations, baptizing them in the name of the Father, and of the Son, and of the Holy Ghost" (Mt. 28:19). "Whose sins you shall forgive, they are forgiven them; and whose sins you shall retain, they are retained" (Jn. 20:23). "Let a man look upon us as ministers of Christ, and the dispensers of the mysteries of God" (1Cor. 4:1). Thus by Baptism, they, in 1815, wipe away the stain of original sin, as well as Christ's immediate successors did. Thus also, by absolution, in 1815, they wipe away the stain of actual sin, as well as the ministers first appointed by Christ. It cannot be conceived that Jesus Christ should grant the power of forgiving sins merely in favor of a single generation, and should then (as if repenting of that grant) deprive all future generations of the same favor and benefit; neither can it be believed, as there is not a word from the mouth of Christ in favor of such a belief. We believe then (even from the written word, without reference to the decision of the church) that all the spiritual powers, originally granted by

Christ to his ministers, still continue with his ministers, and will to the consummation of time. And we believe that anyone, not in possession of those spiritual powers, which Christ himself declares he gave his ministers, cannot be a minister of Christ; he may be a gentleman, he may be a man of learning, he may be what you please, but most assuredly he cannot be a minister of Christ. I shall thank you, dear Sir, to point out to me, how, in thus believing, we are guilty of superstition.

Having explained to you, what we believe of the church and the ministry of Jesus Christ, I shall now, in a brief manner, lay before you some of the particular tenets of the holy Catholic church, those I mean which distinguish that church from all others. I begin with confession.

Article Two: Confession

This I know is the great stumbling block for all those, who, within the last three hundred years, have separated from the holy Catholic church. We believe that the ministers of Christ, those whom we call bishops and priests, have received the power of forgiving and retaining sins, which was given to the Apostles according to John 20:22, 23.

Pray, Sir, is it superstition to believe that our omnipotent and merciful God is as able, and as he was willing, to continue that power in 1815, as he was to give it to his first ministers.

If we believed that man, by his own power, could forgive sin, you would be very justifiable in accusing us of superstition: for who can forgive sins but God, or he who has received that power from him.

We believe that confession is necessarily deducible from the grant of the above power. It can not be conceived how a minister of Christ is to exercise his power of forgiving or retaining sins, unless he has an exact knowledge of the state of the sinner's conscience; this knowledge no one can give him but the sinner himself, as probably ninety-nine out of a hundred are sins concealed from the public eye, sins of thoughts, or desires, etc.

The minister of Christ forgives in the name and by the power of Christ; but, he cannot grant absolution of the sins confessed to him without a moral certainty, that such is the inward state of the sinner, such his repentance, such his purpose of amendment, such his willingness to make restitution of property, character, etc., as to entitle him to the mercy of God, and to forgiveness from above.

The objections made against confession and the power of forgiving sins are so futile, the benefits arising from that sacred institution so manifold and so solid, that it cannot be conceived how so many thousands were and are willing to be deprived of so valuable a blessing.

These benefits are so great, that even some of the most relentless enemies of the church could not refuse their encomiums to that holy institution. There is not, perhaps, a wiser institution, says Voltaire in his remarks on the tragedy of Olympia.

This Voltaire, the greatest enemy that the church ever had, who spent his life in ridiculing the holy scriptures and all the institutions of Christ, who declared an open war against Christ; this Voltaire, at the age of eighty–odd, when in his last sickness, sent for a priest to make his confession to him. Confession is an excellent thing, says the *Philosophical Dictionary*, a curb to inveterate wickedness. In the remotest antiquity, confession was practiced in the celebration of all the ancient mysteries; we have imitated and sanctified this wise practice. It is excellent to induce hearts, ulcerated by hatred, to forgive, and to make thieves restore what they have unjustly taken from their neighbor. The Lutherans of the Confession of Augsburg, have preserved that salutary institution. Luther himself would not suffer it to be abolished. Sooner (says he) would I submit to the papal tyranny, than let confession be abolished (*Collection of Luther's German Writings*, Vol. 3, p. 272).

We find the precept of confession given by almighty God to his chosen people.

"Say to the children of Israel, when a man or woman shall have committed any of all the sins that men are wont to commit, and by negligence, shall have transgressed the commandment of the Lord, and offended, they shall confess their sin, and restore the principal itself, and the fifth part over and above" etc. (Num. 5:6, 7).

It does not appear that the power of forgiving sins had been granted by almighty God to the ministers of the old law. The confession ordered to be made under the law of Moses, may then be considered as a preparation and a figure of that required under the law of grace, which we call sacramental confession, as by the power of God and the merits of Christ, it has the grace of forgiveness and reconciliation annexed to it.

We find the practice of confession in the beginning of Christianity. "And many of those who believed, came confessing and declaring their deeds" (Acts 19:18).

We cannot believe that they came to boast of their good deeds; and therefore we understand that they confessed their bad deeds, commonly called sins.

All the holy fathers of the church, from the earliest dawn of Christianity, bear ample testimony to the general practice of confession. It is difficult to conceive how any man could ever have persuaded mankind to submit to a practice so repugnant to flesh and blood, so mortifying to pride, so humiliating to human nature. The universality of this practice, to which the most powerful kings and emperors, the most renowned military commanders, the most exalted geniuses in all ages and in all parts of the world, have cheerfully submitted, establishes in our minds a conviction, beyond the possibility of a doubt, that confession owes its origin to the founder of Christianity. [7]

---

7. With respect to the belief of the early ages, concerning the
   divine institution of confession, it will be sufficient to quote a

The objections against sacramental confession, I repeat it, are so futile, so trifling, as hardly to deserve any answer.

First objection. How can man forgive sins? I answer, by the power of God.

I answer again with our blessed savior, "That you may know that the son of man hath power on earth to forgive sins," etc. (Mt. 9:6). He does not say, That you may know that the son of God has power on earth to forgive sins; to give us to understand that this power, essentially belonging to God alone, is here communicated to man, the minister of God by excellence, and exercised by him in his own person; and again exercised by him in the persons of his ministers, as he sends them, most assuredly, to do what he did, to preach as he did, to administer reconciliation as he did, etc. "All power is given to me in heaven and in earth". Why this preamble, if he did not mean to give them a supernatural power? "Go ye therefore," etc., (Mt. 28:18,

---

few authorities. "Remember," says Tertullian, "that Christ left the keys of heaven to St. Peter, and through him to the church." (*Scorpiaci*, cap 10). "God," says St. Chrysostom, "has not given to angels the power which he has given to priests, who not only regenerate, but afterwards receive the power of forgiving sins" *(Lib. iii. de Sacerdotio)*. It would be needless to quote Origen in Ps. 13; St. Cyprian *(de Lapsis,* cap. 12); St. Ambrose *(Lib. de Poenitentia,* cap. 2 and 8), and many others. I will now cite a passage from Henry VIII in his *Defense of the Sacraments against Luther,* not so much from any importance to be attached to his authority, as from the reasons which he adduces, being obvious to common sense. "Though confession," says he, "should not have been mentioned, nor even a word said about it by the holy fathers, yet, when I see so great a multitude, for so many ages, confessing their sins to priests, I cannot believe nor think otherwise than that the practice was not introduced by human contrivance, but clearly instituted by a divine precept. Confession, therefore, notwithstanding what Luther may say, appears to me, to have been, established, not by any custom of the people, nor by the institution of the fathers, but by God himself."

19). And "receive ye the Holy Ghost; whose sins you shall forgive; they are forgiven," (Jn. 20:22, 23).

Second objection. The institution of confession is a great encouragement to sin, as papists think they have nothing to do, in order to obtain forgiveness, but to relate their sins to a priest.

Answer. The institution of confession misrepresented *is* an encouragement to sin, granted; but surely, Sir, to form a sound judgment on Catholic doctrines it is not to polluted sources you will apply. I do not know the protestant writer who represents them fairly; yet, it is beyond all doubt, that almost all the knowledge, which protestants have of Catholic principles, is derived from protestant books. And pray what do they all say? Beware of Catholic books, beware of popish priests, beware of priestcraft, beware of popish superstition; thus not one protestant out of a hundred ever has an opportunity of knowing the genuine Catholic principles. As Fletcher very justly observes: the little knowledge, which the protestant possesses of our religion, is borrowed entirely from the declamations of pulpit violence, and the misrepresentations of interested prejudice. In general, Catholic principles are exhibited in all the dark colorings of malevolence, and in all the ludicrous shapes of low ribaldry. In Dryden's words:

> A hideous figure of their foes they draw,
> Nor lines, nor looks, nor shades, nor colors true,
> And this grotesque design expose to public view,
> And yet the daubing pleases!

To return to the second objection, I say that confession, far from being an encouragement to sin, is the greatest check, and the greatest remedy against sin.

It is in confession that the sinner discovers to the minister of Christ, the physician of his soul, all his spiritual maladies, his weaknesses, his temptations, his inclinations, his doubts, the scruples of his conscience, his apprehensions, etc.; and it is there he finds comfort, encouragement, advice, instructions, remedies against temptations, in short, everything that is necessary to cause him to forsake the ways of perdition, and with the prodigal son, to return to his father; it is there Sir, he is told of his obligations, it is there he is made sensible of the impossibility of obtaining forgiveness unless he restores what he got by stealing, cheating, usury, or by any kind of injustice, unless he is reconciled with his adversary, unless he forsakes the occasion of sin. It is there he is reminded of the vanity of earthly pleasure, of the shortness of time, of the dreadful punishments prepared for sinners by the infinite justice of God, and of the incomprehensible blessings which the mercy of God has prepared for his saints. It is there, that in the most pathetic strains, the minister of Christ exhorts the sinner to sincere repentance, and exhibits before his eyes the merits and the sacred wounds of his dying savior, to rouse his desponding confidence. Ah! Sir, is this encouragement to sin? Is this superstition? Great God! Your wrath must have been provoked to a very high degree by the abominable sins committed on this polluted earth, when you permitted so many thousands of sinners to be deprived of so valuable a blessing as that derived from sacramental confession.

Yes, Sir, many thousands of sinners — even the most abandoned sinners — have been reclaimed in the tribunal of penance, and by the pious exertions of Christ's ministers brought back to the practice of virtue. There have been instances of sinners dying in the confessional, their hearts breaking with grief at the thoughts of having had the misfortune to offend their merciful God and savior. Thus, according to Christ's declaration (Lk. 7:47), in one moment they expiated, by the perfection of their love, the sins of many years.

I shall here add one remark made by the celebrated author of the *Philosophical Catechism*. A thing well worth observing (says he) and really supernatural and miraculous is the seal or secret of confession, entrusted every day to thousands of priests, some of whom — alas! — ill qualified for their profession, and capable of any other prevarication, and yet so faithfully kept. Scarcely can ALL church history, during a period of more than eighteen hundred years, furnish one example of infidelity in this point, even among those who, like Luther and Calvin, turned apostates to the church. If anyone reflects on the inconsistency of mankind, on the curiosity of some, and the loquacity and indiscretion of others, on the nature and importance of the affairs entrusted to confessors, the revelation of which would often have astonishing effects, on the means which various interests, avarice, jealousy and other passions fail not to try in order to compass their ends, there will remain no doubt, but that God watches over the preservation of his work (*Philosophical Catechism*, vol. 3, chap. 7 art. 1).

I cannot forbear recommending, for your perusal, a book not very long since published in the city of New York, entitled, *The Catholic Question in America.*

You will there find what respect was paid to that venerable institution (sacramental confession) by a protestant court of justice, at which presided the honorable De Witt Clinton. The Rev. Dr. Kohlman, a Catholic priest in the city of New York, was, by that sacrament, an instrument of restoring stolen property to its owner. Certain persons had been previously arrested on suspicion, and a prosecution instituted against them; and Dr. Kohlman, after restoring the stolen property to its owner, was summoned to give in evidence, and required to disclose the person or persons from whom he had received it. He, in a most respectful manner, stated to the court that not having any knowledge of the theft by any natural or common way of information, it being solely acquired by sacramental confession, it was his duty to suffer any punishment, even death itself, rather than divulge the knowledge acquired in that way. The court unanimously decided in his favor; and, there being no evidence against the defendants, they were acquitted.

In that same book you will find a complete treatise on sacramental confession, wherein by the most respectable testimonies from the holy fathers, it is clearly proved that sacramental confession owes its origin to the divine founder of our holy religion, and has been practiced from the earliest dawn of Christianity, and in all ages of the church, down to our present times. From this short explanation, which I have given, of the Catholic doctrine of confession, you will candidly acknowledge, dear Sir, that the practice of sacramental confession, far from being superstitious, is a very useful one. I shall now explain what the Catholic church teaches and commands us to believe with regard to the holy Eucharist.

Article Three:

The Eucharist, or Lord's Supper.

It is sufficient to read the words of Christ in the gospel to form an accurate idea of what the Catholic church believes on that important subject.

Jesus Christ says, "I am the bread of life" (Jn. 6:5, 48). "I am the living bread, which came down from heaven; if any man eat of this bread, he shall live forever; and the bread which I will give, is my flesh, for the life of the world" (Jn. 6:51, 52). "Unless you eat the flesh of the Son of man, and drink his blood, you shall not have life in you. He that eateth my flesh, and drinketh my blood hath everlasting life; and I will raise him up at the last day. For my flesh is meat indeed, and my blood is drink indeed." "He that eateth my flesh, and drinketh my blood, abideth in me, and I in him." "As the living Father hath sent me, and I live by the Father; so he that eateth me, the same also shall live by me" (Jn. 6:54, 58).

Here you see in plain words what we believe on the subject of the Eucharist. We believe that Jesus Christ is the living bread, the food of our immortal souls (Jn. 6:35, 48). We believe that we must feed on the sacred flesh and blood of Christ, in order to obtain eternal life (Jn. 6:54, 55). We believe that the flesh of Christ and the blood of Christ are our spiritual food indeed, and not in figure (58); and finally, that in the holy Eucharist we receive Jesus Christ himself, the spiritual food of our souls (58).

Divine mysteries being impervious to human reason, we do not arrogate to ourselves the right of philosophizing on the present mystery, nor do we make ourselves uneasy about the means, by which Christ is to enable us to accomplish what he here requires. We do not ask with the Jews: "How can this man give us his flesh to eat?" But with Simon Peter we say, "Lord, to whom shall we go; thou hast the words of eternal life" (Jn. 6:69). Surely, Sir, we ought not to be blamed for believing that Christ meant what he said.

The Jew may be scandalized, the philosopher may smile in his self-sufficiency, but the Catholic, with the humility of a child, submits, not knowing what it is to reason upon impenetrable mysteries. He may stand in silent raptures of astonishment at the depth of God's unfathomable wisdom, but he does not know what it is to doubt, and he has that comfort to know, that before the tribunal of Christ he will be able to bring the very words of Christ in evidence of the orthodoxy of his belief.

Pray, Sir, laying aside all prejudice, will you say that Christ, on the great day of retribution, will condemn me as guilty of superstition for believing precisely what he tells me, *viz:* that I must receive his living flesh and blood; that I really receive both in the blessed Eucharist; that I receive

Christ himself according to his own repeated declaration? You will hardly say so.

On the other hand, what excuse, what plea will anyone have, who, notwithstanding Christ's positive declaration, can see nothing in the sacrament but bread and wine?

Christ said, "you must eat my flesh and drink my blood"; no, no, says limited reason, for how can Christ give us his flesh to eat? Christ says, "my flesh is meat indeed, and my blood is drink indeed". No, no, says corrupted reason, it cannot be so indeed, it must be meant as a figure only. Christ says: "he that eateth me shall live by me". What (says limited reason) what! Eat Christ? That is absurd. That cannot be. And thus does man's corrupted reason do away and make void the sacred words of Christ, and substitute a shadow, a mere nothing, for the most precious gift that Jesus Christ ever bestowed on man.

To a superficial mind there is perhaps something specious in these dictates of limited reason. But, Sir, we must remember that to understand and explain divine mysteries, is not the province of human reason. If we are justifiable in rejecting one mystery, because it is beyond the limits of reason, then we may, nay — in order to be consistent — we ought to reject all divine mysteries as beyond the same limits. Thus we ought to expunge from our creed the mystery of the Trinity and of the Incarnation, the very fundamental principles of the Christian religion. Who indeed, can conceive how there are three really distinct persons in God, and every one of them God, and yet that there is but one God? Even the existence of a God invisible and immense; in every place whole and entire, and yet but one; even the existence of that God, I say, ought to be rejected, if we are justifiable in rejecting any mystery on account of its being impervious to limited reason. Here I would beg leave to observe, that a distinction ought to be made between a thing being against reason and being above reason. If a thing is really against sound reason, we cannot submit to believe it, neither would almighty God require it, as in doing so, he would contradict his own work, which is impossible. If a thing is above reason, that is, beyond the limits of the human understanding: this is by no means a proof of its being false.

With regard to the present mystery, then, if it is really against sound reason, Christ cannot and will not require a belief of it; if it is only beyond the limits of reason, it ought to be believed where the words of Christ are plain. Nay, Sir, its being impervious to reason stamps on it a character of divinity, which essentially belongs to the works of God.

Revelation, similar to the pillar of fire, which the Israelites followed in the desert, has its dark side; but it has likewise its luminous side, whence emanate the purest and brightest rays of truth. In vain would human reason endeavor to penetrate into the dark recesses of the sanctuary; a veil hangs before it, and in granting us the blessing of revelation, it certainly was the will of God to supply the wants, the insufficiency of reason was the will of the Most High, that to him, with the most profound humility, we should make a sacrifice, not of reason itself, but of that vain and presumptuous confidence which we are too apt to have in the dictates of our limited reason. As Mr. Voltaire observes, reason conducts you; advance by its light, proceed a few steps more; but limit your career; on the brink of the infinite, stop short, there an abyss begins, which you must respect.

The most common things, says the celebrated Locke, have their dark sides, where the most piercing eye cannot penetrate; many difficulties are found in natural religion.

Conceive, if you can, how anything can be created out of nothing; how God is present everywhere without being confined by space; conceive what eternity is; conceive, if you can, how in a living man, soul and body are joined together. Is it a wonder then, if in revealed religion, in

God's sanctuary, many mysteries are found, exceeding
the reach of human comprehension, and which it would
even be impious to attempt to fathom the mysteries of
revelation [that] bear no proportion to the measure of
human understanding. Reason leads you to the door of the
sanctuary, but there it leaves you. Reason is now silent and
God speaks, man listens and adores. He sees evidently that
he should believe; he hears God distinctly dictate mysteries,
which he commands him to believe and to revere; but he
understands not those mysteries, which he is commanded
to revere. He is even more satisfied than if he understood
what forms the object of his belief: because, what man's
limited understanding can comprehend, appears to be less
awful, less worthy the divine greatness, than what human
wisdom cannot penetrate.

To return to the mystery of the Eucharist, we grant,
it is, in a great measure, incomprehensible; the most learned
of our divines do not pretend to comprehend it. But, Sir,
it is evident, that God here speaks, and that he speaks in
the most unequivocal terms, that he repeatedly makes use
of the very same expressions: my flesh, my blood, etc. It
is evident that Christ at the last supper tells his Apostles,
Take and eat, etc. This is my body, etc. Drink ye all of this,
etc. This is my blood. It is evident then that we must listen
and adore. A positive refusal to believe would be downright
impiety. But, Sir, if we permit our limited reason to sit in
judgment on the mysteries of revelation, we may soon,
by arbitrary interpretations, get rid of them all; and thus
a belief, framed by the interpretation of limited reason,
amounts to a real and positive refusal to believe. In the
present instance, what could justify us in asserting that in
the Eucharist nothing is given, nothing is received, but bread
and wine? Surely not the words of Christ, for his words and
his repeated words are plainly: my flesh, my blood; surely
not the impossibility of receiving the flesh and blood of
Christ, for it is certainly as easy for Jesus Christ to feed

our immortal souls with his own flesh, as it was for him to assume that sacred flesh. It is as easy for him to conceal his sacred flesh and blood under the forms or appearances of bread and wine, as it is easy for him to conceal his glorious divinity, although everywhere present, from our eyes.

Surely it will not be said that our belief is unreasonable. God is so great, so magnificent, so wonderful in his works; he has done such stupendous things for the happiness of man, that nothing how great, how mysterious, soever, proceeding from so great a God appears to us unreasonable to believe.

Our immortal souls are the images of the eternal Father. Our immortal souls are redeemed by the merits of the divine Son, and washed in his sacred blood.

It is for the sake of those immortal souls that the divine Son assumed human flesh and blood and during thirty-three years, was willing to lead a life of sufferings, and to subject himself to all the torments which the malice of hell and earth combined chose to inflict upon him. It was for the sake of our immortal souls that the divine Son offered his sacred flesh and blood as a victim of propitiation to be immolated on the cross.

Our immortal souls then must be truly great, truly precious, in the sight of God, when so much was done for them. Is it then unreasonable to believe, after all this, that nothing less than the flesh and blood of a God-man is found by our great and merciful God worthy to afford spiritual food and nourishment to those immortal souls, especially as this flesh and blood by being sacrificed, became the life of those souls, which by sin were dead to eternal life?

Will it be found unreasonable to believe that Christ meant precisely what he said? Surely, he came to instruct and not to deceive. When he saw that the Jews were scandalized, and asked, "How can this man give us his flesh to eat?", was not this the opportunity to undeceive them, and to explain himself; in short, to say, I do not mean that you shall eat my flesh and drink my blood, or in other

words, I do not mean what I said. Instead of this, we find
Jesus Christ, after a double amen, insisting no less than six
times in the most unequivocal manner upon the necessity
of receiving his flesh and blood; we find Jesus Christ, at
the last supper, taking bread and wine, and having blessed
them, giving them to his Apostles, and saying, "Take ye
and eat, this is my body, drink ye all of this, is my blood."
We find the great St. Paul (1Cor. 10:16; 11:23, 29) making
use of the very same expressions, and condemning the
unworthy receiver for not discerning the Lord's body.
Surely, Sir, we could not be required to discern the body of
Christ, were it not in the Eucharist.

We afterwards find the whole church of Christ, during
eighteen centuries, that is, during almost fifteen hundred
years before the pretended reformation, and three hundred
after it, believing and teaching everywhere that the flesh
and blood of Christ are received in the holy Eucharist.

In the first age of the church, St. Ignatius, disciple
of St. John the Evangelist, bishop of Antioch and martyr,
speaks in the following manner of certain heretics of his
time: "They abstain from the holy Eucharist and oblation,
because they do not acknowledge the Eucharist to be the
flesh of our savior Jesus Christ, which suffered for our sins"
(*Epist. ad Smyrn*). Therefore, it is not the mere figure of the
body of Christ, as protestants say, but his flesh itself.

In the second age, St. Justin Martyr has the
following plain words: "As Jesus Christ incarnate had
flesh and blood for our salvation, so are we taught, that
the Eucharist is the flesh and blood of the same Jesus
incarnate" (*Apolog. 2 ad Antonium*).

In the third age, St. Cyprian says, the bread, which
our Lord gave to his disciples, being changed, not in shape,
but in nature, by the omnipotence of the word, is made
flesh (*Serm. de Coena Domini*).

In the same age, the learned Origen says, "In the old
law, the manna was meat in an enigma, but now the flesh

of God is meat in reality, as himself says: 'my flesh is meat indeed'" *(Horn. 1. in Levit).*

In the same age again, Tertullian, the great champion and defender of the faith, says, "the bread taken and distributed to his disciples, he made his body" (*Book 4 Against Marcion,* ch. 40).

In the fourth age, St. Ambrose says, "Before it be consecrated, it is but bread, but when the words of consecration come, it is the body of Christ" (*Book 4 of the Sacram.* ch. 5).

In the same age, St. Gregory of Nyssa bears testimony to the same truth, "We truly believe, even by the word of God, that the sanctified bread is changed into the body of God" (*Orat. Catechist* ch. 37).

Also, St. Cyril of Jerusalem, in his fourth *Catechetical Instruction,* says, "Since Christ himself has said of the bread, this is my body, who will, henceforth dispute it? And since he himself has said, 'this is my blood', who will dare entertain any doubt, and say, that it is not his blood? On a former occasion, he changed water into wine, at Cana of Galilee; shall we then consider him less worthy of credit, when he changes wine into blood? Do not judge by the taste, but by faith, and be assured beyond all doubt that what appears to be bread, is not bread, but the body of Christ; and what appears to be wine, is not wine, but the blood of Christ." Could the doctor more clearly express the real presence, or more forcibly exclude the mere figure?

And also St. John Chrysostom, bishop of Constantinople, says, "he that sits above with his Father, even in the same instant of time gives himself to all such as are willing to receive him," etc., "whereas Christ leaving his flesh to us, yet ascending to heaven, there also he hath it" *(L. de Sacerd).*

The same in his sixtieth homily, to the people of Antioch, has the following words: "What pastor feeds his sheep with his own blood! But, what do I say? Pastor! Many mothers there are, who after having suffered the pains of labor, give their babes to strangers to nurse. This Jesus Christ would not suffer, but he feeds us himself, and that with his own blood."

In the fifth age, St. Augustine, that great luminary of the church, and a convert from the Manichean heresy, in his sermon on the 33rd Psalm, makes use of the following expressions: "How David could be carried in his own hands, we find not, but in Christ we do, for he was earned in his own hands, when giving his body, he said, this is my body; for then he carried that body in his own hands etc.".

In short, Sir, it is evident, that in all ages, down to the pretended reformation, the real presence of Christ in the Eucharist has been believed by all Christendom. It is evident, that the same belief has continued throughout the whole Catholic world to our present days.

It is evident that such has always been, likewise, the constant belief of the eastern or Greek church. See the testimonials of seven archbishops of the Greek church, in a book entitled *Perpetuite de la Foi* (vol. 3, p. 569), the testimonies of the archbishops and clergy of the Archipelago (p. 572); of four patriarchs of Constantinople, of the patriarch of Alexandria, and of thirty-five metropolitans or archbishops (*anno* 1672, ch. 6, p. 623); of the churches of Georgia and Mingrelia (ch. 7, p. 634); of the patriarch of Jerusalem, etc. Such is the faith of the Armenians, Moscorites, Syrians, Copts, Maronites, Russians, etc. [8] This

---

8. These testimonies and several similar ones are to be found, not only in that learned work, *La Perpetuite de la Foi*, but also in the *Amicable Discussion*, in the *Letters of a Catholic Doctor to a Protestant Gentleman*, by F. Scheffmacher, and in the *Literal and Dogmatical Explanation of the Ceremonies of the Mass*, by F. Le Bran. They have all the characteristics of authenticity that can be desired, accompanied with the signatures not only of the Oriental bishops, but also of the ambassadors of different European nations. It may be proper here to mention why and how they were obtained. About the middle of

truth appeared so evident to Luther himself that he never could get over it. His words are very remarkable. "If any man (says he) could have convinced me five years ago, that in the sacrament there is nothing but bread and wine, he had wonderfully obliged me, for with great anxiety did I examine this point, and labor with all my force to get clear of the difficulty, because by this means, I knew very well, I should terribly incommode the papists. But I find I am caught without hopes of escaping, for the text of the gospel is so clear, as not to be susceptible of misconstruction." [9]

---

the 17th century, the celebrated Nicolius had composed, in favor of the real presence, a work, in which he adduces, among other proofs, that taken from the constant and unanimous belief of all Christian churches, the reformed ones alone being excepted. As the protestant divines continued to maintain that the eastern churches held the same belief as themselves concerning the Eucharist, different ambassadors and consuls were requested to ascertain the fact. Having, agreeably to the request, made the necessary inquiries, they sent to France the professions of faith of the patriarchs, archbishops, and bishops of the different Oriental churches. All, without exception, expressed themselves in the most positive terms in favor of the real presence which they declared to be their doctrine, and complained of the calumnies heaped on them by the Calvinists who had charged them with holding the contrary; whereas, they condemned it as heretical, and anathematized those who dared maintain it.

9. Luther held Christ to be really present together with the bread in the sacrament, as iron and fire are united in a red-hot bar. This sort of presence is called consubstantiation, and is surely as incomprehensible as the Catholic doctrine of transubstantiation. Calvin himself asserted, against Luther, that the doctrine of Catholics was more conformable to scripture than his. Now, though it is evident that all the difficulties and alleged absurdities attributed to the Catholic doctrine equally attach to the Lutheran, yet what preacher has ever attacked the latter, or what civil disabilities has it brought on its followers, while the former has constantly been a subject of profane ridicule for

Later reformers were not so scrupulous, but soon got over the difficulty, by cutting the Gordian knot.

This indeed, is an easy way to get over all the difficulties we meet in the gospel, a way pretty generally followed by the philosophers of the day. But, dear Sir, I hope you will not accuse us of superstition for taking a safer way, that of simply believing, even where we cannot understand how! In believing the real presence of Christ in the Eucharist, in believing that we receive the flesh and blood of Christ; in believing that we receive Christ himself, in believing that the substance of the flesh and blood of Christ; so far from being guilty of superstition, we have the satisfaction to know that we believe precisely what Christ commands us to believe, what almost all Christendom, these eighteen hundred years, always did believe, and what at present, by far the greatest part of the Christian world, above two hundred millions, including the Greek church, do believe.

I will suppose for a while, Sir, that I am wavering, perplexed, uncertain what to believe on the subject of the Eucharist, and that I apply to you as a minister of Christ in order to have my doubts resolved, my difficulties removed, and certainty fixed in my mind. What would you

---

its enemies, and in some countries, for example, Great Britain, a pretext for depriving its followers of their natural rights? This strange difference of conduct must excite the surprise of every reflecting mind. But, as the celebrated statesman, Canning, well observed, in a debate on the Catholic Question, April 21, 1825, "Sympathy is quite the other way now," continued he, "what is it that we object to in the Catholic belief? One doctrine is that of transubstantiation. Yet, do we not admit into our religious creed that other doctrine, consubstantiation? Which, if anyone read Luther's polemic discourse on this subject, he will perceive it to bear so strong an affinity or relationship to the former, as not to be able to ascertain very easily their discrepancy or difference. Yet the opponent to the Catholic claims will consider the man who professes to believe in consubstantiation a faithful subject, and denounce the other as a traitor."

tell me, what security could you offer in order to induce me to reject the overwhelming weight of authority which undoubtedly favors the Catholic doctrine of the Eucharist, and to persuade me that I ought to believe there is nothing in the sacrament but bread and wine? You will appeal to my senses, my eyes, my taste, etc. I confess indeed Sir, that the senses of my body discover nothing in the sacrament but bread and wine, and that I do not see, nor taste the flesh and blood of Christ. But Sir, Christ tells me, blessed are they that have not seen and have believed (Jn. 20:29).

I would then incline to say with St. Thomas Aquinas:

> *Visus, tactus, gustus in te fallitur*
> *Sed auditu solo tuto creditur*
> *Credo quidquid dixit Dei filius*
> *Nil hoc Verbo veritatis verius.*

> Not to sight, or taste, or touch be credit,
> Hearing only do we trust secure,
> I believe, for God the Son has said it —
> Word of truth that shall ever endure.

With nearly all Christendom for eighteen centuries, I will sooner believe the testimony of my divine savior than the testimony of my senses; to speak more correctly, I am not obliged to disbelieve the testimony of my senses, for you know, Sir, that what we perceive of anything by our senses, is not the substance of the thing itself, but mere accidents, such as form, color, taste, size. Now it is very evident that God, to whom nothing is impossible, may very easily change the substance of a thing and yet continue the accidents, or cause it to make upon my senses the same impression which it did before. This is precisely what the Catholics believe of the Eucharist.

Good God! Shall we say that Christ has no other way to make his words good, and to give us his flesh and blood, than to reach them to us in their natural form or appearance? Humanity shudders at the thought, and common sense naturally suggests the reason why that sacred food of our souls is given us under the form of the most simple food of the body. You will tell me, perhaps, that according to our doctrines, the body of Christ must be present in a great many places at the same time, which is impossible.

In answer to this objection, I refer you to the system of the most celebrated protestant philosopher, Mr. Leibnitz, who, besides many others, from the most generally acknowledged principles of metaphysics, and from observations made in natural philosophy, clearly shows that this seeming mystery, the existence of the same body in many places, cannot be proved impossible. But, Sir, admitting it to be impossible for a body in its present corruptible state, can the same be said of a glorified body, which St. Paul calls a spiritual body? Can it be said especially of the glorified body of Christ? Pray, Sir, do you know anything at all about the nature of glorified bodies? I must confess I do not; and whilst we are totally ignorant about the nature of a glorified or spiritual body, it appears to me vain to form any opinion about what is possible or impossible for such a body. When I see the glorified body of Christ passing through a door which was shut (Jn. 20:19), I am willing to believe, that the same body may be present in thousands and millions of places at once; I am willing to believe that that same body may feed my soul, and yet continue glorious in heaven, if such is the will of God, although I cannot comprehend, far less explain how it can be.

Archbishop Cranmer owns that Christ may be in the bread and wine, as also in the doors that were shut (*Answer to Gardner & Smith*, p. 454).

Melancthon says, "I would rather die than affirm that Christ's body can be but in one place."

I am sensible, Sir, that human reason once seated on the tribunal to judge of the truth or falsehood of revealed mysteries, and guided only by itself, will find a great many more objections. But, Sir, as the raging waves, after having beaten against the majestic rock which rises from the bottom of the sea, return in harmless froth; so likewise will all the weak productions of human reason, when beating against the majestic fabric which Christ has raised.

I beg leave here to quote the testimony of three celebrated protestant divines in favor of the Catholic doctrine: "The adoration of the Eucharist," says Mr. Thorndike, "was the practice of the ancient and true church, before receiving" (*Epil. L.* 53. c. 30 4). "And I," says the protestant Bishop Andrews, "with St. Ambrose, adore the flesh of Christ in the mysteries" (*Andrews to Bel.* ch. 8). "The external adoration of Christ in the Eucharist," says the protestant Bishop Forbes, "is the practice of sounder protestants, and to deny such adoration is a monstrous error of rigid protestants" (*Forbes de Euchar. L.* 2). [10]

---

10. A striking difference may be observed in the style of protestant controvertists. Those among them who have been deservedly ranked the first for talents, learning, and good sense, are much more temperate in their language, than others who, in the estimation of the public, fall far short of them in the above qualities. In writers of the latter class, do we so often find such expressions as: the dogma of the real presence is absurd; the adoration of Christ in the sacrament is idolatrous and superstitious. The example of wiser and better men should make them pause before they indulge in the effusions of rashness or malevolence. Before exposing themselves to the danger of blaspheming that which they know not; first, they should reflect that God can reveal nothing absurd; and, secondly, they should fully and impartially examine the proofs of God's having revealed the dogma which they deride. Were our opponents to proceed thus, they would regard the real presence as an adorable mystery, instead of rejecting it as absurd. For what greater evidence of its divine revelation can be required than the authority of the scriptures, the doctrine of the Apostles, the testimony of all ages, and the consent of all Christian nations until the epoch of the reformation, and, even now, the protestants alone excepted? Finally, the belief of the church in her origin, and the ages immediately succeeding, when her doctrine is allowed to have been pure, and the impossibility that this dogma, if not divinely

You will object, perhaps, [to] the following words of Christ: "It is the spirit that quickeneth, the flesh profiteth nothing; the words that I have spoken to you, are spirit and life" (Jn. 6:64).

St. Augustine, who lived about fourteen hundred years ago, explains these words in his twenty-seventh treatise

---

revealed, could have obtained so firm and constant belief, render it certain that it must have come from Jesus Christ himself. The following questions and answers are taken from *A German Lutheran Catechism*, printed in Chambersburg, in 1815, by Johann Herschberger, for William Warner, bookseller, of Baltimore.

Q. What is the last supper of our Lord Jesus Christ? A. The last supper of Christ is a holy sacrament, a godly word and sign, in which Christ gives us truly and substantially, with bread and wine, his body and blood, and assures us of the forgiveness of our sins, and life everlasting.

Q. What do you receive, eat, and drink in the holy last supper? A. With bread and wine, I do eat and drink the true body and the true blood of Jesus Christ, as St. Paul says: "The chalice which we bless, is it not the communion of the blood of Christ? And the bread which we break, is it not the communion of the body of Christ?" (1Cor. 10:16).

And again, from the 5th article on the sacrament of the altar. Q. What is the sacrament of the altar? A. It is the true body and blood of our Lord Jesus Christ in the bread and wine, for us Christians to eat and drink, instituted by Christ himself (1Cor. 10:16, 17, 11:23, 29).

In both catechisms, the doctrine of the real presence is evidently implied by the words, taken in their obvious sense, as they ought to be, since catechetical instruction, being designed for the young and ignorant, and therefore adapted to the capacity of such, are naturally supposed to contain the plainest exposition of what is to be believed. It may, at first, appear strange, that protestants should, in their language, approach so near to Catholic doctrine. The reason of this is that our doctrine is so conformable to scripture, that they, though differing from us in sentiments, yet affect to hold nearly the same language as we, in order to avoid the palpable contradiction of their professed rule of following the scriptures in their plain and literal sense.

on St. John: "What means, the flesh profits nothing, says St. Augustine? It profits nothing as they understood it for they understood flesh, as it is torn in pieces in a dead body, or sold in the shambles; and not as it is, animated by the spirit. Wherefore it is said the flesh profiteth nothing, in the same manner as it is said knowledge puffeth up (1Cor. 8:1). Must we then fly from knowledge? God forbid. What then means knowledge puffeth up? That is, if it be alone without charity; therefore, the Apostle added, but charity edifies. Join therefore charity to knowledge, and knowledge will be profitable, not by itself, but through charity; so here also the flesh profiteth nothing, viz; the flesh alone. Let the spirit be joined with the flesh, as charity is to be joined with knowledge, and then it profits much. For if the flesh profiteth nothing, the Word (Christ) would not have been made flesh, that he might dwell in us." So far St. Augustine.

Besides flesh and blood is often mentioned in scripture for the corruption of our nature, as when it is said, "flesh and blood cannot inherit the kingdom of God" (1Cor. 15:50); and "flesh and blood hath not revealed it unto thee" (Mt. 16:17). And in this sense the flesh profiteth nothing to discover and firmly believe what Christ announces; but it is the spirit and grace of God that quicken and giveth life to our souls, by inspiring us with a full assent and obedience to divine revelation. Faith is undoubtedly a gift of heaven, and that we may not be deterred by our corrupted reason and senses from believing divine mysteries, we need the light and assistance of God himself. This our divine savior plainly declares in these words: "Therefore did I say to you, that no man can come to me, unless it be given him by my Father" (Jn. 6:66). So that the foregoing words the flesh profiteth nothing, rather suppose and confirm the truth of the real presence.

But God forbid that we should say the flesh of Christ profits nothing; this would be a blasphemy, and it is evident that Christ asserting that flesh profits nothing, did not mean his flesh, for this would be contradicting his own assertion: "my flesh is meat indeed."

Our doctrine on the Eucharist is further confirmed by the ancient figures or types of that sacrament. They were manifold. I shall notice only three of them, *viz:* the paschal lamb, the blood of the testament, and the manna.

1. The paschal lamb. That this was a figure of Christ, the Lamb of God, is acknowledged on all hands. The paschal lamb was killed at the going out of the land of Egypt on the journey to the land of promise. The Lamb of God is killed, and we are delivered from a more-than-Egyptian darkness, and introduced into the road to the real land of promise.

The paschal lamb is eaten (Exod. 12:8); so likewise must the Lamb of God be eaten to accomplish the figure. The paschal lamb had no blemish (Exod. 12:5); the Lamb of God is pure and immaculate by excellence. The blood of the paschal lamb was a sign of salvation (Exod. 12:13): The blood of the Lamb of God is salvation itself. The sacrament of the Eucharist was instituted by our savior immediately after eating the paschal lamb with his disciples. The figure was then accomplished, and the substance substituted for the figure.

2. That the blood of the testament, the blood of victims solemnly sacrificed to God, was a figure of the blood of Christ in the sacrament, appears evident from the words of Christ in administering that sacred blood.

Moses said to the people, "This is the blood of the testament, which God hath enjoined to you" (Exod. 24:8: Heb. 9:20). Jesus Christ said to his disciples, "This is my blood of the new testament" (Mt. 26:26).

3. That manna was a figure of the sacrament of the flesh and blood of Christ, appears in John (6:58), "Your fathers did eat manna and are dead; he that eateth of this bread shall live forever" — likewise, in 1 Corinthians (10:3).

manna came from the Lord (Exod. 16:15). The holy Eucharist is also given by our Lord and savior (Mt. 26).

Manna was given to the Israelites as their food during the whole time of their journey through the desert until they reached the land of promise. The holy Eucharist is given to us as the spiritual food and nourishment of our souls, during the whole time of our mortal pilgrimage, until we reach the true land of promise, our heavenly home. We cannot believe, dear Sir, that the figure is better than the thing it represents; St. Paul tells us on the contrary, that the old law had nothing but "a shadow of good things to come" (Heb. 10), "that all its sacrifices and sacraments were but weak and beggarly elements" (Gal. 4:9), and that "it was annulled, by reason of its weakness and unprofitableness" (Heb. 7:18).

Now, Sir, if the sacrament of the Lord's supper is nothing but bread and wine, it is evident that the figure — manna — is far better than the thing prefigured; for manna comes from heaven; bread comes from the baker's oven. Manna had a very pleasant taste, and was in many respects miraculous; our bread is a common and natural food.

I have said enough, I think, to convince you, dear Sir, that we are not guilty of superstition in believing as we do, on the subject of the holy Eucharist, and that our belief on that subject is founded on the plainest words of divine revelation, and not contradicted by reason: add to this, that it is supported by the greatest authority on earth.

Admitting for a while that the words of Christ were not very plain, or were susceptible of different interpretations, where are we to apply in order to know with certainty the true sense of the words? Are we to adopt the sentiments of any of the reformers? If so, which are we to select for our guide? Luther held that the bread is the body of Christ; Osiander, that the bread is one and the same person with Christ; Calvin, Zuinglius, etc., that it is only a figure of the body of Christ. Nay, so far did this diversity of opinions go, that after little more than half a century from the commencement of the reformation, controvertists counted not less than two hundred different interpretations of the words, "This is my body." The numerous sects of the present day are not less at variance with one another with respect to this point. What other effect then can such contrariety of belief have, than to bring more strongly to our recollection that observation of Tertullian: It is natural for error to be ever changing. But Christ tells us to apply to the church, which he has provided with the unerring light of truth forever. This holy church commands us to believe that in the Eucharist, as given by Christ at the last supper, and as consecrated since by legally ordained ministers, are really contained the flesh and blood, the soul and divinity of Jesus Christ Christ, God and man (Council of Trent, *de Euchar. Sacram. Sess.* 13, c. 1,2).

The words used by the confession of Augsburg seem to convey the very same idea. The true body and blood of Jesus Christ are truly present under the form of bread and wine in the Lord's supper, and are there given and received.

Were we to judge from the approved catechisms of several protestant sects, they would seem to hold the same doctrine. The church of England in her catechism, declares that the body and blood of Christ are verily and indeed taken and received by the faithful in the Lord's supper.

A seemingly weighty objection against the real presence of Christ in the Eucharist is found in the following words of our savior, "Do this for a commemoration of me" (Lk. 22:19); and in the words of St. Paul, "...as often as you shall eat . . . and drink . . . you shall show the death of the Lord until he come" (1Cor. 11:26).

We do not understand how those words can be considered as excluding the real presence of Christ. Whilst man is in his present state of imperfection, carnal, weak, under the influence of his senses, of his imagination, and of so many passions, he is very apt, even whilst engaged in the most solemn of all duties, saying his prayers, or celebrating the divine mysteries, to forget himself, and to perform those duties, through habit, mechanically, and of course, without benefit to himself.

Because Christ — the subject of our adoration — is not visible in the Eucharist, our attention may very easily be diverted from him to created objects, which affect our senses or imaginations, when we celebrate those mysteries. In order to guard us against that misfortune, we are particularly commanded to direct our attention to our divine savior, to his death upon the cross; we are not to receive his flesh and blood mechanically, but, whilst we receive them, to remember the infinite love of Jesus Christ in immolating that sacred flesh and blood for our salvation, and in feeding our souls with the same.

The command then to remember the death of Christ when we celebrate and receive the Lord's supper so far from excluding the real presence of Christ, is rather founded upon it.

Having now explained to you, dear Sir, the doctrine of the Catholic church concerning the blessed Eucharist, this leads me naturally to the explanation of the sacrifice of the Mass.

Article Four: The Sacrifice of the Mass

It is in the Mass that the holy Eucharist is consecrated. The main objection against this sacrifice is its being considered a second sacrifice, whereas it is acknowledged by all Christians that the sacrifice of the cross, in which Jesus Christ immolated himself for the salvation of our souls, is the only sacrifice of the new law, and a very sufficient one, as by it, and by it alone, the redemption of man was consummated and God's justice satisfied.

The objection arises from a misunderstanding. The Mass, so far from being a second sacrifice, is only a continuation — and at the same time, a commemoration — of the great sacrifice of the cross.

Do this in commemoration of me, says Christ at the last supper to his Apostles, and, of course, to their successors. It is in the Mass, dear Sir, that this precept of Christ is fulfilled. It is there that the bread and wine are consecrated; and by consecration, changed into the body and blood of Christ. In this consecration the blood is mystically separated from the body — as Jesus Christ did separately consecrate the bread into his body, and the wine into his blood — which includes a striking representation and commemoration of that real and violent separation, which took place upon the cross.

By this consecration, as I have shown before, Jesus Christ becomes really present upon the altar under those signs or forms which represent his death.

Now Jesus Christ being present in the Eucharist, by virtue of the consecration which he himself appointed, "presents himself", says St. Paul, and "appears for us, before the face of God" (Nah. 9:24). Here then is a continuation of the great sacrifice of the cross; here Jesus Christ continues to present to his heavenly Father the merits of his passion and death; he perpetuates the memory of his obedience, even to the death of the cross which includes an acknowledgment of God's supreme dominion; of course here is a true and real sacrifice, and yet not a second sacrifice, but only a continuation of the great sacrifice of the cross. Thus the prophecy of Malachi is fulfilled; "For from the rising of the sun, even to the going down, my name is great among the Gentiles: and in every place there is sacrifice, and there is offered to my name a clean oblation" (Mal. 1:11).

The sacrifice here alluded to cannot be that offered on Mount Calvary on the cross, as that was only offered in one place, of course, it must be the holy sacrifice of the Mass; because this is offered in almost every part of the globe, and because Jesus Christ, who there perpetuates the memory of his passion and death, is the only one that can offer a clean oblation to God.

When we consider what Jesus Christ operates in this mystery; when by faith we behold him actually present with these signs of death, we unite ourselves to him in this state; we offer him to God as our only victim, and as the only one, who, by his blood, can merit for us mercy; protesting, at the same time, that we have nothing to offer up to God but Jesus Christ, and the infinite merits of his death. We consecrate all our prayers by this sacred offering, and, in presenting Jesus Christ to God we are taught to offer up ourselves also in him and by him to his divine majesty, as so many living victims. Pray, dear Sir, does this doctrine savor of superstition?

Here then is the great sacrifice of Christians — differing widely from that which was in use in the old law — a spiritual sacrifice, worthy of the new covenant; where the victim, though present, is perceptible only by faith; where the immolating sword is the word, which mystically separates the body from the blood; where the shedding of the blood is of course mystical, and where death intervenes but in representation: a most real sacrifice, however, inasmuch as Jesus Christ is truly contained in it, and presented to his Father under these symbols of death. But still a sacrifice of commemoration, which, far from withdrawing us, as is objected, from the sacrifice of the cross, attaches us to it, by all its circumstances, since the former is not only totally referred to the latter, but in fact has no existence, except by this relation, from which its efficacy is entirely derived.

Such is the express doctrine of the Council of Trent, which teaches that this sacrifice was instituted only to represent that which was once offered upon the cross; to perpetuate the memory of it to the end of time; and to apply its saving virtue to us, for the remission of those sins which we every day commit (Sess. 22, c. 1). The church then, far from believing the sacrifice of the cross to be by any means defective, is on the contrary, so convinced of its perfection, that it looks upon everything done in consequence, as intended merely to commemorate it, and apply its virtue.

We believe then, the holy sacrifice of the Mass to be the greatest act of religion that can be performed, the only one perfectly worthy of God, as in that sacrifice Jesus Christ, equal to his Father, is both the high priest and the victim: he is the high priest, inasmuch as he immolates and offers up the victim, which is himself, to his Eternal Father, he is the high priest forever according to the order of Melchisedech (Ps. 190:4).

Forever. Although he immolated himself but once in a bloody manner, in the Mass he perpetuates this sacrifice day after day in an un-bloody and mystical manner. *According to the order of Melchisedech*: because as Melchisedech brought forth bread and wine, for he was the priest of the most-high God (Gen. 14:18), so does Christ, the high priest of the new covenant, bring forth bread and wine, and having by his omnipotence changed them into his flesh and blood, continues under those forms of bread and wine to offer himself up, to present to his heavenly Father the merits of his passion and death, and likewise under these forms to feed and nourish the souls of men.

Whoever is the least versed in the history of the church and the writings of the holy fathers, will readily acknowledge, that the Mass was always considered as the great sacrifice of the new covenant, and that the practice of celebrating Mass is as ancient as Christianity.

In all the liturgies of the ancient churches, we trace the words sacrifice, immolation, altar, priesthood, host, victim, namely Christ really present, and consequently, all the conditions of a true and perfect sacrifice. Now, the liturgies exhibit to us the belief of the whole church, even in the first ages, since they are themselves very ancient. They are ascribed to St. James, St. Mark, St. Basil, and St. John Chrysostom, and have been carefully preserved, not only by the Latins and Greeks, but also by the Nestorians, Eutychians, etc., who departed from the church 1,400 years ago.

It is the same with the holy fathers. St. Irenaus, bishop of Lyons, in the second century, says, "Christ took that which is naturally bread, and gave thanks, saying, this is my body, and he taught the new oblation of the new covenant, which the church receiving from the Apostles, everywhere presents to God. This Malachias had foretold," (*Ad. Haer. lib.* 4. cap. 23). In the third century, St. Cyprian, bishop of Carthage, says, "Who is the priest of the most high in a more perfect manner than our Lord, who offered a sacrifice to God, and offered the same that had been offered by Melchisedech, namely, bread and wine, that is, his body and blood?" *(Epist. 68 ad Caecilium).*

In the fourth century, St. Cyril of Jerusalem says, "When we offer the sacrifice, we pray for our departed brethren; believing that their souls receive much assistance from the awful sacrifice of our altars" (Catech. 5).

St. John Chrysostom, Bishop of Constantinople says, "The wise men worshipped him in the manger, thou seest him not in the manger, but on the altar" (1Cor.).

"Again, from its being offered in many places, are there then many Christs? No: for as he who is everywhere offered is one body, and not many bodies, so the sacrifice is one" *(Hom. 17, in Hebr.).* In the same age, St. Ambrose says: "When we sacrifice, Christ is present" (5 in Cap. 1 Lk.).

St. Augustine of the fifth age, says: "When now we see this sacrifice offered to God in every place by the priesthood of Christ, according to the order of Melchisedech, and the Jews' sacrifice cease, why do they yet expect another Christ?" *(De Civitate Dei,* c. 35.), and in Book 9 of his *Confessions* (c. 3), he tells us his mother Monica desired on her deathbed to be remembered at the altar, where she knew the holy sacrifice to be offered, wherewith the indictment against us was blotted out.

In another place he says: "Christ is at the same time both the priest that offers, and the host (or victim) which is offered; and he would that the sacrifice which the church daily offers, should be the sacrament and the representation of this mystery; because the church being the body of that divine head, it offers itself by him." All these holy fathers and bishops of the church lived some 1,100, some 1,200 years before the pretended reformation, at a time when even the most learned protestants own that the church of Christ had not yet gone astray. In the sixth age, that is, about one thousand years before the reformation, St. Gregory the Great, by whose means England was converted, has the following remarkable words, in a sermon which he preached on Christmas day: "Whereas by the grace of God, we shall this day celebrate Mass three times, we cannot speak very long on the gospel" *(Homil. 8. in Evangel)*.

Such was the practice of the church thirteen hundred years ago, and such is the practice of the church at present in 1815; on Christmas day every priest celebrates Mass three times.

If then, dear Sir, we are guilty of superstition in celebrating Mass, and believing as we do of the Mass, it is a great comfort to us to find, that our superstition is no other than that of which were guilty all the holiest and wisest bishops of the most remote antiquity. It is a great comfort to us to know, that the church had already existed more than 1,500 years before it was found out, that to celebrate Mass and to believe that Christ is really present in the Eucharist, are superstitious practices and doctrines.

Before I conclude this important subject, I should not omit explaining the practice of the Catholic church of giving communion under one kind or form.

Article Five:
Communion Under One Kind or Form

Upon this head we are accused of depriving the laity of an essential part of the sacrament. From the moment, dear Sir, the real presence of Christ in the Eucharist is admitted, there can exist no difference on this subject. It must be a matter of perfect indifference whether we receive the holy communion under one or both kinds. [11]

"Christ rising from the dead," says St. Paul, "dieth no more" (Rom. 6:9). Consequently wherever Christ is, there also is Christ's body; wherever the flesh of Christ is, there also is his blood, his soul and divinity; and where his blood is, there is also his flesh, etc. To say that Christ is divided between the two kinds or forms, so as for one form to contain the one-half, and for the other form to contain the other half

---

11. If the precept of Christ, "drink ye all of this," regard not the Apostles only, who alone were present, and were then ordained priests, for offering, under both kinds, this holy sacrifice, which was to be continued by their lawful successors, but be extended to all persons indifferently, the absurd consequence will be, that all are priests. Moreover, did we Catholics hold the mere figurative system, we could not deny that there would be some reason for receiving the liquid as well as the solid substance, as the former may appear to represent more aptly the blood, and the latter the body. But believing as we do, Christ to be really present, we believe that he is equally and entirely present under each species, and consequently, is equally and entirely given to the faithful, whichever they receive. The Catholic clergy, far from thinking that they wrong the laity by withholding the cup, always act conformably to this belief. Hence, when any of them are prevented by corporal infirmity, or any other cause, from offering the holy sacrifice, and wish to communicate, they receive under one kind. The same is observed at the hour of death, when the viaticum is always administered under one kind to the clergy as well as to the laity.

of Christ, would be impious. But it is said, that in giving communion under one kind, and depriving lay people of the chalice, we transgress the commandment of Christ, who, at the last supper said, "Drink ye all of this," etc.

In answer to this we say, that when Christ spoke to his Apostles at the last supper, it is certain that none were present but the Apostles. The precept then was directed to the Apostles — the first priests, here ordained by our Lord — in obedience to which they, and their successors, celebrate the holy mysteries — to this day — always receive under both kinds.

St. Paul very clearly states that communion may be validly received under either kind alone: "Wherefore, whosoever shall eat this bread, or drink the chalice of the Lord unworthily, etc." (1Cor. 11:27). I know, dear Sir, that your protestant translations say eat and drink, instead of eat or drink; but if you compare the Catholic translation with the genuine original Greek, you will find it correct. The sufficiency of one kind in the holy communion is clearly acknowledged by the Calvinists of France in two of their synods. The Synod of Poiters, held A.D. 1560, has the following words: "The bread of the Lord's supper ought to be administered to those who cannot drink wine, upon their making a protestation that it is not out of contempt, when they also obviate all scandal by bringing the cup as near to their mouth as they possibly can" (Synod of Poiters, chap. 12, article 7th of the Lord's supper).

The same was again approved and confirmed by the Synod of La Rochelle, A. D. 1571.

After all I have said, dear Sir, you will conceive that Catholics are not guilty of superstition in believing as they do on the subject of the Lord's supper and the Mass.

They are compelled to believe so by the combined weight of heavenly and earthly authority, which overrules the dictates and judgment of our corrupted senses, and of our weak and limited reason; and to all the arguments of human reason, or if you choose, philosophy, we answer with St. Paul, "Our faith does not stand on the wisdom of man, but on the power of God" (1Cor. 2:5).

I must confess that I am less surprised to see a person (with the Socinians) rejecting all mysteries, than to see him admit one and reject another, though the latter is perhaps more clearly expressed in the written word than the former.

Although I detest the impiety of the Socinian, yet I cannot but acknowledge his consistency, and should I ever have the misfortune (which God in his tender mercy forbid) to forsake the unerring guide, which now overawes and silences my reason into perfect submission, and should I ever become so much blinded by a more than diabolical pride, as to make my limited and corrupted reason the sole arbiter of my faith, I think it would suggest to me the rejection of all mysteries, of everything incomprehensible to that reason, and thus lead me at once into the paths of Socinianism. The same reason that would suggest to me the absurdity of eating the flesh of Christ, would likewise suggest the absurdity of three distinct persons in the divinity, which is essentially one.

If you cast your eyes around you (without traveling many miles from home), do you not see, in many respectable members of society, the deplorable consequences of trusting to the light of reason, and refusing submission to unerring authority? Do you not perceive in many of those, whose reason has been developed by a liberal education, a perfect indifference (if not a kind of contempt) for the mysteries in general, and even in particular for those very mysteries, which by all societies are considered the fundamental principles of Christianity? In proportion as the powers of their understanding have been improved, they seem to have acquired a greater right to set up their reason as a judge over the divine mysteries, and thus to abuse the noblest gift of God to purposes of impiety.

The whole system of the Christian religion; the greatest of all the works of God, one and indivisible, must be believed in the whole and in all its parts; neither does it require less impiety to reject one part of that divine system known to be revealed by Jesus Christ, than to reject the whole. Now, Sir, from what you see, I mean the rejection both in principle and practice, of so many mysteries among protestants, and this is only a natural consequence of making limited reason the arbiter of faith; how long, do you suppose, will it be until faith will be entirely extinct? Will the present generation of children, after coming to the age of maturity, remember that their parents were Christians? Will the next generation even enjoy the benefit of Baptism? I am acquainted with many youths of both sexes, who, although born of protestant parents, never received the benefit of Baptism. Why so? — because their protestant parents, guided by the light of reason, could not see into the necessity of Baptism, and thus probably judged it an idle ceremony. Thus is the child's eternal fate left to rest on the private opinions of their parents on religious mysteries, as if our merciful God had left us in a state of uncertainty, in those matters principally, in which certainty is absolutely necessary.

After this digression, which a sincere zeal for the salvation of souls has occasioned, I shall continue to explain a few remaining articles of Catholic faith. Having explained the Catholic doctrine of the Mass, this leads me to the Catholic doctrine of purgatory and prayers for the dead.

Article Six:
Purgatory and Prayers for the Dead

What has induced the gentlemen of the pretended reformation to discard purgatory from their creed, and to renounce the practice of praying for the deceased, I am at a loss to know. To any man of information, it must be notorious that the belief and the practice are older than Christianity, almost universal, and far from being impervious to human reason, must, upon a candid examination, meet the approbation of reason.

The Catholic church, the supreme tribunal of our faith, teaches that there is a purgatory, a place of temporal punishment after death, and that the souls therein detained are helped by the prayers of the faithful, and especially by the holy sacrifice of the Mass (*Concil. Trident. Sess. 25, Decret. de Purg*). This decree of the church, assembled in general council, is sufficient for a Catholic to regulate his faith on the present subject, and to convince him fully of the existence of a purgatory, and of the usefulness of prayers for the dead. Still it is a satisfaction to a Catholic, already convinced by the authority of the church, to find that even the plain words of scripture, and the plainest dictates of reason, are in perfect unison with the declaration of the church. Long before the coming of Christ, the people of God prayed and offered sacrifice for the dead. Witness the collection of money made by Judas Machabaeus, the defender of God's sanctuary; and making a gathering, he sent twelve thousand drachmas of silver to Jerusalem for sacrifice to be offered for the sins of the dead, thinking well and religiously concerning the resurrection it is there fore a holy and wholesome thought to pray for the dead, that they may be loosed from sins, (2Mach. 12:43, 46). I know that protestants reject the Machabees. But you will permit me to observe that this rejection, made by modern reformers, can bear no weight when made in opposition to all antiquity, in opposition to the universal church, the only one extant at the time of the pretended reformation.

In the earliest ages of Christianity we find the holy fathers quoting the Machabees, as well as other scriptures. Witness St. Clement of Alexandria (*lib. 6, Stromaf.*; *Origen, lib. 2, de Principiis,* cap. 1); St. Cyprian (*lib. de Exhortatione Martyrii*); St. Jerome (*cap. 23; Isa.*); St. Augustine (*lib. 8, de Civitate Dei,* cap. 36). St. Isidore Hispalensis says, "The books of the Machabees, although separated by the Hebrews as apocrypha, are by the church of Christ honored and proclaimed as divine books" (lib. 6). The General Council of Trent (Sess. 4) declares the two Machabees to be divine books.[12]

The belief of a middle state is supported by many other texts of the Old and New Testaments.

---

12. The Council of Trent, in defining the divine inspiration of those books, has only followed the constant and unanimous tradition of the church, and the examples of other councils, some of which were even general. For those books had been reckoned among the sacred writings by the General Council of Florence, held in 1439, under Eugenius IV; by a council of seventy bishops, held in Rome in 494, under Pope Gelasius; by Pope St. Innocent I in his famous epistles, written in 405, to St. Exuperius, bishop of Tolouse; by the third Council of Carthage, held in 397, at which St. Augustine assisted; by St. Augustine himself, in his work on *Christian Doctrine,* book 22 chap. 23, and in the *City of God,* book 18, chap 36; in a word, by many other fathers. The books of Machabees must be allowed, even by those who do not receive them as canonical, to be, at least, authentic records; as such, then, they bear undeniable testimony of the belief and practice of the Jews of the present day, who, surely, have not borrowed them from Catholics. Seeing, then, the doctrine of purgatory and praying for the dead to have been held by God's people 150 years before Christ, what are we to think of the candor of those who assert it to be an invention of the dark ages?

"Thou also by the blood of thy testament, has sent forth thy prisoners out of the pit, wherein is no water" (Zach. 9:11).

That pit cannot be hell, as out of hell there is no redemption. Consequently it must be a place of temporal punishment from which redemption is had by the blood of the testament.

"Every man's work shall be made manifest: for the Lord shall be revealed by fire: and the fire shall try every man's work, of what sort it is. If any man's work abide, which he has built there upon, he shall receive a reward. If any man's work burn, he shall suffer loss: but he himself shall be saved, yet so as by fire" (1Cor. 3:13-15).

This text hardly requires any comment. From it appears plainly that, although the works of man have been substantially good, and pleasing to almighty God, yet on account of many deformities, the effects of human frailty and corruption, man must be cleansed by a purging and punishing, yet saving, fire before he can be admitted into that sanctuary; into which nothing defiled can enter, (Apoc. 21:27). "But I say unto you, that every idle word that men shall speak, they shall render an account for it, in the day of judgment" (Mt. 12:36). Dear Sir, you will hardly say that every idle word will consign man to the everlasting punishments of hell! If so, who will be saved? There must then be some temporal punishments prepared after this life for trifling faults, which we call venial sins.

According to the same Evangelist there are sins that "shall not be forgiven neither in this world nor in the world to come" (Mt. 12:32). Does not this intimate that some sins may be atoned for in the world to come?

Make an agreement with thy adversary quickly, whilst thou art in the way with him: lest perhaps the adversary deliver thee to the judge, and the judge deliver thee to the officer, and thou be cast into prison. "Amen I say to thee, thou shall not go out from thence, until thou pay the last farthing" (Mt. 5:25, 26).

The last text I am going to quote establishes the doctrine of a third place so very plainly, that it appears strange how it can be misunderstood.

"Christ also died once, for our sins, the just for the unjust, that he might offer us to God, being put to death indeed in the flesh, but brought to life by the spirit, in which also he came and preached to those spirits who were in prison: who in time past had been incredulous, when they waited for the patience of God, in the days of Noe, when the ark was building" (1Pet. 3:18-20).

It will hardly be supposed that Christ preached to the damned spirits in hell, as it is acknowledged on all hands, I believe, that there is no redemption for them. How then can the above text be understood, unless by admitting a place of temporal punishment, in which were confined those, who, in the time of Noe, were incredulous, and who had not fully satisfied the justice of God before departing this life.

The doctrine of the existence of a third place is founded on the belief that very often, after the guilt and the eternal punishment are taken away by the mercy of God, upon the sinner's sincere repentance, there still remains, on account of the defects of that repentance, something due to the infinite justice of God, something to be expiated either in this world or in the next. Nothing indeed can be more clearly established in scripture.

Adam was cast out of the earthly paradise, himself and all his posterity punished with death and many miseries, after his sin of disobedience had been forgiven, and his right to heaven restored to him.

David was punished with the death of his child, after his enormous crimes were forgiven, after his sincere repentance (2Kings 12). "O king," saith Daniel to Nabuchodonosor, "redeem thy sins with alms," (Dan. 4:24).

If temporal punishments have often been indicted by the justice of God, after the guilt and the everlasting punishments were remitted, it follows of course, that if the person die before he has suffered that temporal punishment, he dies that much indebted to God's justice and must, undoubtedly, discharge that debt before he can enter into heaven.

The writings of the holy fathers of both the eastern and the western church, most clearly prove that from the earliest dawn of Christianity, the belief of a purgatory was general in the church. Tertullian, who lived in the second age, says, "No man will doubt but that the soul doth recompense something in the places below" *(Lib. de Anima* c. 58). And again, in his book *de Corona Militis,* "We make yearly oblations for the dead."

St. Clement in the same age tells us, "St. Peter taught them, among other works of mercy, to bury the dead, and diligently perform their funeral rites, and also to pray and give alms for them" *(Epist. 1, de S. Petro).*

In the third age, St. Cyprian says, "It is one thing to be cast into prison, and not to go out thence 'till he pay the last farthing, another, presently to receive the reward of faith; one thing to be afflicted with pains for sins to be expiated, and purged long with fire, another, to have purged all sins by sufferings" *(Epis. 52, ad Antone).* In the same age Origen says, "Though a release from prison be promised (Mt. 5), yet it is signified, that none can get out from thence, but he who pays the last farthing" *(In Epist. ad Roman, and Horn. 35, in Lk).*

In the fourth age, St. Ambrose, "But whereas St. Paul says, "yet so as by fire," he shows indeed that he shall be saved, but yet shall suffer the punishment of fire, he may be saved, and not tormented forever, as the infidels are with everlasting fire" *(Cap. 3, Epis. ad Cor).*

In the same age, "This is that," says St. Jerome, "which he saith, thou shalt not go out of prison, till thou shalt have paid for even thy little sins" (Mt. 5).

In the same age, St. Cyril of Jerusalem says: "We beseech God for all those who have died before us, believing the observation of that holy and dreadful sacrifice, which is put on the altar, to be the greatest help of the souls for which it is offered" (*Catech. Mystagog. 5*).

Again, in the same age, St. John Chrysostom says, "These things were not in vain ordained by the Apostles, that in the venerable and dreadful mysteries of the Mass there should be made a memory of those who have departed this life; they knew much benefit would hence accrue to them" (*Homil. 3, in Epist. ad Philip*). It would fill volumes to quote all those passages from the holy fathers which prove the belief in a third place, and prayers for the dead, to be coeval with Christianity. Those whom I have quoted lived twelve, thirteen, and fourteen centuries before the pretended reformation, and were of course better judges of genuine apostolic tradition than the late reformers could be.

If these holy and learned doctors, some of whom were the immediate successors of the Apostles, did not think themselves guilty of superstition in praying for the dead, but declared that in doing so, they followed and obeyed the ordinances of the Apostles; neither are we guilty of superstition in believing and doing as they did.

An objection against purgatory is found in the following words of scripture: "If the tree fall to the south, or to the north, in what place soever it shall fall, there it shall be" (Eccle. 11:3).

Admitting that the scripture here speaks of the soul after death, which indeed is highly probable, how does this make a case against purgatory?

We believe that there are only two eternal states after death, *viz*, the state of glory and the state of damnation. If the soul departs in the state of grace, it shall be forever in that state, although it may have some venial sins to satisfy for, which may for a while retard the consummation of its happiness. If it dies in the state of mortal sin, and an enemy of God, it shall be ever in torments. Here are two everlasting states, which may be meant by the north and south of the above text. This is the interpretation, of St. Jerome, Pope St. Gregory the Great, St. Bernard, St. Thomas, etc. It is besides so satisfactory that it is surprising that protestants, instead of admitting it, vainly endeavor to discover in the text the nonexistence of purgatory. How anyone can see in it the exclusion of our doctrine, I cannot conceive.

I shall now undertake to prove, that the belief in a place of temporal punishment, after death, far from being unreasonable, is perfectly agreeable to the dictates of sound reason, and here I shall borrow the words of the *Philosophical Catechism* (Art. 7 sect. 4, N. 480).

Here is what a Christian orator and philosopher might say: the soul of man ceasing to dwell upon earth, is summoned to appear before the tribunal of God; his works and virtues speak for him. The law, which he has religiously observed, stands up in his defense to get him crowned in the assembly of the saints. A slight transgression, a foible hardly perceptible, a small failing, inseparable from mortal nature, is perceived in a crowd of meritorious deeds. You, who acknowledge a just God, who adore a merciful God, and yet a God inimical to all iniquity, incapable by nature of admitting into his abode anything sullied with guilt, say: what is to be the fate of this soul, righteous indeed, though stained with sin; a friend to God, yet bearing in its bosom an enemy to God? Shall its sins be placed along with its virtues? Its weakness and its fortitude be crowned alike? Its Christian works confounded with the works of natural frailty? No, you will never think it; nor have even the adversaries of the tenet of purgatory ever ventured to say it openly. But, must this unfortunate soul be eternally reproved without mercy or resource? Shall the purity of its faith, the liveliness of its hope, the good works without number or measure it has performed, plead for it in vain? Far be it from us to think it. By thinking so, we should attack the infinite excellence and perfections of the sovereign Lord of this world. No; never will God rank in the same category, inadvertence and malice; a distraction in prayer and the total neglect of it; an officious lie and a detestable perjury; the man with a few blemishes, and the miscreant sunk over head and ears in profligacy; he will purify the one and reprobate the other; he is at once the God of all justice, and the God of all sanctity. A holy soul, but sullied by a stain, shall not enter his mansion, because he is the God of sanctity; and yet shall enter, because he is the God of justice, He, therefore, will reform it, will complete the luster of its virtues, establish the purity of its works, and then will place it in his glory. There is the solid foundation of the belief of a purgatory, and such is the conclusion we are to draw from the incontestable attributes of our Judge and our God. Hence it is that of all the tenets of the Catholic church, the most widely diffused, and the most generally admitted, is the tenet of purgatory. The knowledge of a God, both just and holy, has united the most inimical religions, and the most opposite to one another, in the belief of a purgatory — that is, of a certain delay put to the eternal reward — during which the just man is still more sanctified. An offended God does not damn, for venial sins, because his wrath does not extend to the offender's death; nor a remunerating God confer his rewards immediately, because his liberality is restrained by the faults of a just, yet guilty, man. This the sages of antiquity have taught in their books, Plato and Timaeo; this the profane, but sublime, poets have sung in their hymns (Virgil's *Ænaid*, L. 6: V. 730); this the nations, misled by Mahomet, profess in their Koran; in this the Hebrews, both ancient and modern, agree with the Christians; and the Greeks, severed from the church by a long and obstinate schism, pray for the dead.

Here then is the greatest part of mankind, all that believe in revelation (except those who follow our late reformers), and numbers of those who are guided by reason alone, are agreed in the belief of a place of temporal punishment, and in the practice of praying for the dead.

If then the protestant continues to assert that he cannot find either purgatory or the practice of praying for the dead in scripture, the Catholic church answers, that they find both the doctrine and the practice very clearly in holy scripture.

If the protestant peremptorily decides that the belief in purgatory is absurd, and the practice of praying for the dead ridiculous — we in our sober senses, possessed of common sense, as well as that of our good protestant neighbors; enlightened as well as many of them by a liberal education; endowed with genius and talents, capable of the most profound disquisitions; in short endowed, many of us, with all the perfections of the understanding which nature can give, or education improve — we answer, that we find the belief in a place of temporal punishment, and the practice of praying for the dead, perfectly reasonable.

Here then is reason opposed to reason, common sense to common sense, genius and talents to genius and talents; the reason, common sense, etc., of very many in favor of purgatory opposed to the reason, common sense etc., of comparatively few against purgatory.

Who shall decide, and decide so as to put the question forever to rest? None but the great tribunal which Jesus Christ established on earth more than eighteen hundred years ago. When infusing into his ministers the spirit of truth, he promised that that spirit should never depart from them to the end of time. This tribunal, as I have proved above, has decided in our favor, and it is because that supreme and infallible tribunal has decided so, that we believe as we do.

Just as I was going to close the present subject, a little pamphlet fell into my hands, the author of which calls himself an independent minister, in which I find the following objection against purgatory: "This doctrine of purgatory casts a reproach on Christ as a savior of sinners, representing his obedience and suffering as insufficient to atone for their sins."

This objection, dear Sir, will appear very trifling to you when you know that the Catholic church teaches that the merits of Jesus Christ are of themselves far more than sufficient to atone for all the sins of mankind. But Jesus Christ requires our cooperation; and it depends upon the degree of our cooperation, whether those infinite merits of Christ are applied to us in a more or less abundant measure. It is in the order of grace as in the order of nature, "In the sweat of thy face shalt thou eat bread" (Gen. 3:19). God's omnipotence alone gives growth to our grain; yet without casting a reproach on that omnipotence we may safely assert that, caeteris paritbus, in proportion as we plough and sow, in that proportion we shall reap. So, likewise, although Christ's merits and satisfaction for sinners are of infinite value, yet the benefit we shall reap of those infinite merits will be proportionate to our endeavors in subduing our corrupt nature, our sinful inclinations, and conforming to the will of God.

"He who soweth sparingly shall reap sparingly; and he who soweth in blessing shall also reap of blessings" (2Cor. 9:6).

He, then, who soweth so sparingly in this world as to remain, in his dying moment, indebted to the divine justice, will, after his death, be compelled to pay to the last farthing what, by more strenuous endeavors, he might have paid in this world.

I believe, Sir, I have fulfilled my promise of proving that we are not guilty of superstition in believing a purgatory, and praying for the dead. I shall now try to prove, that we are no more guilty of superstition in honoring the saints, and applying to their intercession.

Article Seven: Honoring the Saints and Applying to Their Intercession

Few of the tenets of our holy religion are attacked with more virulence than the present one; but pray, Sir, how is it attacked? By misrepresentation it is exhibited in a most odious form, and then this phantom, the offspring of a heated imagination, or perhaps of a malicious heart, is attacked by the most violent abuse, the very worst of bad arguments; it is attacked with the powerful arms of ridicule and low ribaldry.

According to the bold assertions delivered from protestant pulpits, and propagated from protestant presses, we worship the saints, we make gods of them, we consider them as our mediators, we give them the honor belonging to God alone, etc.

The General Council of Trent expressly teaches that "The saints who reign with Christ offer up their prayers to God for men, and that it is good and useful to invoke them, and in order to obtain from God, blessings, through his son Jesus Christ our Lord, who alone is our redeemer and savior, to have recourse to their prayers, help and assistance" *(Conc. Trid. Sess. 25)*.

Again, "Although the church does sometimes offer up Masses in honor and in memory of the saints, yet it is not to them, but to God alone, who has crowned them, that the sacrifice is offered up: therefore, the priest does not say, I offer up this sacrifice to thee, Peter, or thee, Paul, but to God himself, giving thanks to him for their victories, imploring their patronage, that they may vouchsafe to intercede for us in heaven, whose memory we celebrate on earth" *(Conc. Trid. Sess. 25, c: 2)*.

You will readily acknowledge, dear Sir, that there is a wide difference between divine worship and simple honor or reverence. Divine worship belongs to God alone, honor and reverence may be paid to many of God's creatures.

Thus, even by God's commandment, we honor our parents, our superiors in church and state, we honor persons respectable for their rank, dignity, virtue, talents, etc., and all this without robbing God of that honor and reverence justly due to him.

If then, it is no sin to honor poor mortals who are yet in this place of trial, of whose eternal fate we are very uncertain, why should it be sin to honor those whom the great God has been pleased to honor with a seat of eternal glory in his kingdom? All the power, riches, and glory of this world are nothing in comparison to a single ray of glory emanating from the lowest saint in heaven.

What honor does not a monarch receive over the whole earth? And perhaps he is a very great sinner, perhaps a victim of God's eternal vengeance; how much more honor and reverence is even the least saint in heaven entitled to? The Council of Trent, ordering sacrifice to be offered to God alone, confines divine worship to God, but at the same time recommends the saints to be remembered and honored, and their intercession, in our behalf, to be implored.

The catechism of the Council of Trent (part 3) explains the prodigious difference there is between the manner of imploring the assistance of God, and that of imploring the assistance of saints; "We pray to God," it says, "either to grant us good things, or to deliver us from evil: but because the saints are more agreeable to him than we are we beg of them to plead on our behalf, and to obtain of God for us whatever we stand in need of." Hence it is, that we make use of two forms of prayer, widely different from one another; for, in speaking to God, we say, *have mercy on us*, whereas, in addressing ourselves to a saint, we say no more than *pray for us*.

It is a very ancient and common practice among Christians to ask one another's prayers, and to pray for one another. "I beseech you," says St. Paul, "that you also help me in your prayers to God for me" (Rom. 15:30). "I make my prayer," says St. John, "that thou mayest prosper as to all things, and be in health etc." (3Jn. 2).

The holy Apostles then, in applying to the intercession of others, or praying for them, did not think they were guilty of derogating from any of the divine perfections, or of attributing to mere creatures what belongs to God alone. Neither are we guilty of derogating from the perfections of God, when we apply to one another's intercession. Why then should we be guilty of derogating from the perfections of God, by applying to the intercession of his saints in heaven, admitting that the saints are able to hear our prayers, and willing to offer their intercession in our behalf? You will readily acknowledge, dear Sir, that their intercession must be more efficacious than the intercession of our fellow mortals. If, then, praying to the saints is by the gentlemen of the reformation considered as superstitious, it must be, because the saints are considered too far from us to hear our prayers; or because they are thought unwilling to apply in our behalf. Such, indeed, is the objection I find in a book called the *Morning Exercise Against Popery*, which is a collection of sermons preached by twenty-four protestant ministers, with the avowed purpose of detecting and confuting errors of the Roman Catholic church. This practice is irrational, says Mr. Mayo, in his sermon against invocation of saints and angels (p. 525); there is nothing more absurd. Consider, says he, their incapacity to hear the prayers that are directed to them. That this is the case of the glorified spirits is evident, because 1) They are not omnipresent; they are circumscribed and finite creatures, and can be but in one place at once. 2) They are not omnipercipient; if they should hear what men say with their mouths, they cannot perceive or understand what men say in their hearts. Here is logic indeed!

The saints and angels are not everywhere, do not know everything, therefore they do not hear our prayers, far less perceive our thoughts. Such and no better will be the way of reasoning of any person who has no other guide than reason blinded by prejudice.

Beginning where he should end, he will lay down as self-evident the very matters in dispute, without any better proof than his own bold and presumptuous assertion it is certain, it is absurd, it is self-evident, etc.; and thus starting from false principles, his conclusion can be no better.

Mr. Mayo, and I suppose all the gentlemen of the reformation, take it for granted then, that saints and angels do not hear our prayers, far less perceive our thoughts. Now, Sir, abstracting for awhile from the decision of the Catholic church, which for Catholics is sufficient, and taking the present question on your own ground, what does scripture say? "There shall be joy before the angels of God upon one sinner doing penance" (Lk. 15:10). The angels then see our thoughts.

"Take heed that ye despise not one of these little ones, for I say to you their angels that are in heaven, always see the face of my Father" (Mt. 18:10). The angels then know when we are injured, and pray to God in our behalf; "and the saints are as the angels of God in heaven" (Mt. 22:30). "Equal to the angels," (Lk. 20:36). "When thou didst pray, said the angel Raphael to Tobias, I offered thy prayer to the Lord" (Tob. 12:12).

"The angels are all ministering spirits, sent to minister for them who shall receive the inheritance of salvation" (Heb. 1:14). Also that God gives the saints great power in the government of this world is plain from the following:

"He that shall overcome, and keep my works to the end, to him will I give power over the nations, and he shall rule them with a rod of iron" (Apoc. 11:26, 27).

That angels and saints actually pray for us is likewise plainly stated in scripture: "The angel of the Lord answered and said, O Lord of hosts, how long wilt thou not have mercy on Jerusalem, and the cities of Juda, with which thou hast been angry these three score and ten years?" (Zach. 1:12). "The four and twenty ancients fell down before the Lamb, having every one of them harps, and golden vials full of odors, which are the prayers of the saints" (Apoc. 5:8). "And Judas Machabeus saw in a vision Onias, that had been high priest, holding up his hands and praying for the Jews, and pointing also to another, in these words: this is a lover of the brethren, who prayeth much for the people and for the holy city namely, Jeremias, the prophet of God" (2Mach. 15:12, 13, 14). They had both been dead many years.

That the practice of honoring and praying to the saints is as ancient as Christianity is evident from the testimony of the holy fathers in all ages. The belief of the first age on this point, will appear from St. Ignatius, who requesting, a little before his martyrdom, which happened in 107, the prayers of the Trallians for himself and his church, adds thus, "that my soul may intercede for you, not only in this life, but hereafter in the presence of my God."

St. Justin the martyr, who lived in the second age, says, "We venerate and worship the angelic host, and the spirits of the prophets, teaching others as we ourselves have been taught."

"I will begin to fall down on my knees," says the learned Origen, who lived in the third age, "and pray to all the saints to succor me, who dare not ask God, for the exceeding greatness of my sin. O saints of God! With tears and weeping I beseech you to fall down before his mercy for me a wretch" (in *Lament.*).

And again, "all the saints departed, still bearing charity towards the living, it will not be improper to say, that they have a care of their salvation, and help them with their prayers to God for them, etc." (*Homil. 3, in Cant.*).

St. Ambrose, who lived in the fourth age, says: "That my prayer may be more efficacious, I call upon the intercession of the Blessed Virgin Mary, I ask the prayers of the Apostles, the assistance of the martyrs and confessors"

(*Prep. for Death*). And, again, "It is our duty to pray to the angels who have been given us to be our guardians. We should address our prayers to the martyrs, whose bodies still remaining among us are pledges of their protection. Neither let us blush to ask their intercession under our infirmities, since they, even when they conquered, knew what infirmities are."

In the same age lived St. Basil, who expressly refers this practice to the Apostles, where he says, "I invoke the Apostles, prophets, and martyrs to pray for me, that God may be merciful to me, and forgive me my sins, since this has been ordained by tradition from the Apostles, and is practiced in all our churches."

In the fifth age, St. Augustine says, "We do not pray for the holy martyrs, but we recommend ourselves to their prayers" *(Tract. 84, in Joan)*.

Instead of quoting any more of the holy fathers, I cannot forbear giving you here the opinion of the learned protestant Bishop Montague on this subject, "I do not deny," says he, "but the saints are mediators, as they are called, of prayer and intercession, but in general, and for all in general. They interpose with God by their supplications and mediate by their prayers" *(Antid.* p. 20). The same Bishop Montague owns that "The blessed in heaven do recommend to God in their prayers their kindred, friends, and acquaintances on earth; and having given his reason," he says, "this common voice with general concurrence, without contradiction of reverend and learned antiquity, for aught I ever could read or understand; and I see no cause or reason to dissent from them touching intercession, in this kind," (*Treat. Invoc. of Saints.* p. 103). He owns also that "It is no injury to the mediation of Christ, to ask of the saints to pray for us. Indeed I grant Christ is not wronged in this mediation; it is no impiety to say, as they of the Roman church do, holy Mary pray for me; holy Peter pray for me" (p. 118); and again, "I see no absurdity in nature, no incongruity unto analogy of faith, no repugnancy at all to sacred scripture, much less, impiety, for any man to say, holy angel guardian pray for me."

It is true, the same protestant bishop seems in another place to express a doubt whether the saints can hear or know our prayers.

"Could I come at them," he says, "or certainly inform them of my state, without any question or much ado, I would readily and willingly say, holy Peter, blessed Paul, pray for me; recommend my case unto Christ Jesus our Lord. Were they with me, by me in my kenning, I would run with open arms and fall upon my knees, and with affection, desire them to pray for me."

The only difficulty, then, with this good bishop is his uncertainty whether the saints can have any knowledge of the petitions made to them, but this difficulty seems to be completely removed by the declaration of scripture, that there is joy in heaven at the conversion of a sinner. St. Augustine *(Lib. de Cura pro Mort.* c. 26), moves the same difficulty, confessing it above the reach of his reason, to understand how the saints relieve those that call upon them. Yet he, with all the holy fathers and doctors of the church, maintains that the saints do certainly assist us, and intercede for such as call upon them.

Divine mysteries, as I have already observed, always offer difficulties to the human understanding. The present difficulty, however, is not altogether insuperable to human reason; on the contrary, dear Sir, the Catholic belief on the present subject must, upon examination, meet the approbation of reason.

Would it not be unreasonable, even impious, to assert that the saints and angels assisted with the light of grace and glory, do not know as much as the infernal spirits, who are deprived of both. Now, Sir, it is certain that evil spirits have knowledge of us, and in a great measure know not only our actions, but even our thoughts.

"The devil cometh," says Christ, "and taketh the word out of their heart, lest believing they should be saved" (Lk. 8:12). "When an unclean spirit is gone out of a man, he walketh through dry places, seeking rest, and findeth none. Then he saith, I will return into my house from whence I came out. And coming he findeth it empty, swept, and garnished. Then he goeth, and taketh with him seven other spirits more wicked than himself, and they enter in and dwell there: and the last state of that man is made worse than the first" (Mt. 12:43, 44, 45). Moreover, since the evil spirit is said by St. John, to be "the accuser of the servants of God" (Apoc. 12:10), and by St. Peter, to be "like a roaring lion going about, seeking whom he may devour" (1Pet. 5:8).

Is it unreasonable to believe that blessed spirits have at least as much power in protecting man, as infernal spirits in destroying man? Is it unreasonable to believe that the blessed spirits who surround the throne of God, have at least as much zeal for the salvation of man, as infernal spirits for his damnation? Finally, is it unreasonable to suppose that the blessed in heaven are as able and willing to plead in our behalf, as evil spirits are to accuse us?

The secrets of hearts have been in many instances known to mortals. Thus, Eliseus, in his house, knew the king's intention to take his head (4Kings 6:32). Thus, the same Eliseus knew what passed between his servant Giezi and Naaman, when he himself was absent (4Kings 5:26).

St. Peter knew the sacrilegious fraud acted privately between Ananias and Sapphira (Acts 5). What was possible for feeble mortals, by the light of grace, should that be impossible for the blessed saints, who have both the light of grace and glory? Of whom St. Paul says, they see and know God face to face, even as they themselves are known (1Cor. 13:12). Much more might be said on the subject, yet enough has been said to convince the candid reader that Catholics are not guilty of superstition in honoring those whom God himself chooses to honor, and in expecting much from the intercession and protection of those blessed angels and saints, who surround the throne of God, and whose thoughts, desires, affections, charity, zeal, etc., are in perfect unison with God's holy will and infinite charity.

It can be no superstition, then, to believe that the saints desire our salvation, because God desires it. It can be no superstition to believe that the saints know our thoughts and desires (which even the devils know), the scripture declaring that the repentance of the sinner on earth causes joy among the blessed in heaven (Lk. 15:10). It can be no superstition to expect much from the protection of those, who, by the spirit of God are declared to be appointed ministering spirits for our salvation (Heb. 1:14). And who are again declared to have power, and to be rulers of nations (Apoc. 2:26). It can be no superstition to apply to the intercession of those, who in holy writ are declared intercessors in our behalf (Zach. 1; 2Mach. 15). It can be no superstition to believe that the intercession of the saints in heaven will be of more avail towards deciding the fate of men and nations, than the intercession of ten mortals would have been in deciding the fate of a city (Gen. 18:32), or the intercession of one man (Job) in deciding the fate of his three friends.

Permit me, dear Sir, to ask one question. Are you very certain that the Lord, whose decrees are inscrutable, has not perhaps made your salvation dependent on the intercession of some certain saint or saints? Are you altogether certain that your own prayers will prove sufficient to obtain now, and in your last hour, a full application of the merits of your dying savior? The Lord, it is true, is merciful beyond expression, but he calls himself a jealous God; are you certain, that the Lord is not offended, that his wrath is not kindled to the highest degree, at seeing those neglected and despised upon earth, whom he so much exalts and honors in heaven.

Are you certain that those will ever be associated, in the enjoyment of eternal glory, to the blessed saints in heaven that had no communication with them on earth?

The Apostles Creed, I believe in God, etc, makes mention of the communion of saints, which is the ninth article of this creed. Pray, which church is it that really, and not in words alone, holds and believes this communion of saints in every sense of the word?

Forgive me, dear Sir, if my zeal for the salvation of my protestant fellow mortals causes me sometimes to overstep the bounds of my subject, and of my original plan, which was to exculpate Roman Catholics from the guilt of superstition. Before concluding, I must here observe with respect to this false and odious charge, that it was first made to serve the interested views of those who judged it expedient to excite clamor and prejudice against the Catholic religion. They well knew the falsehood of what they asserted, but wanting sufficient virtue to prefer truth to temporal advantages, they hesitated not to employ the vilest slanders to attain their end. The same are still propagated by many, either from the same base motive, or because they suppose this the surest and readiest means of bringing themselves into notice, or of acquiring influence in their respective societies, by thus gratifying the prejudices of their hearers. The conduct of the latter is scarcely less culpable than that of the former. It is a very weak excuse for those who now calumniate our religion to say that they, finding those charges already made by others, take them for granted, without inquiring whether they are true or false. Such a mode of proceeding would be extremely unjust towards even an individual, and it is much more so, towards the far largest body of Christians in existence. Our adversaries are so much the less excusable in imputing to us doctrines which we detest, as they might easily ascertain what we really hold, especially since so many approved works, containing the principles of our belief and practice, are before the public, and may be easily had. Some of them have so far misrepresented our invocation of the saints, as to charge us with substituting the worship of demons for that of God. The falsehood of this charge of idolatry, is evident from the simple statement of our doctrine on this point: we believe that it is good and profitable to invoke the prayers of the saints, to whom God can, by innumerable ways, reveal those addressed to them; and therefore, it is unimportant to know what may be the particular means employed by him for this end. By praying to them, we attribute no divine perfection to creatures, as the idolaters did, since we acknowledge even in the greatest saints, no degree of excellence but what comes from God; no virtue, but what is the gift of his grace; no knowledge of human affairs, but what he is pleased to communicate to them; in fine, no power of assisting us, except by their prayers. Moreover, that the saints are not raised above the rank of creatures, by ascribing to them the knowledge imparted, however, by God, not only of the things passing in this life, but even of our thoughts, is evident from the examples of the prophets, who knew not only things present but what is yet more wonderful, future things, the knowledge of which God seems to have particularly reserved to himself. Hence, several eminent protestant writers, who have viewed, in its proper light, the doctrine of Catholics on this point, have totally given up the groundless charge of idolatry and superstition. For example, Bishop Montague, quoted above, and Thorndike, prebendary of Westminster, warns his brethren "not to lead people by the nose, to believe they can prove papists to be idolaters, when they cannot" (*Just Weights*, p. 10).

I shall now in a few words explain the doctrine of the holy Catholic church respecting images, pictures, and relics.

Article Eight: Images, Pictures, and Relics

Much indeed needs not be said on that subject to those who are candid and provided with the least share of common sense; to those, who with seeing eyes will not see, and with hearing ears will not ear, too much has been said already.

The General Council of Trent declares that, "The sacred bodies of the holy martyrs and of other saints, who were living members of Christ, and the temples of the Holy Ghost, which bodies will by him be raised to eternal life and glorified, ought to be venerated by the faithful on earth" (Conc. Trid. Ses. 25). Also, that the images of Christ, of the Blessed Virgin, and of other saints, are to be retained, especially in churches, and that due honor and veneration is to be given to them, not that any divinity or any power is believed to reside in them. The Catechism of the Council of Trent adds, *"istud maxime cavendum, ne quod Deo proprium est cuiquam praterae triburmit"* (T. 2, p. 603); particular care must be taken, that to none be given what belongs to God alone. Here is nothing but what every Christian must approve as conformable to the word of God, and to reason. St. John the Baptist venerated the very latchets of our savior's shoes (Mk. 1:7).

The Israelites venerated the brazen serpent, a type or figure of Christ (Num. 21:9).

By the command of God, two images of cherubim were made and placed on the ark (Exod. 25:18). The primitive Christians venerated the very shadows and garments of Sts. Peter and Paul, and received particular blessings thereby (Acts 5:15; 19:12).

Roman Catholics venerate the images of Christ, of the Blessed Virgin, and of the saints, on account of their prototypes. None of them are so stupid as to believe that any divinity, any power or virtue resides in any of those images.

How many, both protestants and Catholics, keep the picture of General Washington, and exhibit the same in the most conspicuous place of their houses, certainly with a view of showing honor to the memory of the deceased general. Nobody, in his senses, ever thought of condemning that practice as superstitious.

How many protestants hang upon the walls of their houses the pictures of their deceased parents and friends? How many a protestant child will honor the picture of a deceased parent with a costly frame: look at that picture-with sentiments of respect and veneration, perhaps bedew it with tears of sorrow and gratitude, nay, with the most sincere affection press it to its lips? Sir, will you accuse that child of superstition?

Let prejudice subside, and now substitute a Catholic in the room of the protestant, and the picture of Christ crucified, in the place of the picture of the deceased parent; pray, dear Sir, will you not permit that Catholic to exhibit his crucifix in the most conspicuous part of his house? Will you not permit him to look at his crucifix with respect and veneration? Will you not permit him to bedew his crucifix with tears of sorrow and gratitude? Nay, with the most sincere love and affection to press that crucifix to his lips? And suppose that Catholic should allow an honorable place to the picture of the most Blessed Virgin mother of our savior, and likewise to the pictures of the holy Apostles, and of the other servants of Christ, would you condemn him? Would you accuse him of superstition? I cannot think so.

I have spent many happy moments before the celebrated picture of Guido Reni, in the gallery of Dusseldorf in Germany, which represents the Assumption of the Blessed Virgin, and I must confess that I was struck with awe. I found myself in a deep contemplation, my soul, as it were, withdrawn from its earthly habitation, and elevated towards the mansions of eternal bliss. The heavenly looks of the Virgin, as expressed in the picture, pointed out to me the proper object of my affections. With the deepest sentiments of my unworthiness, I had the most exalted ideas of the dignity of man, and it was with regret I left the spot, when called away to my lodgings.

Religious pictures in general, are well calculated both to enlighten and edify. To enlighten by exhibiting the most remarkable and prominent facts belonging to the history of religion; to edify by kindling up the fire of devotion.

What place then could be found more proper for religious pictures than the church, the house of God, the sanctuary, where the tremendous sacrifice is offered, and where the sacraments, the divine mysteries, are administered. That place, above all others, is the place of devotion, and it is there, that by hearing the word of God, by offering up our prayers; by meditating on divers religious subjects represented by our pictures; meditating on the religious and moral virtues of the saints, whose images are before us; meditating especially on the great sufferings of Christ, as represented by our crucifixes, on his immense love for sinners, etc., it is there, I say, and by such means, that our piety is both enlightened and inflamed.

Superstition! Amiable superstition indeed, which is productive of so much good! And does not zeal for the cause of religion suggest a sincere desire, that the crucifix and other religious pictures would be substituted in the place of many of those pictures that often adorn the walls of our people of fashion, to the detriment of both religion and morals? Would not that zeal which attacks our religious pictures, and exhibits them most shamefully as the objects of our superstitious worship, be more meritoriously employed in condemning those indecent, immodest, and truly scandalous pictures, which by defiling the imagination, and tarnishing the purity of the heart, are so calculated to extinguish devotion, or the love of God altogether, and therefore to produce an effect the very reverse of that produced by religious pictures: and if the commandment of God, "thou shalt not make to thyself any graven images," etc., ever was intended to be understood in the literal sense, was it not principally with regard to such images of pictures, as have a tendency, by defiling the imagination, and corrupting the heart, to withdraw from the great creator that affection, honor, and worship which are due to him alone, and to place them on the most unworthy of God's creatures. This, in my opinion, is the most dangerous kind of idolatry, the most universally practiced, both by bad Catholics and bad protestants. It is thus the idolatry of the pagans chiefly originated; never would altars have been erected to Bacchus or to Venus had not corrupted man bestowed his heart and affections on the infamous objects of his passions.

Ah Sir! permit me to say it, this is not one of the least of Satan's infernal stratagems, in order to drag millions of souls into the gulf of perdition to raise the hue and cry against popish pictures. Popish idolatry, to sound the trumpet of alarm from the rising to the setting of the sun, and to attack the pious practice of keeping crucifixes and religious pictures, with sharp and poisonous shafts of low ribaldry and sarcasm. I say this is not one of the least of Satan's infernal stratagems, in order to divert the attention of corrupted man from the far more dangerous idolatry in which his own heart is engaged, having bestowed all his attention, his affection, his devotion the unworthy objects of his criminal passions, and feeling for his God nothing but the most perfect indifference.

That gentlemen who call themselves ministers of Christ, who pretend to no inconsiderable share of learning, and who are, or might be well acquainted with the doctrine and practice of the Catholic church, in regard to crucifixes and pictures, should join in this work of destruction, should willfully misrepresent this pious and edifying doctrine and practice, and that they should, with unabashed zeal, attack this pretended popish idolatry, a mere phantom, instead of directing their united efforts against that real idolatry, which is driving millions of souls into the gulf of perdition, is truly astonishing, and affords an additional proof of what I have already advanced: that sinful man, if he should become so presumptuous as to attempt reforming the most holy, the most perfect of all the works of God, the church will, in just punishment for his sacrilegious presumption, be deprived of the heavenly light of God's grace; with seeing eyes he will not see, he will call right wrong, and wrong right, and "blaspheming what he does not know, he will perish in his own corruption" (2Pet. 2:12).

With regard to relics or remains of saints, we honor them in the same way as we do religious images, according to the practice of antiquity. If this practice scandalizes you, Sir, why do you permit your protestant hearers to show honor and respect to the remains, or relics, of their deceased friends? Protestants, are not the remains, or relics of your deceased honored with decent burials, accompanied by many ceremonies? Are not their tombs decorated with costly monuments; are not the remains, or relics, of many protestants embalmed at very great expense, and sometimes even with great labor conveyed many thousand miles to the country of their nativity, to be deposited with great pomp and ceremony in the burying ground of the family? Is not this paying respect and honor to remains and relics?

Such respect and honor are frequently shown by both Catholics and protestants without incurring the guilt of superstition, though shown to the remains or relics of men often notorious for their impiety! To the remains or relics of men who — though entitled by their services to the gratitude of their country — in all their lifetime, never seemed to remember their savior, except to blaspheme his holy name; men who have left us — to say the very best — in the most cruel uncertainty with regard to their future and everlasting destiny, having nothing to found our hopes on, but the late, commonly too late, repentance of the agonizing sinner!

Now, Sir, if such honor and respect may be shown to the relics of men, whose souls have received that sentence which their deeds deserved, and are actually a prey to God's eternal vengeance, why shall it be a sin, why superstition, to show honor and respect to the relics of men who, having been the best among the good, the holiest among the holy, are now enjoying in the bosom of God, the fruits of their penance and charity, sanctified by the merits of their savior? Why shall it be superstition to venerate and honor the relics or remains of the Apostles, whose sacred bodies underwent such great fatigues, labors, and sufferings, in order to administer salvation to the different nations of the globe? Why superstition to respect and venerate the sacred remains of so many thousands of martyrs whose souls and bodies were altogether employed in promoting the glory of God, and the salvation of their fellow mortals, who died under the most excruciating torments, victims of their faith and charity?

How much almighty God is pleased with the honor rendered to the relics of his deceased servants and saints, he has repeatedly proved by making these very relics instruments of miracles.

The very touch of Eliseus' bones raised a dead man to life (4Kings 13:21).

The napkins and handkerchiefs, that had but touched the body of St. Paul, cast out devils and cured diseases (Acts 19:12).

Nay, the very shadow of St. Peter cured diseases in such as honored it (Acts 5:15).

St. Augustine — a holy father respected by both protestants and Catholics — certifies, that at the relics of St. Stephen there were so many miracles wrought, that if all should be recorded, they would fill many volumes (Book 22, of *The City of God*).

When we consider that the body of a Christian — in a great measure — is made partaker of those blessings which by the holy sacraments of the church are conveyed to his soul; that at the general resurrection it will likewise partake of that divine glory, with which the mercy of God will reward his faithful servants: then we must readily confess that a great deal of honor, respect, and veneration is due to the remains or relics of a saint.

The water of regeneration, administered in baptism, sanctifies the body as well as the soul, and renders it susceptible through the merits of Christ for eternal glory. In the holy sacrament of Confirmation, the soul and body are sanctified again by the presence of the Holy Ghost and the anointing with the holy chrism.

By means of that body we eat the flesh of Christ, who thus communicates himself to the soul. Thus, a body — nothing but clay, and by the sin of Adam nothing but corruption — becomes, through the merits of the redeemer, a sanctified body, the temple of the Holy Ghost (1Cor. 6:19): the mansion of Christ, destined to become at the general resurrection a spiritual body, a glorified body, resplendent with light and glory forever (1Cor. 15:43, 44).

Is it superstition, dear Sir, to show great respect and veneration to those remains or relics, which God himself is pleased to honor so highly? But you have been told, or you have read somewhere, that Catholics worship relics! Of this I do not doubt, for I have been told so repeatedly, and have read it in several protestant books; yet, although I lived fifteen years in a Catholic country, and have been acquainted with numbers of Catholics, both of the clergy and laity from almost every Catholic country in Europe, I never knew one so stupid as to worship relics. The most ignorant can easily distinguish the supreme worship due to God alone, from the respect to be shown to the relics of the saints, his servants. If this relative respect may, as we have shown, be lawfully paid to the memorials of all distinguished persons, why may it not be equally so to those of the saints? Veneration has been maintained for them in all ages of the church, for we know that the primitive Christians carried away the relics of St. Ignatius, St. Polycarp, and other martyrs immediately after their execution, and carefully preserved them as more valuable than gold and precious stones. It appears from St. Gregory of Nyssa, who lived in the fourth age, that the relics of the saints were deposited in the churches. Hence, according to the custom of venerable antiquity, those precious relics are kept in costly shrines under and about the altars, and highly venerated, as having been, even in their corruptible state, the temple of the Holy Ghost (1Cor. 6:19), and as being intended for eternal glory, when reunited to the soul.

I shall now dismiss the subject, trusting that I have said more than enough to convince you and your candid hearers, that we are by no means guilty of superstition, in respecting and honoring the images and relics of saints. The principal article of importance left for me to explain is what we believe of the pope.

Article Nine: The Pope

We believe that Jesus Christ, who would have his church to be one, and solidly built upon unity, hath instituted the primacy of St. Peter to support and cement it. To St. Peter alone, our blessed savior said, "thou art Peter [a rock] and upon this rock I will build my church" (Mt. 16:18).

To Peter alone, our blessed savior said, "I have prayed for thee that thy faith fail not; and thou being once converted confirm thy brethren" (Lk. 22:32).

To Peter alone, our blessed savior proposed three times the following question: "Simon, son of Jonas, lovest thou me?" (Jn. 21:15-17); and upon Peter's answer in the affirmative, he tells him twice "feed my lambs" and the third time, "feed my sheep".

Finally, although Jesus Christ tells all his Apostles collectively, "Whatsoever you shall bind on earth, shall be bound also in heaven, and whatsoever you shall loose upon earth shall be loosed also in heaven" (Mt. 28:19). Yet Peter is the only one who receives the power separately and individually; "I will give to thee the keys of the kingdom of heaven, and whatsoever thou shall bind upon earth" (Mt. 26:19).

The name of Peter is generally mentioned before the names of the other Apostles, although it appears that others were called to the Apostleship before him; and we find, upon all important occasions, Peter taking the lead among the Apostles. In the choice of an Apostle to supply the vacancy occasioned by the prevarication of Judas (Acts 3:4-6); in the defense before the high priests (Acts 4); in the judgment against Ananias and Sapphira (Acts 5); in the calling of the Gentiles to the church of Christ (Acts 10); likewise in the first council held at Jerusalem (Acts 15:7).

This primacy of jurisdiction, which was given to St. Peter we acknowledge in the successors of St. Peter, the bishops of Rome, to this present day. Their names are all upon record, and any person versed in the history of the church, and the writings of the holy fathers, will candidly confess, that a primacy of jurisdiction has always been acknowledged in the bishops of Rome.

St. Irenaeus, in the second age, says, that all churches, round about, ought to resort to the Roman church by reason of its more powerful principality (C. 3. c. 3).

In the third age, St. Cyprian says, we hold Peter the head and root of the church, and he calls the church of Rome, St. Peter's chair (Epist. 55).

In the fourth age, St. Basil calls St. Peter that blessed one, who was preferred before the rest of the Apostles (*Serm. de Judicio Dei*).

In the same age, St. Epiphanius says, he chose Peter to be the chief of his disciples (*Heres. 51*).

In the same age, again, St. Cyril of Jerusalem, says, Peter the prince, and most excellent of all the Apostles (*Catechis. 2*).

In the same age, St. Chrysostom says the pastor and head of the church was once a poor fisherman (*Homil. 55 in Mt*). In the same age, Eusebius Emissenus calls St. Peter not only pastor, but the pastor of pastors *(Serm. de Nativ. S. Jo)*.

Again, St. Ambrose says, Andrew first followed our savior, yet Andrew received not the primacy, but Peter (2Cor. 12).

In the fifth age, St. Augustine calls Peter the head of the Apostles, the gatekeeper of heaven, and the foundation of the church (to wit, under Christ) (*Epist. 88*).

The first General Council of Nicaea, A.D. 325, defined that he who holds the See of Rome is the head and chief of all the patriarchs as being the vicar of Christ our Lord over all people, and the universal church of Christ; and whosoever shall contradict this, is excommunicated.

The same is declared by the General Council of Chalcedon (Sess. 15, Can. 58, A.D. 451); and in all subsequent general councils down to the last — the General Council of Trent, A.D. 1545 — the bishop of Rome, with the unanimous consent of all the bishops always presided.

Several learned protestant divines own this primacy of the church of Rome, and acknowledge its usefulness.

Hugo Grotius, a celebrated protestant divine, who was very industrious in examining into the root of all protestant divisions, and very zealous in composing them, positively declares in his last work written shortly before his death, "There can be no hopes of uniting protestants among themselves, except they are united together with those who are in communion with the See of Rome" *(Close of last reply to Rivet)*.

Melancthon likewise confesses that "The primacy is even necessary for preserving unity."

"What is the reason", says the above quoted Grotius (*Reply to Rivet*, ad Art. 7), "that those among Catholics who differ in opinion, still remain in the same body, without breaking communion, and those among the protestants who disagree, cannot do so, however they speak much of brotherly love? Whoever will consider this aright will find how great is the effect of primacy."

"As certain bishops preside over many churchs", says Melancthon, "so the bishop of Rome is president over all bishops. And this canonical policy, no wise man, I think, does or ought to disallow, for the monarchy of the bishop of Rome is, in my judgment, profitable to this end, that consent of doctrine may be retained. Wherefore an agreement may easily be established in this article of the pope's supremacy, if other articles could be agreed upon" *(Cent. Epist. Theol. 74).*

Mr. Thorndike, another celebrated protestant divine, confesses that "A pre-eminence of power and not of rank only has been acknowledged originally in the church of Rome," (*Epic.* L. 3, cap. 20, p. 179).

I have in my possession a letter, written by Martin Luther to Pope Leo X, dated A.D. 1518, and printed among the other works of Luther, in Jena (A. p. 1579, Vol. 1. p. 74). This document is of so much the more importance as it proves beyond the possibility of a doubt that Martin Luther, the father of the pretended reformation, at the date of the letter, acknowledged the bishop of Rome as the head of the church, and his lawful superior, and that if he afterwards rejected the same authority, it was evidently the effect of passion, spite and malice, produced by the sentence of excommunication, which the pope pronounced against him; in this we are confirmed by the indecent, scurrilous, and malicious language made use of by Luther after his excommunication, whenever he speaks of the pope.

I shall only quote two passages of Luther's letters to the pope, the beginning and the conclusion.

> *Epistola Luther ad Leonem X. Rom. Pont. Beatissimo patri Leoni Decimo Pont. Max. F. Martinus Lutherus Augustinianus aeternam saluter.*
>
> *Auditum audivi de me passinum Beatissime Pater, quo intelligi, quosdam amicos fecisse nomen meum gravissime coram te et tuis faetere, ut quia auctoritatem et potestatem clavium, et summi pontificis minuere molitus sim — sed rem ipsam, Beatissime Pater, digneres audire ex me."*

In English:

> Epistle of Luther to Leo X, Roman pontiff. To the most holy father Leo the tenth, sovereign pontiff, brother Martin Luther, of the order of St. Augustine, wishes eternal welfare.
>
> I am informed, most holy father, that you have heard of me the very worst, and understand that certain friends have brought my name into very bad repute before you, etc., saying that I am trying to lessen the authority and power of the keys and of the sovereign pontiff — but deign, most holy father, to hear the whole business from me ...

Luther concludes the letter with the following words:

> *Quare, Beatissime Pater, prostratum me pedibus tuae beatitudinis offero cum omnibus, quae sum et habeo. Vivifica, occide, voca, revoca, approba, reproba, ut placuerit; vocem tuam, vocem Christi in te praesidentis et loquentis agnoscam* etc.

In English:

> "Therefore, most holy father, prostrate at the feet
> of your holiness, I offer myself and all I have. Vivify,
> kill, call, recall, approve or reprove as you please in
> your voice I acknowledge the voice of Christ, who
> presides and speaks to you, etc. [13]

I shall not be detained in defending the temporal
power exercised by some popes. That the pope has any
such power was never an article of faith. It is true that
this power has been assumed and exercised. Yet candor
requires that we should view history as it is in itself, and
not as it appears through the prism of misrepresentation.
When ignorance and barbarity, which were the natural

---

13. Such was the language of Luther till his doctrine was condemned,
when he shook off all authority, and set up the tribunal of his own
private judgment. No sooner had he done so than his disciples,
proceeding on the same principle, undertook to prove that his
own doctrine was erroneous. Carlstadt, Zuinglius, Oecolampadius,
Muncer, and several others of his followers, wrote and preached
against him and against each other with the utmost virulence.
In vain did he claim a superiority over them; in vain did he denounce
hellfire against them; he had the mortification to see his assumed
authority, as well as threats, totally disregarded by them. His followers continued to act in open defiance of him, till their mutual abuse
became so scandalous as to fill the more moderate among them
with grief and shame. Experience convinced them that for preserving unity of faith, and regularity of discipline, a fixed supreme
authority is required. Capito, minister of Strasburg, writing to
Farel, pastor of Geneva, thus complains to him, "God has given
me to understand the mischief we have done, by our precipitancy
in breaking with the pope," etc. Dudith, another reformer, writing
to Beza, says, "In what single point are those churches which have
declared war against the pope, agreed amongst themselves?"

consequences of the dissolution of the Roman Empire, and of the invasion of the barbarians, had spread all over Europe, national and civil wars were the order of the day. Nations were arrayed against nations, kings and emperors against each other; myriads of petty chieftains, each one with his retinue, were laying waste the whole face of Europe. No safety was to be found, but destruction, violence, murder, and bloodshed were to be met with everywhere. Among the laity there were none who knew how, or were willing, or able to administer justice. In that general desolation, it was but natural that both the people and their chiefs should turn their attention towards the See of Peter, on which sat men to whom their eminent virtue and science gave a moral influence which placed them above all their contemporaries. All were anxious to take refuge under their protection. It was not the popes who sought for power, but it was power which forced itself, as it were, upon the popes. The people were like children calling on their common father to preserve them from destruction. Had the pope turned a deaf ear to their call, he would have been accused of egotism and indifference; he protected them, and he is accused of ambition, of thirst of power, etc., as well might a young man who has become of age, accuse his guardian of ambition, because, during his infancy, he watched over his interests.

It is a remarkable fact, that whenever the pope has exercised that temporal power, which is the object of so much and so bitter censure, he has exercised it for the interest of the people against their oppressors, by deciding that they were no longer, in conscience, bound to obey those princes who, instead of acting the part of fathers towards their subjects, had become their insufferable tyrants. It is also remarkable, that on those memorable occasions, when the pope is said to have deprived princes of their dominions, it was never for his own benefit, and they never acquired an inch of ground for themselves.

In short, the exercise of that power was grounded on the general jurisprudence of those times, and princes themselves contributed and gave sanction to it, by frequently applying to the Holy See for the settlement of their temporal concerns. Thus, the accusation of ambition, pride, etc., against the popes disappears when the facts are accurately investigated and truly stated.

What is called the patrimony of St. Peter is an estate which the pope owes to the munificence of his powerful friends, and which he has possessed for upwards of a thousand years; and when he has taken up arms, it has been either to protect it against aggressors, or to rescue it from the hands of those who had invaded it unjustly.

I shall never try to defend the conduct of all our popes. Peter denied his master; is it a wonder then if among so many of his successors, some should be found guilty of prevarications? Some, no doubt, were far from being edifying in their conduct. Christ foresaw it; what he says of the Pharisees and Jewish doctors may be said of them. "The Pharisees and Scribes have sitten upon the chair of Moses. All therefore whatsoever they shall say unto you, observe and do; but according to their works do ye not" (Mt. 18:2, 3).

Although in their capacity as men, some popes have exhibited proofs of their weakness and corruption, yet as heads of the church, they have all during these eighteen hundred years taught one and the same Catholic doctrine.

If the abuse of power were conclusive against the title of him who exercises it, there would be no longer any authority upon earth. On the contrary, I may safely advance, that the real or supposed abuse of power by some popes, not only proves nothing against the solidity of their title, but is an argument in favor of its existence.

If we take a retrospective view of the history of the world, we shall find that abuses of power have almost always been attended with the destruction of the power in which they originated. Thus the abuse of regal power turned Rome into a republic; the abuse of republican power, turned republican Rome into imperial Rome. Thus the abuse of imperial power turned Switzerland and other countries of Europe into republics, by abolishing the authority abused. Thus the abuse of English power turned the United States into a republic, by abolishing in these States the power of England.

What is the reason then that the abuses of papal power, supposing them to be as great and numerous as you represent them to be, have not been attended with the same consequences; the destruction of the papal power itself? Why does that power, after a lapse of eighteen hundred years, still continue to be acknowledged by three-fourths of Christendom.

Christ gives the answer to this interesting query; "Thou art Peter, and upon this rock I will build my church, and the gates of hell shall not prevail against it" (Mt. 16:18).

Attacked with the most relentless fury for ages by the combined efforts of hell and earth, by fierce enemies in and out of the Catholic church apparently on the brink of destruction, its downfall has often been prophesied.

Many of the sovereign pontiffs fell victims to those persecutions. The majestic rock of St. Peter remained, Peter was put to death. Pius the VII was banished and kept in close confinement. During the period of about eighteen hundred years, from Peter to Pius VII, the chair of St. Peter has still been occupied, and we have upon the records of the Catholic church, the names of more than two hundred and fifty sovereign pontiffs, who followed one another in regular succession on the chair of St. Peter, a great number of whom died martyrs for their faith, very few of whom can be said to have been scandalous.

Mr. Hume, who certainly will not be suspected of partiality for the Catholic religion, owns that although the popes sometimes misused the authority they had, they most commonly made a laudable and humane use of it, by promoting peace among Christian princes, by uniting them against the hordes of barbarians who were extending every day their bloody conquests, by repressing simony, violence and every kind of excess, which overbearing, cruel masters committed against their weak, oppressed subjects; it served to make, of the whole Christian world, one great family, whose differences were adjusted by one common father, the pontiff of the God of concord and justice. A grand and affecting idea that, of the most extensive and the noblest administration that could be thought of.

From what I have stated, you will plainly see, dear Sir, that all that can be alleged of the criminal conduct or abuse of power of some popes, makes nothing against the Catholic church. It only proves that popes are subject to human frailties in common with the rest of mankind; that with the Roman orator, they have a right to say, *homo sum, humani nihil a me alienum puto*, and that no power or authority, how great soever; no character, how sacred soever; affords sufficient security against the corruption of human nature, and the influence of the passions.

Far from affording an argument against the Catholic church, I rather think that the corruption of popes, and of the clergy, admitting it to exist even beyond the limits our adversaries would fain wish to suppose, affords a powerful argument in favor of the Catholic church.

Any person possessing the least knowledge of the nature of man, and versed in the history of religion, will own that religious opinions have but too often originated in the passions and the corrupted heart of man, their dictates being too often mistaken for those of cool and impartial reason. Neither will it be denied that the great variety of religious systems (which may be counted by hundreds) contradicting and condemning one another, owe their origin to the variety of human passions and interests. Before the coming of Christ, the objects of religious worship were more

spiritual, or more carnal, according to the impulse given
to the hearts of men, by their respective passions,
either towards spiritual or carnal objects. The world,
embracing Christianity, has introduced into the church
its corruption and its passions. Although men ruled by
the same passions are, by the overwhelming force of
evidence, prevented from mistaking the main object of
their worship, which is Jesus Christ, yet being under
the influence of these various passions and interests
they pretend to find out various ways of going to
Jesus, ways more easy, more smooth, in short more
congenial to each one's passions and inclinations; ways
more spiritual or more carnal, ways all differing from
the old narrow road which alone was pointed out by
Jesus Christ as leading to him. Now, Sir, starting from
this undeniable position, and admitting popes, clergy,
and if you choose, laypeople of the Catholic church
by millions, to have been very much corrupted, the
popes and clergy to have been ruled by pride, ambition,
covetousness, and all the passions that corrupted
hearts are subject to; to have set up and enforced the
most extravagant claims, to have with Satan equaled
themselves to the most high; if notwithstanding this
sink of corruption, if not withstanding the wonderful
irritation and opposition which such tyrannical claims
and acts must have produced, if notwithstanding this
dreadful conflict of passions and clashing of interest,
the Catholic church has still continued to this day,
during a period of eighteen centuries, to preserve its
perfect unity, has still continued to acknowledge the
same power, and the same head, though guilty of such
enormous abuses, must we not confess, that here is the
hand of the most high?

Travel over all the Catholic countries of Europe.
Why has the demon of discord, who has so many
times overturned their governments by the most

dreadful revolutions? Why have the furious tempests raised by human passions, that have divided, destroyed, leveled with the ground; so many human institutions that seemed to bid defiance to time? Why have they not been able to divide, to destroy Catholic unity, to hurl the pope from the See of St. Peter, to emancipate Catholics from the tyrannical yoke (as it is called) of the Roman pontiffs?

The answer is plain. The Catholic church, the See of St. Peter, and Catholic unity, are all the work of God, which man cannot destroy.

Popes, bishops, and priests, as individuals, are subject to all the passions, and form of themselves nothing but a dead body, which, like any other human body, would soon become a prey to corruption and dissolution, were it not, according to the promise of Jesus Christ, animated, vivified and preserved forever in perfect unity by the Holy Spirit of Truth. The Holy Ghost being the soul of that body, keeps it alive, keeps it, head and members, in unity and harmony. Being himself the foundation of truth and holiness, he dispels the mists of falsehood and corruption, which the malice of Satan and the passions of individuals, whether clergy or laypeople, often cause to arise in order to obscure the bright and pure rays of divine revelation. Thus, the abuses in the church, whether in the members or the head, are reformed by the church, and the words of Christ accomplished: the gates of hell shall not prevail against it.

I shall take but little time to refute the false and ridiculous charge of those who accuse our popes of granting indulgences to commit sin, requiring a certain sum of money, greater or smaller, according to the kind of sin for which the indulgence is granted.

That such a charge is frequently published in protestant books, and from protestant pulpits, you will not deny. Now, all Catholic books, sanctioned by the church, no matter where or when published, tell you plainly, that an indulgence is nothing but a remission or relaxation of certain temporal punishments, remaining due to sin, after the guilt and eternal punishment are remitted, as in the case of David, to whom Nathan said, "The Lord hath taken away thy sin; nevertheless the child that is born to thee shall surely die" (2Kings 12:13, 14).

Such indulgences are granted upon the sinner's sincere repentance, and satisfaction for his past sins, the Apostles and their successors having received from Christ full authority to forgive the sins of those who are judged worthy of forgiveness. There is no doubt, but owing to the perverseness of many individuals among the clergy, the most shocking abuses have taken place sometimes in the dispensation of indulgences. However, as these abuses were not sanctioned, but reprobated by the church, as you can see if you read Chapter 9 of the 21st Session, and *Decretum de Indulgentiis* of the 25th Session of the Council of Trent, they of course make nothing against the holiness, purity, and infallibility of the church of Christ, and only prove that all human flesh is subject to infirmities.

I believe, dear Sir, that I have fulfilled my promise, and proved to everybody's satisfaction, that Roman Catholics are not guilty of superstition in submitting to the spiritual jurisdiction of St. Peter and of his successors, the sovereign pontiffs or bishops of Rome.

Permit me to add a few words more on another important subject upon which our doctrine is grossly misrepresented, I mean the doctrine of the Catholic church on toleration.

Article Ten: Toleration

We are represented as the most intolerant set of men upon earth. The most cruel, the most uncharitable intolerance is laid to our charge;[14] but this charge against us probably proceeds from a misunderstanding of our doctrine on that subject.

The question here is not about civil toleration. Catholics and protestants are united in considering civil

---

14. A favorite topic with most protestant writers is to charge the Catholic church with a spirit of persecution. They constantly describe her as intolerant, and as claiming the right of punishing those who differ from her with fire and sword. This is a malicious accusation, intended to excite hatred against her. The Catholic church neither does, nor ever did claim any such right. Persecuting laws, it is true, have been made and acted upon by several Catholic princes, who, for the most part, judged such necessary to preserve the ancient order of things, and prevent the anarchy which attended reforming principles. Is it fair then, to ascribe what has been done, chiefly from motives of state policy, to the persecuting spirit of the church? But has not persecution been practiced by protestants in every country in which they have acquired power; and this not only against Catholics, but even fellow protestants? Witness the conduct of the first settlers in New England. It may here be asked, can our accusers show in the statutes of any Catholic country, any to be compared with the demoralizing and inhuman penal laws of England and Ireland? What Catholics have for centuries suffered from religious persecution in the latter country alone, may be safely said to counterbalance all that protestants have suffered on the score of religion through out the rest of the world. Such writers then as represent the Catholic religion as essentially intolerant, and the protestant as alone admitting toleration, shows anything but candor. It would seem that they either have unaccountably forgotten the existence of the above laws, still in several instances acted upon, or imagined their readers so ignorant, as not to know that such existed.

toleration an invaluable blessing, especially in a country like ours, where there were so many different denominations at the time its constitution was formed. We all agree in believing that no authority, merely human, possesses any right of controlling the consciences of men.

The question then before us is concerning theological toleration, *viz.*, whether almighty God can approve of so many different religious systems which we find established upon earth; whether all these different religious systems can be considered as so many different ways to heaven. If so, we ought to be in favor of universal toleration.

The Catholic church teaches that Jesus Christ established but one church for the salvation of man, and that out of that one church salvation is not to be had.

The written word is very plain on this subject: "There shall be made one fold and one pastor," (Jn. 10:16). "I beseech you, that you all speak one thing, and that there be no schisms among you, but that you be perfect in one sense and one judgment" (1Cor. 1:10).

Christ prayed that his disciples might be one (Jn. 17:11).

"One Lord, one faith, one baptism" (Eph. 4:5). "He that believeth not shall be condemned" (Mk. 16:16). "Without faith it is impossible to please God" (Heb. 11:6).

"I believe in one holy Catholic and Apostolic church," says the Nicene Creed, which is admitted by both Catholics and protestants.

This is the Catholic faith (says the creed of St. Athanasius, likewise admitted by Catholics and protestants) which, if anyone does not faithfully and firmly believe, he cannot be saved.

Several creeds and professions of faith, which I have carefully perused, very plainly and unequivocally assert that out of the church, which is but one, salvation cannot be obtained: so says the church of England, so says the church of Scotland, etc. What, indeed, can be more reasonable. And what, on the other hand, more unreasonable, more absurd, than universal toleration? To be convinced of it, it is only necessary to examine what true religion is.

True religion is an institution of which God himself is the founder. It is an institution in which God makes known to man what he must believe, and what he must do in order to obtain salvation. It is a system, not the offspring of human reason, not the result of human philosophy, not the ingenious contrivance of human talents and learning; it originates in the fountain of eternal and infinite wisdom, and was by the supreme authority of God, established on earth, to control both the understanding and the will of man, dictating to his understanding what he must believe, and to his will what he must submit to do in order to obtain salvation. It will not be denied that God has as much right to control our understanding, to require a submission of our understanding to the belief of whatever mysteries he chooses to reveal, as he has to control our will to submit to his commandments. It will be also acknowledged, that God alone can save man, that God alone can institute a religion worthy of himself, and adequate to supply all the spiritual wants and necessities of man, a religion, in which all those heavenly blessings are administered which transform the carnal into a spiritual man, and finally into a citizen of heaven. God alone can draw man out of the mire of original corruption, and he alone has a right to determine by what means this wonderful change from depravity to innocence is to take place. None can attach to the weak element of water the power of performing this astonishing change.

None but God can wash away the iniquities of man, restore to him his sanctifying grace, and none except him, has a right to determine the means by, and the conditions upon which, this blessing of reconciliation and forgiveness is to be granted.

None but God can feed and nourish the soul of man, or arm that soul with power sufficient to overcome his spiritual enemies, and to persevere to the last breath in the performance of his duty, and in the service of his creator.

In short, Sir, whatever blessings we stand in need of, none but God can convey them, or determine the precise manner in which we are to obtain them. To say that man, even the wisest man, may, by the force of reasoning, contrive a religious system, calculated to answer the above purposes, is to equal him to God.

Religion, then, is that divine institution of God's own creation, in which is shown to man the way to glorify God, and to procure everlasting happiness to his own soul. In it are established by Jesus Christ certain rites or ceremonies, as so many channels to convey to our souls those manifold blessings, which we stand in need of. Those rites are called sacraments, and must be precisely the very thing that Jesus Christ instituted. If they are only of the institution of man, they are no longer entitled to religious respect as man has not the power to annex heavenly blessings to the performing of certain external acts. I shall explain this general position by a few examples.

Jesus Christ has annexed, to the pouring of water on a person, and the pronouncing of the words, "I baptize thee in the name of the Father, and of the Son, and of the Holy Ghost," the grace of cleansing that person from the guilt of original sin. So we are told by the church, the infallible interpreter of God's word.

Pray, Sir, would it be in the power of man to substitute some other words and ceremonies, and to make them equally efficacious in conveying the same blessing? I believe not.

Jesus Christ has annexed to the words, *absolvo te a peccatis tuis* (I absolve thee from thy sins), when pronounced by a lawful successor of the Apostles, the power of really remitting sins, provided the sinner is well disposed. So we are told again by the infallible interpreter of God's word. Pray, Sir, would it be in the power of man to give the same efficacy to some other words of his own contrivance? I think not. Jesus Christ has annexed to the imposition of hands by legally consecrated bishops, and to the pronouncing of certain words, the power of communicating the Holy Ghost, which rite we call the sacrament of Confirmation. So we are told again by the church. Is it in the power of man, by some other ceremonies and words of his own contrivance, to impart the Spirit of God to his fellow-mortals? Certainly not.

It is obvious then, that none but the one system of religion, which Jesus Christ himself established is entitled to any religious respect whatever, in that one alone are to be found the true scripture, the true interpreter of scripture, the true word of God, the true sacrifice, the true sacraments; only in that one system of religion are to be found the true ministry of Christ, the power of the keys, etc. Reform that system of religion in one only point and you deform it, you change the work of God into the work of man. Denominate this doctrine uncharitable, cruel, barbarous, or what ever you please, it is beyond all doubt the doctrine of truth and common sense; and of course, the only one which genuine charity will make use of, because it is the duty of charity to lead along the thorny paths of truth, and not along the enchanting and flowery roads of falsehood and deception. I here appeal not to your learning, not to your genius and talents, but only to your common sense, which enables you to know that black is not white; and I ask you, whether it be uncharitable to teach that contradictory systems of religion cannot all proceed from the Holy Spirit of Truth; whether it be uncharitable to say, that of a hundred religious systems contradicting one another in some point or other, only one can possibly be true, only one can proceed from the spirit of truth? When we hear one minister preaching up the necessity of Baptism for salvation, and another promising salvation without Baptism, is it uncharitable to say that one of them is the minister of error, and not of Christ? When we hear one minister declare infants not admissible to Baptism, and another, on the contrary, insisting on the necessity of baptizing infants, is it uncharitable to say that one must be a teacher of error?

Is it uncharitable to say, that if Calvin is right, Luther must be wrong; if Arminius teacheth the truth, Gomar must be a teacher of falsehood; if Socinus is the teacher of pure and undefiled truth, Luther, Calvin, Arminius, Melancthon, Fox, Zuinglius, etc., must all be ministers of error.

Or will it be more charitable (adding blasphemy to deception) to say, as the independent minister appears to do, (p. 58), that all these different teachers, although contradicting one another in most essential points, are all ministers of the God of truth? He makes mention of no less than seventy-odd names of persons who were raised, he says, by the almighty, from the seventh to the sixteenth century, to oppose the errors of the church of Rome, many of whom differed more from one another in matters of faith, than they did from the Catholic church. It appears then that he, with many more of his colleagues, admits but one criterion of the true faith, *viz.*, that of protesting against the holy Catholic church. Thus when Luther pleads the necessity of baptism, and the real presence of Christ in the Eucharist, he will say, the man is right. When Fox rejects Baptism, Eucharist, and all other sacraments, he, with the political Tinker, will say again, *the man is right*. When Calvin, differing from both, sees nothing in the Eucharist but signs or symbols of the flesh and blood of Christ, again he will say, the man *is right*.

When Wickliff rises up against almost all divine and human institutions, and tries to establish his abominable system of liberty and independence, which caused so much blood to flow, here again, *the man is right.*

The independent minister, and I believe, all our modern ministers, those I mean, who would appear liberal, charitable, and I suppose, fashionable, will tell you, that all those men, and many more, were true ministers of God. They will tell you, forsooth, that they evinced their divine mission by opposing, by protesting against the church of Rome.

Thus is common sense sacrificed at the shrine of spite and malice, and a most impious, blasphemous system, a compound of the most palpable contradictions, obtruded on the ignorant and the prejudiced, as the pure religion of Jesus, under the name of *protestant religion.*

Here are toleration and liberality extending to all sorts of creeds, but excluding the greatest number of the Christian people.

You will hardly call such a toleration and liberality charitable, as on the one hand it makes too many exceptions, as on the other hand, as I have proved, it is not founded upon truth, and cannot meet the approbation of common sense; it is a deceptive kind of charity, it calls out "peace, peace," and there is no peace; it lulls the unhappy sinner into false security, and under the pompous names of reformation, protestantism, etc., leads him far away from the only true church of Jesus Christ.

Catholic intolerance is both rational and charitable; it is founded upon the immovable rock of eternal truth. Sure of the assistance of Christ forever, sure of being directed by the spirit of truth into the one truth forever, the holy Catholic church has at all times condemned as heresy any doctrine contradicting her doctrine.

As a tender mother and faithful spouse of Jesus Christ, she has always, in the spirit of charity, endeavored to preserve her children from the delusive and flowery paths of heresy; and in the most sorrowful accents, she prays, she entreats those that have left her, to return to her pale. She perseveres in fervent prayers for the conversion of her strayed children, and would fain carry them back upon her shoulders to the only one fold of Christ. Is not this genuine charity?

Moreover, whilst the holy Catholic church, guided forever by the Holy Ghost, fulminates her anathemas against all kinds of heresies or false doctrines, she feels nothing but charity and compassion for so many individuals born in heterodox societies. She charitably supposes several of them honest in their errors, invincibly ignorant of the true church, and consequently excusable in the sight of God. But still she deplores their misfortune of being deprived of so many means of salvation, not to be found out of her pale.

Catholic intolerance then, exhibits stronger features of genuine and practical charity, than protestant toleration and liberality. Yet I must confess its sound is harsher, and by no means so melodious as the siren song of deception and flattery, which calls every system, *the true church of Christ,* provided it protests against the Catholic church. The observation made by Tertullian in his time was that the sole principle of unity amongst heretics is the hatred of Catholicity. The same may be truly applied to the numerous sects of the present day, which seem to have no other link of unity than their hostility to the parent church, which they have all abandoned. This seems their only rallying point, for whether we look to the old world or the new, we will see the singular spectacle of men differing from one another in faith, as widely as earth from heaven, yet uniting in opposing that of Catholics. Nay, this animosity has long since been judged the criterion, not only of protestant orthodoxy, but of protestant loyalty, since the British legislature required of the members of both houses of parliament, as a necessary condition before taking their seats, to swear that they believed the Catholic worship to be superstitious, idolatrous, and damnable! Provided they held this fundamental point, they were at perfect liberty to hold any other religious opinion, or none if they pleased.

Conclusion

I have endeavored to explain the most essential articles of Catholic faith, in order to prove that we are not guilty of superstition, and I hope that with the candid, I have succeeded. Those who are not sincere, who with seeing eyes will not see, I cannot expect to convince. Many points of minor importance I have omitted, not wishing to swell my defense into a large volume. Thus, I have said nothing about the Sign of the Cross, about holy water, blessed salt, blessed candles, and many more things made use of by Catholics. It is surprising indeed, that people who call themselves Christians, should be scandalized at the sign of their redemption. Freemasons have their signs, and many other societies have their signs; soldiers have their signs and counter signs; pray, why should the soldier of Jesus Christ not be permitted to arm himself with the sign of the standard of Christianity, under which our chief conquered the powers of hell, and under which alone the Christian soldier is to conquer? Tertullian testifies (in his book *de Corona Militis*) that the practice of making the Sign of the Cross is most ancient and most common in the church of Christ.

Pray, how will those feel, who despise and ridicule that practice, when they shall SEE THE SIGN OF THE SON OF MAN appear in heaven? (Mt. 24:30).

As for holy water, blessed salt, and many other things blessed by the prayers of the church, I do not understand how they can become any subject of scandal to anyone believing in the power of Christ.

If inanimate things have been cursed by God's infinite justice in punishment of the sin of our first parents (Gen. 3:17), that curse cannot be removed and changed into a blessing but by the power and the merits of Jesus Christ. This supreme power, confided by Christ to his ministers (Mt. 28:18), is exercised by them in blessing water, salt, and many other things for the use of man.

Where is the superstition in believing that those elements, created for the use of man, but cursed by a justly irritated God, may be blessed again and sanctified by the prayers of the church, through the merits of Jesus Christ?

Instances are so very common of the good effects produced by the use of holy water, blessed salt, and many other blessed things, that it would take volumes to publish them all. I have been frequently applied to by parents, whose children were afflicted with the most strange and unaccountable symptoms, and have found that, after all the powers of medicine had been tried in vain, a little blessed salt, or some other things, blessed by the prayers of the church, through the merits of Jesus Christ, very often performed a complete cure.

If you were to read the memoirs of those missionaries, who, with unabated zeal, and often at the expense of their blood, converted millions of idolaters in Canada, South America, the East Indies, China, Cochin China, Siam, Persia, you would find instances, by hundreds, of the efficacy of the Sign of the Cross, holy water, etc., in banishing evil spirits, and destroying that power which those infernal spirits frequently exercise over the souls, bodies, and property of those who are guilty of idolatry, of which we find so many instances in the New Testament.

God has chosen the weak things of this world, that he might confound the strong (1 Cor. 1:27). The efficacy of blessed things is so well known to many protestants that it is not very uncommon to see protestants apply to Catholic priests for holy water, blessed salt, blessed candles, etc.

To believe that any miraculous power or virtue naturally resides in that water, salt, or any other of God's inanimate creatures, would be superstition indeed, but to believe that the infinite power and goodness of Jesus Christ, exercised by the church, may apply a certain blessing to those inanimate creatures, so as to render them productive of certain happy effects when applied to man, is no more superstition, than to believe that the waters of the Jordan, through the power of God, became instrumental in curing the leprosy of Naaman (4Kings 5:14).

Our age, dear Sir, is the age of incredulity, commonly called the age of philosophy. It is almost fashionable to disbelieve, to reject with disdain and contempt everything which we cannot perceive our carnal senses, or compass with our limited and much corrupted understanding. At the hour of death, at the entrance of eternity, when the senses shall have lost their baneful influence, and corrupted reason shall have been almost extinguished, we shall remember that God, who can do what he pleases, to whom the laws of nature are subject, who can and does, for his own glory and the salvation of man, subvert those very laws, as he did through the ministry of Moses, when he opened the Red Sea, as he did again through the ministry of Joshua, when he stopped the sun in its course. We shall then remember that, there is a God of truth, who ought to be believed, who must be believed, and as much so, when what he reveals is incomprehensible, as when it is ever so plain; as much so, when what he reveals appears contrary to the laws of nature, as when his revelations are in unison with those laws.

Permit me, Sir, to close my subject by contracting into as narrow a compass as possible, and exhibiting before your eyes, under one point of view, all the sublime mysteries of our creed, which have been explained to you one by one.

"I believe in God the Father almighty, creator of heaven and earth." As father, he loves us, as God, his love for us is infinite, and as almighty, he can do whatever he pleases to show his love in practice.

"And in Jesus Christ, his only Son, our Lord," both God and man, our only redeemer, only as man subject to sufferings, and only as God able to satisfy God.

"Who was conceived by the Holy Ghost, born of the Virgin Mary." Jesus Christ then was both God and man, whilst enclosed in the womb of the Virgin Mary. The Virgin Mary, is of course, the mother of Jesus Christ, both God and man, and consequently she is entitled to the highest honor which it is possible for man to exhibit to the most honorable and the most perfect of God's creatures.

"Suffered under Pontius Pilate, was crucified died and was and buried." Suffered out of infinite love for man, the most cruel torments that the malice of hell and earth could inflict on him; suffered unto death, that we may live.

"He descended into hell; the third day he arose again from the dead." He descended not into the hell of the damned, but as St. Peter explains it (1 Pet. 3:18, 19, 20) into that prison, or place of temporal punishment, in which were detained many souls, that had departed before the coming of Christ.

"He ascended into heaven; sits at the right hand of God the Father almighty." There his merits are continually pleading in our behalf; there he is our high priest forever, according to the order of Melchisedech; there he continually guides and protects his church, being with his ministers to the end of time, protecting them against the spirit of error and darkness, according to his repeated promises (Mt. 28:20; Jn. 16:13; etc.).

"From thence he shall come to judge the living and the dead"; to give everlasting life to those who had the true faith, being members of the only true Catholic church, and who led a holy life; and to punish with everlasting torments those who did not believe (Mk. 6:16); those who, through their own fault, were not members of his only true Catholic church, and those who led an ungodly life (Mt. 16:27).

"I believe in the Holy Ghost"; who proceeds from the Father and the Son, and is equal to them; who was promised by Jesus Christ to his church (Jn. 16:26, 16:13); who actually came upon the Apostles on Whitsunday (Acts 2:1, 4); who has enabled them and their successors to this day, and will enable them to the end of time, to persevere in the true and genuine doctrine of Jesus Christ, without deviating from it in one single point (Jn. 16:16, 17–18).

"The holy Catholic church"; that church of which Jesus Christ is the architect, built upon a rock, to stand forever, in spite of all the efforts of hell (Mt. 16:18, 28:20); that church "*is the house of the living God*" (1Tim. 3:15); "*the kingdom of Christ*" (Lk 1:33; Dan. 2:44); "*the sheepfold of Christ*" (Jn. 10:16); "*the body of which Christ is the head*" (Col. 1:18; Eph. 5:23); "*the spouse of Christ*" (Eph. 5:24 31); "*that church is always subject and faithful to Christ*" (Eph. 5:24); "*always without spot, wrinkle or blemish, always holy*" (Eph. 5:27); "*always loved and cherished by him*" (Eph. 5:25, 29; 5:31, 33); "*that church is the pillar and ground of the truth*" (1Tim. 3:15); "*always one*" (Cant. 6:8, 9; Jn. 10:16; Eph. 4:4, 5); "*always visible*" (Isa. 2:2, 3; Mich. 4:1, 2; Mt. 5:14); "*always and infallibly teaching the truth, the whole truth, and nothing but the truth*" (Mt. 16:18, 28:19, 20; Jn. 14:16, 17, 26, 16:13; 1Tim. 3:14, 15; etc.).

That church, of course, can never stand in need of reformation. The very attempt of man to reform this, the most perfect, the most noble of all the works of God, is a most daring, a most sacrilegious, most blasphemous act of impiety, of which no precedent can be found, except in the attempt made by Satan to equal himself to the Most High, for which he was precipitated into the eternal abyss. This holy Catholic church is spread over the universe, which makes it Catholic, teaching everywhere the same doctrine, because she is wholly inspired and directed by the holy spirit of truth (Jn. 14:16, 17, 26), and always guided by Christ (Mt. 28: 20). The ministers of that church form but one body, of which St. Peter and his successors were by divine authority constituted heads (Mt. 16:18, 19; Lk. 22:32; Jn. 21:15, 16, 17).

"Communion of saints." In the church of God, there is a communion of its members in holy things, being partakers of the same spiritual blessings, sacraments, etc., which Christ empowered his church to administer. We likewise communicate with the blessed saints in heaven. They are already landed on the shores of eternal peace. We are yet tossed by the raging billows of a tempestuous sea. We stretch out our hands to them for help; we beg their intercession to obtain a safe landing. We meditate on their virtues; we are encouraged by their examples; we confide much in their charitable intercession (Apoc. 5:8; Zach. 1:12; 2Mach. 15:12, 14; Tob. 12:12; Heb. 1:14; Apoc. 2:26, 27; Lk. 15:10; Mt. 18:10). Whilst we look up to the saints in heaven for their help and assistance, we offer up our prayers and intercession for those of our fellow members, who having died before they had fully satisfied the justice of God, have yet to suffer for a time, before they can be admitted into that sanctuary where nothing defiled can enter (1Cor. 3; 1Pet. 3:18-20).

"The forgiveness of sins." This forgiveness of sins, originating in the infinite power and mercy of God alone, and granted solely in consideration of the merits of Christ, is administered to us by the ministers of Christ in the holy Catholic church, first in the sacrament of Baptism; and then again in the sacrament of Penance, upon our sincere repentance and conversion, and upon sincere confession (Mt. 18:18; Jn. 20: 22, 23: Acts 19:18, Jas. 5:16, etc.).

"The resurrection of the body, and life ever lasting, Amen." A glorious resurrection of soul and body, by which we are to become members of the church triumphant of Jesus Christ, will be granted to those only, who have been true members of the only one and true church militant of Christ on earth. And those who had not the holy Catholic church, the spouse of Christ, for their mother, will find to their everlasting sorrow, that they have not Jesus Christ for their Father and savior.

Permit me now, dear Sir, to address you in the spirit of charity, and to entreat you to meditate seriously on the following solemn truths:

The day is fast approaching, when you and I will be summoned before the dreaded tribunal of Jesus Christ; I, in the capacity of a Roman Catholic priest; you, in the capacity of a protestant minister; both claiming the title of minister of Christ. What will become of that one who shall not be able then to substantiate his claim, and establish his title. We may be suffered by a God of infinite mercy and patience to establish the most unfounded, the most extravagant titles before men; but will the illusion be suffered to continue before the tribunal of eternal justice? And will not the bright rays of pure and undefiled truth forever dissipate those foul and thick mists of corruption, which in this world enabled us to dupe ourselves and others? Will not the two-edged sword of truth cut off all those difficulties which our own corruption had raised as a bulwark against the authenticated revelations of Jesus Christ? Will not the bright and dazzling rays of glory, that shall emanate from the throne of the omnipotent judge, be the most incontestable proof of the divinity of his revelation, and of the truth of those mysteries, against which proud and corrupted reason suggested so many difficulties?

When the sacred code shall be opened, by which all Christians are to be tried, will it be permitted there, think you, to allege the foolish dictates of human philosophy, in opposition to the plain revelations of that sacred code? Will it be permitted there to talk about reforming the most noble work of the great God? Will it be permitted there, by way of apology, to tell Jesus Christ that he broke his repeated promises? That he had promised to be with his church to the end of time, and yet that he had forsaken that church and permitted it to go astray? That he had promised the spirit of truth to it to guide it into all the truth forever, yet he had withdrawn that spirit of truth, and permitted the church to become a sink of errors and idolatry? Will it be permitted there to call the plain ordinances of Jesus Christ, papist superstitions? Will it be permitted there (by way of apology for not complying with his ordinances) to tell Jesus Christ that such and such things were impossible? That no man could forgive sin, not even those who most plainly and distinctly had received that power from him? Will you be permitted there, think you, to tell Jesus Christ to his face, that it was impossible for him to give his flesh and blood under the appearance of bread and wine? Will you there be permitted to allege the testimony of your corrupted senses and limited reason, in opposition to the plain and repeated assertions of infinite wisdom? Will it be permitted there, think you, in the face of the cross, that sign of the Son of Man, to ridicule those, who signed themselves with that holy sign? In short, Sir, will it be permitted there, to deceive yourself and others any longer? Corrupted reason sat upon the tribunal in this world, and with more than satanic presumption summoned before it the tremendous mysteries clearly and distinctly revealed by an omnipotent God, to be judged, to be approved or condemned, according to its own whimsical notions, and more so according to its corrupt inclinations. The case will be then reversed, infinite power and wisdom will occupy the judgment seat; proud reason, with all its boast of philosophy, will stand confused, appalled, convicted, and be forever silenced. Will it be permitted to say, by way of apology, I rejected such and such mysteries because I could not understand them, or because they

appeared to me impossible? But, you were not required
to understand them, you were only commanded to listen
and adore; and this you could have done as easily as so
many millions of persons as wise as yourself. Ah! Sir,
believe me, believe a person who is sincerely concerned
for the salvation of your soul; the very garb which at
present is considered by you as a mark of distinction
and honor, will, before the dreadful tribunal, on the day
of God's eternal vengeance, be the terror and despair
of your soul, and its everlasting condemnation; I mean
the garb of protestantism. You protested! Against what?
Against the church of Christ! Against divine ordinances!
Against divine and tremendous mysteries? Against all
that is sacred? This was not enough. Under the title of
minister of Christ, you taught thousands to do the same,
to ridicule and blaspheme what they did not understand,
and by misrepresenting the holy mysteries of the Catholic
church, you prevented their return to that only sheepfold
of Christ, from which the pride and corruption of some
arch-heretics of former times caused their ancestors to
depart. Thousands and thousands of these unfortunate
laypeople will have a lawful excuse to allege before the
tribunal of impartial justice, namely, the misrepresentation
of their teachers. Many of them will find their acquittal
in the plea of invincible ignorance. Will this plea be
of any avail to those who with seeing eyes would not
see? To those who, without mission from above, without
deputation from the Catholic church of Christ, presumed
to step into the sanctuary and to arrogate to themselves
that sacred title which the Catholic church alone can give,
she being exclusively the depository of the power of
Jesus Christ on earth?

For God's sake, dear Sir, if you value the glory of God,
and the salvation of your soul, give up protesting against
the Catholic church; in it alone you will find salvation.
As sure as God lives, it is the true church of Christ. May

the day of judgment be for me the day of God's eternal vengeance if the Roman Catholic church is not the only one true and immaculate spouse of Christ. May my soul be doomed to suffer for you to all eternity, all those torments, which you would deserve by following all the pretended superstitions of the church of Rome.

Hush into silence your prejudices; listen and adore; humble yourself with St. Paul to the very dust; pray for light, and you shall see it brighter than the dazzling rays of the midday's sun. Ask for grace to overcome human respect and all carnal considerations, those obstacles which Satan raises to prevent the conversion of millions; that grace will be imparted to you. Seek the kingdom of heaven, by which in scripture language is often meant the church of Christ, the Catholic church, as yet in a state of suffering, persecuted, ridiculed, tried like gold in the furnace, as yet wandering through the dreary and frightful desert, but on its way to the land of promise; you will find it, and with it you will enter the mansions of eternal peace. That you and all your hearers may obtain that blessing of blessings, is the sincere desire, and shall be the constant prayer of

Your humble and obedient servant,

Demetrius A. Gallitzin

An Appeal to
the Protestant Public

Religious controversies, when carried on in the spirit of charity, and with candor, are certainly of great utility; as they tend to dispel the clouds of error, which obscure or deform the truth, and to unite those whom a diversity of opinion keeps at variance. Unfortunately, however, for the cause of religion, religious controversies do not often proceed from a spirit of charity, and are but seldom expressed in the sweet accents of harmonious suavity, in consequence of which, the breach is made wider.

When I published my *Defense of Catholic Principles*, I was actuated by charity and zeal for the salvation of my brethren in Christ, and I did not intentionally make use of any expression calculated to hurt the feelings of any. I was not the aggressor, but compelled by duty to repel the rude and unprovoked attacks of an enemy of our holy religion. I find by his late publication that he is one of those,

> Who prove their doctrine orthodox,
> by apostolic blows and knocks.

For this reason, and for some others, which I am now going to state, I shall not address any more letters to the protestant minister, but direct my future publications on religious subjects, to a protestant friend.

The protestant minister, has spent nearly two years in gathering and publishing his *Vindication*, in which he endeavors to exhibit Roman Catholics to the eyes of the public as a superstitious and idolatrous people; and I must own, that in the execution of his design, he has acquired a claim on the gratitude of the whole body of Catholics, and especially of the Catholic clergy having furnished us with new proofs of the weakness of his cause, and of the impossibility of overthrowing, by fair argument, the principles of Catholics.

The most solid arguments by which I have established our principles, he has not ventured to attack, but passed them unnoticed, knowing them to be unanswerable.

He has generally attached himself to some of the weakest proofs only, which I had adduced in favor of our principles; but which alone, would not be sufficient to establish them.

In my *Defense of Catholic Principles*, I have attached myself to the most essential points of religion only; those on which depends your salvation. And the proofs on which I have established these fundamental points, are principally taken from scripture.

Many of you, my protestant brethren, have been candid enough to acknowledge that these proofs are unanswerable, and leave no chance for a reply. Convinced by these arguments, and giving way to the grace of God, some few among you have applied to me, and testified an eager desire to renounce their errors, and become members of the Catholic church. What does the protestant minister do? In order to draw your attention from the main subject, he introduces numbers of subjects of minor importance, which he exhibits in the most odious colors, and in all the ludicrous shapes of low ribaldry.

Although he denies the existence of infallibility in the whole body of Catholic prelates, yet he seems to claim that infallibility for himself: for how can he otherwise expect that the least respect or attention can be due to his interpretations of scripture, especially when he takes the liberty to take hold of the sacred text, as he would a nose of wax, and squeeze it into whatever shape he pleases, to make it answer his purpose. In reading his *Vindication*, you must have admired his ingenuity, as an interpreter of scripture.

"The gates of hell shall not prevail against the church" (Mt. 16). That means, says he (page 14), that death shall not prevail against the genuine members of the church.

"Unless you eat the flesh of the Son of man, and drink His blood, you shall not have life in you" (Jn. 6). This means, says he (page 24), that we must believe in Christ.

"This is my body, etc. This is my blood, etc." (Jn. 6). That means, says the protestant minister, This is not my body, this is not my blood for it is nothing but bread and wine (page 27, 28).

"Receive ye the Holy Ghost; whose sins you shall forgive, they are forgiven" etc. (Jn. 20:22-23). That means nothing at all, for, says the protestant minister (page 19), where is that power (of forgiving sins) given to a sinful creature, and one who has to answer for his own sins?

Jesus said, "Son, be of good cheer, thy sins are forgiven thee," (Mt. 19). That means only, says the same minister, (pg. 20), that the temporal punishment of sin was released.

"The church of the living God," says St. Paul (1 Tim. 3:15), "is the pillar and ground of truth." That means, says the protestant minister (pages 15, 16), only the church of Ephesus.

Christ says, "Blessed are they that have not seen and have believed," (Jn. 20:29). That means nothing for the minister tells you (page 29), that the foundation of our faith must rely on the truth of our senses.

The Apostle St. Paul, says, "if any man's work burn, he shall suffer loss, but he himself shall be saved, yet so as by fire," (1Cor. 3:15). That means, says the protestant minister, yet so as out of the fire (page 47).

I freely confess, my dear brethren, that I am no match for the protestant minister; for he hath the holy scripture at his command, can squeeze it into any shape, or make it say what he pleases; he therefore, can never be at a loss. I, on the contrary, am so convinced of my ignorance, of my inability to interpret scripture, that I, in all cases, confine myself to that interpretation which the holy Catholic church gives me: because my savior, Christ, has promised that the Spirit of Truth shall remain with his Apostles forever, (Jn. 16:16-17). And because Christ, when he sent his Apostles to begin the work of the ministry, preaching, baptizing, etc., promised to be and remain with them "until the consummation of the world" (Mt. 28:20). And finally, because the same Christ, the divine architect, who built the church, built it upon a rock, and promised that the gates of hell should not prevail against it" (Mt. 16:18). The sense of which declaration is explained by Christ himself (Mt. 7:25), where speaking of a house raised by a wise man, he says, "it fell not, for it was founded upon a rock." Now I am so confident that Christ has kept all these promises, that I feel perfectly happy and safe in taking the Catholic church as my only guide in the interpretation of the holy scripture, and in all matters of salvation. Thus I am confined within certain narrow limits, beyond which I cannot step, and therefore am no match for the protestant minister, who is not constrained by any limits whatever; for he tells us plainly, and repeatedly, that the scriptures alone, no matter how interpreted; for everyone is to interpret for himself as well as he can, are our only rule of faith.

This is not all. I do not wish to give the gentleman any offence, or to hurt his feelings, knowing that charity is the principal virtue of a Christian, nay the very soul of religion. However, truth being the sole object of a writer, who undertakes to defend the true religion, he is of course obliged to point out the many misrepresentations by which it is deformed, and the falsehoods by which it is rendered hateful or ridiculous. To perform this task is highly unpleasant; as zeal for the cause of truth, which animates the writer, may easily be mistaken for malice or ill-will. God knows I feel nothing but charity for the protestant minister. His endeavors in misrepresenting the Catholic doctrine, the odium and ridicule he throws on the Catholic clergy, by representing them as impostors, sorcerers, sleight-of-hand men, cruel executioners, blood-suckers, roasting the bodies of men, etc. excites in me nothing but compassion, and a fervent desire that God may open his eyes before it is too late.

I would fain wish to persuade myself that he errs through ignorance, in which case I certainly should address a second letter to him, in order to undeceive him; but no, I am compelled to believe, that he willfully and knowingly advances falsehoods in order to render the Catholic religion hateful and ridiculous, and establish his own system. You, my dear brethren, will be able to judge whether I be right or wrong. I shall at present only mention a few of the most palpable falsehoods advanced by the protestant minister, intending to be more particular in my future publications.

Page 20. He tells you that the pope and his priests think it no blasphemy to thrust the souls of men into purgatory, and either to roast them there for hundreds of years, or, if their friends are rich enough, to bring them out in a shorter time.

As the protestant minister has read the Catholic doctrine of purgatory, he, of course, knows the lines quoted above to be false.

Page 75. He tells you that our holy water is composed of water, salt, a live coal put into it, and the priest's spittle.

As the minister tells us (page 140), he is acquainted with the missal or Mass–book, which contains the blessing of the water, he therefore is guilty of a willful falsehood in the above assertion. He is guilty of telling no less a falsehood, when he tells you (page 140), that the Catholic priests have with all their might endeavored to suppress all attempts of translating the Roman Mass–book, breviary, etc.

Sir, thousands of English prayer books, used by the Catholics of America, and hundreds of thousands by the Catholics of England, Ireland and Scotland, contain the whole Mass, word by word, in the English language; and there are besides other books printed for laypeople, which contain in the English language, all the different Masses and offices for the most solemn days and times of the year, such as Advent, Lent, Holy Week, Easter Week, Pentecost, etc., translated from the Roman Mass–book and breviary. Many more such translations are to be found in the hands of Catholics living in Catholic countries, such as France, Spain, Portugal, Italy, the greater part of Germany, etc..

I have translations of the kind in both English and French, and I do most solemnly call upon you, my dear brethren, to produce any one person among yourselves, who understands French and Latin, and I shall in order to satisfy you, give him a chance to compare said translations with the Latin Mass-book. This will also give you an opportunity of finding out how horribly the protestant minister imposes on you, and with how little conscience he calumniates the Catholic church, when he speaks (p. 140) of the filth and abominable corruption contained in our Mass–books, etc., and hid under the cover of an unknown tongue.

How much will you be surprised when you shall find that nearly nine-tenths of the contents of the Mass–book and breviary are taken from the holy scriptures, and that the remainder is a short account of the holy lives of some of the principal saints, proposed for imitation, together with some prayers to obtain their intercession with almighty God, that we may be enabled to follow their steps, and thus to be admitted to enjoy, in partnership with them, the blessings of eternal life.

Page 104. The minister in laying before you the Catholic creed, as published by Pope Pius IV, has the following words, "I do believe that the saints reigning together with Christ are to be worshipped and prayed unto." And again, pretending to quote the Council of Trent, "the sacred bodies of martyrs, etc., are to be worshipped."

Here again is a willful corruption. The *Roman Ritual,* which contains the said creed or profession of faith for receiving converts into the church, does not say worshipped, but honored: "That the saints reigning together with Christ, are to be *honored"* etc. I pledge my word to you, dear brethren, to show you these words in the *Roman Ritual* any time you apply to me. The Council of Trent does not say that the sacred bodies of martyrs, etc. are to be *worshipped* but *venerated,* as having been in this life, according to St. Paul, (1Cor. 3:16-17), "temples of the Holy Ghost," and according to the same (1Cor. 5:15), "members of Christ." What shall I say of the minister's assertion (page 100) that the church allows not only the deposing, but also the killing of 'crowned heads.' I hope you will forgive me, my dear brethren, if I denominate this a most wicked malicious lie, invented by Satan, the father of lies, and his ministers, to lead you astray from the holy Catholic church.

I shall not at present pollute my pages with any more of the protestant minister's misrepresentations and falsehoods; they shall all be noticed in due time. Let me here only remark, that as those falsehoods are generally advanced without any proof, they of course ought to bear no weight. It is a general principle of law and justice that every person is to be considered innocent until proved guilty. And the more heinous the crime is, with which a person is charged, the stronger the proofs ought to be before he can be considered guilty. This principle is not admitted by the protestant minister in his most fixed determination to raise the utmost hatred against the Catholic church, and to render it ridiculous and contemptible. And in order to accomplish his design, he charges the church with all the crimes committed by some of its members.

So, because Clement and Ravaillac, two monsters in human flesh, were guilty of murdering two French kings, he tells you it is the principle of the Catholic church to murder kings.

So, likewise (page 63) because certain ignorant friars wrote that even God himself is subject to the Virgin Mary, and such like blasphemies, therefore he tells you that the Catholic church approves and teaches those blasphemies.

What would you think of me, my friends, if I should assert that the protestant religion approves of murder; for a certain protestant minister murdered one of his elders some years ago in Bedford. Or, if I should assert that the said religion approves of drunkenness, for some of its members, and even some of its ministers, are in the habit of getting drunk.

Unfortunately, there are too many members of the Catholic church, whose conduct widely differs from their speculative principles; who have nothing of Christians but the name; and who are capable of committing the most atrocious crimes. The church condemns their conduct, admonishes them to repent, denounces to them the judgments of God, if they do not repent, but she is not invested with the power to compel their amendment.

The protestant minister shows a particular want of generosity in his lengthy account of the wickedness and extravagant claims of some of the popes. After the acknowledgment and concession I have made on that subject, (pages 147, 157 of my *Defense*), he ought to have been ashamed to say even one word on the subject. The prevarications of popes can no more be charged to the church than the treason of Judas or the fall of St. Peter; and therefore if all his assertions against our popes were true, this would be no argument against the Catholic church. Throughout the whole of the minister's *Vindication*, I find a total want of sincerity and candor, a perversion and misrepresentation of my arguments, and the most sedulous and persevering endeavors to bury the fundamental and essential tenets of Catholic faith under a load of irrelevant matter.

As an instance of his want of sincerity, and I must add, of a gross imposition on the public, I beg leave to refer you to page 9, line 29, of the *Vindication*, where the minister tries to make you believe that I said scripture should not be read, whereas he very well knows that I only said that holy writ (although certainly God's word). was not intended to be our supreme judge in matters of faith etc..

Where he could not by any solid arguments overthrow the Catholic doctrine itself, he has only attacked its abuses, for which the church cannot be made answerable; for the most holy things have been, and will be abused. He has made use of vile and scurrilous language, unworthy a Christian and a gentleman, of which I need not give here any particular instance.

He has willfully perverted the words of our general councils and the sense of our doctrine, in order to make it ridiculous and contemptible.

He has even perverted the meaning of plain English words, to answer the same purpose, trying to make you believe that to venerate signifies worship, etc..

He has been guilty of advancing most palpable falsehoods, as in the case of the holy water, etc. He has carefully, and in very many instances, concealed from your view most essential parts of the truth.

Finally, such are his anger and ill–will against Catholics that he cannot bring himself to call them by their proper name. Nothing will do for him but papists, Romanists, Romish, in the true style of British statutes.

These are a few of my reasons for not addressing any more of my letters to the protestant minister.

Should he ever be willing hereafter to recall the many falsehoods he has advanced; to confute by solid arguments the Catholic principles; to do it in a decorous manner, in a manner becoming a Christian and a gentleman, without comparing the pope to an old cow, without calling the priests impostors, sorcerers, conjurors, etc. without introducing irrelevant matters, such as the scandalous conduct of some popes, etc., I shall then consider it my duty to resume the correspondence with the protestant minister. And I believe that a controversy carried on in a mild dispassionate way, proceeding on both sides from a spirit of charity, attacking only principles, not men, would go a great way towards dispelling the clouds of error that have too long obscured the truth, would silence the spirit of bigotry and malevolence, and would reunite in the bonds of charity those whom the infernal spirit of religious discord, often mistaken for religious zeal, has too long kept at variance.

My brethren, we are all the children of God. We are all brothers and sisters in Jesus Christ. Let us forever banish hatred and malice from our hearts, and be guided only by the Spirit of Truth and Charity, which Jesus Christ sent to His Apostles and disciples, which formed them into one church, and which Christ promised should remain with them until the consummation of the world.

A Letter to a Protestant Friend on the Holy Scriptures

Being a continuation of
the Defense of Catholic Principles

The foolishness of God is wiser than men:
and the weakness of God is stronger than men.

— 1 Corinthians 1:25

Prince Demetrius Augustin Gallitzin

the son of the proudest and most powerful nobleman of the Russian empire, was born on December 22, 1770, at The Hague, where his father was the Russian ambassador. His father was a member of the Greek church, but his mother was a Catholic. For several years the young prince was brought up in the Greek faith, but was confirmed a Catholic, August 28, 1786.

When the time came for him to make a tour of the continent, "revolution had converted Europe into a vast battlefield, and the prince was sent to the United States, to make the acquaintance of Washington and Jefferson and to study the institutions of this country. He sailed from Rotterdam for America in August 1792. Two months had hardly passed in the intimacies of life with Archbishop Carroll — then bishop of Baltimore — until he resolved to relinquish a princely fortune and forfeit the highest rank of nobility, and had devoted himself, body and soul, to the service of God and the salvation of souls in America. Gallitzin was the second priest ordained by Bishop Carroll, and commissioned, as a true pioneer of civilization, to carry the word of God and the means of salvation through the untouched forests of the New World.

In the apostolic trips which frequently took him from Maryland into the then far west, on the table–lands of the Alleghany range Gallitzin alighted on a settlement made up of a few Catholic families. In the midst of this Catholic nucleus, he resolved to establish a permanent colony, destined in his mind as the center of his missions. Several poor families, whose affections he had won, determined to follow him; and, with the consent of his bishop, he took up his line of march from Maryland in the summer of 1799. As soon as the small caravan had reached its new home, the settlers addressed themselves to the work before them. It was called Loretto, and is still known by that name. Father Lemcke says of this settlement: "Out of the clearings of these untrodden forests rose up two buildings, constructed out of the trunks of rough-hewn trees: of these, one was intended for a church, the other a home for their pastor. On Christmas Eve of the year 1799, there was not a winking eye in the little colony. The new church, decked with pine, laurel and ivy leaves, and blazing with such lights as the scant means of the faithful could afford, was awaiting its consecration to the worship of God. There, Gallitzin offered up the first Mass, to the great edification of his flock, and to the great astonishment of a few Indians, who had never dreamed of such a pageantry." There the energetic missionary labored, amid privation and disappointment, for nearly half a century. In spite of his vast and varied labors, he found time to write and give to the world his *Defense of Catholic Principles and Letter on the Holy Scriptures.* They exerted an immense influence, even among the higher classes of society, but especially so among the humble members of the community, for whom they were destined. His biographer says: "The curiosity of readers enlarged their circulation everywhere; and I myself have found Gallitzin's works as perfectly thumbed as any spelling book, in spots where I never dreamed of meeting with them."

Years passed on, and the pioneer could mark the slanting shadows of declining life, when a young missionary came over from Europe to share his toils. This was Father Lemcke, a Benedictine, who, after having been his assistant, became his successor and is now residing in Elizabeth, New Jersey. Father Lemcke set out from Philadelphia, and, after several days' rough traveling, reached Munster, where an Irish family received him kindly. In that village he procured a guide, and started for Loretto. "As we had gone," says he, "a couple of miles through the woods, I caught sight of a sled, drawn by a pair of vigorous horses, and in the sled a half-recumbent traveler, on every lineament of whose face could be read a character of distinction. It occurred to me that some accident had happened to the old gentleman dressed in a threadbare coat and dilapidated hat that compelled him to resort to this singular mode of conveyance. Whilst I was taxing my brain for a satisfactory solution to the problem, my guide turned round, and, pointing to the old man, said, "Here comes the priest." I immediately coaxed our nag up to their sled. "Are you really the pastor of Loretto?" said I. "I am, sir." "Prince Gallitzin?" "At your service, sir," he said with a laugh. "You are probably astonished at the strangeness of my equipage! But there is no help for it. You have already found out that in these wild regions you need not dream of a carriage road. You could not drive ten yards without danger of upsetting. I am prevented by a fall, which I have had from riding on horseback, and it would be impossible for me to travel on foot. Besides I can carry along everything required for the celebration of Mass. I am now going to a place where I have a mission, and where the holy sacrifice has been announced for today."

In 1839, the old missionary's health failed him. The load of years and the thousand hardships weighed heavily upon him. His body gradually bent, his step became unsteady, his voice failed him, and the last scene of this eventful life closed on May 6, 1841, when the missionary-prince left this world, accompanied by the prayers of his parishioners gathered around him: for every apartment of the house, and the chapel attached to it, were thronged with a wailing, weeping, and praying community. This supreme hour revealed the depth and the sincerity of the love which dwelt in every heart for this man of God. On the day of his funeral, whole populations swarmed from every point within fifty miles to pay to the good father a last tribute of that affectionate respect which had attended him through life. Such is a brief sketch of one of the pioneers of Catholicity in this country.

Preface

The following *Letter to a Protestant Friend*, I give to the public at the request of some respectable friends, who are of opinion that it may be of benefit to other protestants besides the one to whom it is directed. In my *Address* (sic) *to the Protestant Public*, I have stated my reasons for not addressing the protestant minister anymore. His ungentlemanly language, together with the many falsehoods he advances in order to expose the Catholic cause to the hatred and contempt of the public, plainly show that he is not actuated by motives of charity, and that he is blinded by passion; and of course, not open to conviction. However, truth compels me to acknowledge, that I am, nevertheless, indebted to him for affording me a considerable degree of assistance in converting protestants to the Catholic faith. *His Vindication of the Doctrines of the Reformation* gave the finishing stroke to several of them, who after reading Catholic principles in Catholic books, were very curious to know what arguments protestant writers could have to oppose to those principles. They read the *Vindication* with the greatest attention, and read it again. What was the result? They came to me, and prayed to be admitted members of the Catholic church. On the first Sunday of October (after having made their sacramental confession) six of them made their public profession of Catholic faith, before the altar at St. Michael's church of Loretto, according to the rites and ceremonies prescribed by the *Roman Ritual*, renouncing their errors, and promising before God and the congregation, to live and die in the Roman Catholic church. Since that time several more protestants have applied to me, and testified an eager desire to become members of the holy Catholic church of Christ. If I had any favor to ask of the protestant minister, it would be that he would please continue to write against the Catholic church, and to vindicate the doctrines of the reformation. I promise to make a good use of his writings, and to draw from them a great deal of useful information, for the conversion of all sorts of protestants to the Catholic faith.

There are some precious acknowledgments made by the protestant minister in his *Vindication of the Doctrines of the Reformation,* which should be very sufficient to open the eyes of protestants to the imminent danger they are exposed to, whilst living in a state of separation from the holy Catholic church of Christ. I shall only notice two of those acknowledgments.

First: (p.13) He tells us plainly that no such a thing as infallibility was ever intended by Jesus Christ to be given to the church; in other words, it was never intended by Jesus Christ that we should know to a certainty whether we believe right or wrong; for the mysteries of revelation are so transcendently above the reach of the human understanding, that none but a divine infallible guide can possibly prevent our going astray in investigating those profound mysteries, or give us a certainty that we do not misunderstand the words or mistake the sense of our blessed savior.

Protestants! Here is a plain acknowledgement made by one of your ministers, and I dare say, confirmed by the whole of them, that the church or churches you and they belong to are not infallible. Pause a little, if you value your souls, and meditate seriously on the consequences of that acknowledgment. It appears then, that your believing right or wrong is left to chance; that your ministers can give you no security that they deliver unto you the true interpretation of the word of God, or the sense of the Holy Ghost; and that you shall never know to a certainty whether you believe right or wrong until you find yourselves before the judgment of him who has declared that "he that believeth not shall be condemned" (Mk. 16:16).

Second: (p.117) Speaking of the divisions in the protestant communions, he acknowledges that there is "a criminal schism somewhere" among them.

Protestants! Read the words of St. Paul (Eph. 5:25-27) and you will find that the church is the spouse of Christ, as holy as Christ could make it, and far from having in its bosom a criminal schism somewhere, has not even the least blemish anywhere. From your minister's own acknowledgment, the protestant church, then, is not the church of Christ; and from his own acknowledgment, he knows there is a criminal schism somewhere, but he is not able to tell where it is. Protestants if you wish to know where it is, read the *Defense of Catholic Principles,* and read the following *Letter to a Protestant Friend,* and you will find that the whole reformation is a criminal schism, or a separation from the only true Catholic church of Jesus Christ, which (although having many wicked members, both among clergymen and laymen), yet was always itself holy, immaculate, and infallible in its faith and moral doctrine.

The acknowledgments made by your protestant minister give the reformation a mortal stab. They give rise to very serious reflections; reflections that have opened the eyes of many, and have caused several protestant ministers in New York and elsewhere to forsake the pretended reformation, and to join the Catholic church.

Protestants! As long as I live I shall consider it my duty to try to undeceive you; to remove the prejudices in which you have been raised; to counteract the schemes by which the ministers of the pretended reformation have ever tried to render the Catholic church odious and ridiculous. I shall never cease calling upon you in the name of your and my savior, to forsake the criminal schism in which you live, and to return to the pale of the Catholic church, from which your ancestors departed.

The protestant minister accuses me, in his preface, of kindling up a flame that had long since been extinguished, because I do not choose to let him say what he pleases against the Catholic church. Is this fair? Is this candid? Without any provocation on our part, and at a time when the country was in danger, when the enemy was in the heart of the country, our capital threatened, etc., at that very time (the general government having appointed a day of fasting, humiliation, and prayer) it was expected that the ministers of religion would exhort their hearers to repentance, and call upon them in the name of God, to unite in defending their country. How does he fulfill that sacred duty? "Look," says he, "look through all the countries of our popish and heathen neighbors, and see if the former have changed their superstition, or the latter their gods, which yet are no gods," etc., and again a little farther, "We are Americans, we are protestants."

The above expressions are well calculated to disunite, to kindle up a flame, to raise scorn and contempt on one side, anger and ill will on the other side. I should think myself guilty of a gross neglect of duty were I to suffer such expressions to pass unnoticed, or not to contradict the many falsehoods he advances in order to ridicule the Catholic doctrine. On the other hand I shall give him full liberty to advance whatever he pleases against my person. He tells us in his preface that he took no notice whatever of a piece which I published in the *Huntingdon Gazette*, in order to refute his expressions, "Because," says he, "it was too despicable to merit a reply." If he had added that my person itself is very despicable, I should feel obliged to acknowledge the correctness of his expressions, and I

hope, with the grace of God, that I shall never feel any
anger or resentment against his person, were he even
to say much worse of me. The truth is, I feel within my
breast inclinations to every kind of evil, and if there is
any evil which I do not commit, I must entirely attribute it
to the grace of God. My talents also, are very slender and
trifling. It is no wonder, then, if their productions should
be despicable. Indeed, if I did not depend on the goodness
of my cause, which is the cause of Jesus Christ, I should
never have the presumption to step forward in its defense.
However, the same God that enabled an ass to speak, that
enabled the illiterate to convert the universe, that caused
ignorance to overcome wisdom, and weakness to triumph
over power, may also enable my ignorance to detect and
expose the cunning and artful stratagems of falsehood
against truth, and to say something to the purpose, in
defense of the Catholic cause. In truth, it does not require
a very great share of knowledge or very extraordinary
talents to refute the many falsehoods advanced against
the Catholic doctrine. When we hear it said by thousands
of protestants that the pope is Antichrist, although the
scripture plainly tells us that Antichrist will only reign
three and a half years, (specifically forty-two months):
when we hear it said that Catholic priests have horns;
that Christ was crucified by the Roman priests; that
protestants turning to the Catholic church are made
to curse their mothers' breasts; that the popes sell out
licenses to commit sins; that Catholics think it no sin to
murder protestant kings; that Catholics do not think it
a duty to keep faith with protestants; that they think it
meritorious to massacre protestants; that their holy water
is made of the priest's spittle, etc.; that money will bring
any souls out of purgatory, etc. When we hear these, and
many more lies asserted among protestants of every
denomination and of every nation, we are not at a loss
to know where those lies originate. Thank God, there are

some protestant ministers who are men of conscience, and who, from principle, never will say a word against the Catholic church when they preach or instruct; some of them indeed have lost their places by this their moderate disposition; for, such is the taste of many protestants, that the most eloquent sermons appear to them insipid unless they are set off with some invectives against popery.

Protestants! It is a common saying, and a very true one, that "honey catches more flies than vinegar." If your minister really believes that we are going astray, along the broad road of perdition, why does he not address us in the sweet accents of charity? Why does he not exhort his hearers to pray for our conversion? Why does he not publish little tracts, written in the spirit of mildness and charity, and wherein he, in a gentle manner, proves the fallacy of our real principles, without attributing to us principles and doctrines which (he well knows) never belonged to us? We are made of the same flesh and blood as you; we are subject to the same infirmities; we are easily, too easily, provoked by insults and calumnies; and when provoked, feel very little inclined to listen even to the good instructions or advice of him that insults or provokes us.

It certainly is a gross violation of the maxims of religion to substitute noise for sense, insult for argument, accusation for conviction; and it is also a departure from the rules of wisdom and prudence.

Insult is the instrument with which bad causes attack good ones. If it be in the power of reason to convince, why have recourse to abuse and invective? The celebrated Vossius says that he one day observed to a protestant minister at Dort, in Holland, that it was wrong to impose upon the people, though it were even in regard of popery. "What then!" said the minister, "do you mean to take part with the papists? "No; believe me, you cannot abuse them too much; it is our duty to make the people detest them." Vossius informs us also, that he heard the same observations from the ministers at Amsterdam; "If we leave off preaching that the pope is Antichrist," said they, "the people will leave our communion."

Here is a candid acknowledgment.

The Catholic church must be abused forsooth, because it has truth on its side, and truth is hateful to error.

It must be misrepresented, because fairly represented it is divine; its beauty, its sublimity, its awful majesty prove its divine origin.

Protestants! It must be held out an object of your execration and contempt, in order to keep you from becoming members of that holy church of Christ. Let a man err as he pleases, let him reject all revelation, deny the divinity of Jesus Christ, or even the existence of a God; let him be notorious for his blasphemies or impieties, still there is charity for him — for the Roman Catholic there is none.

Most of protestant ministers in all countries unite in bawling out against popery, in calling the pope Antichrist, the church a sink of idolatry and superstition; and take pains to leave such unfavorable impressions on the minds of their hearers with regard to the Catholic church, that they scorn the very idea of investigating its principles, and would be ashamed to be suspected of entertaining a favorable idea of it.

The question naturally occurs, if the Catholic faith is really so ridiculously contemptible, so foolishly absurd, why in the name of good sense keep so much fuss about it? If we despise an enemy, we pass him by in contemptuous silence, thinking him beneath our notice. Now it is notorious that ever since the pretended reformation, protestant ministers of all sorts, and in all protestant countries, have continually kept up the most clamorous noise against it. It is not easy to conceive the extravagance of the sanctified violence with which the zeal of protestant ministers was wont to assail us. The pulpits of the reformation re-echoed with abuse the most coarse, the most illiberal; oratorical eloquence was exhausted in proving the absurdity of our principles by attributing to us principles that were not ours; and the presses of the reformation were groaning with lies, and overflowing the world with volumes of antidotes against popery. In the name of sense, why so much fuss, these three hundred years past, about a thing that is said to be so very contemptible, far below the notice of any man of sense?

Protestants! By this manner of proceeding, your ministers have, in spite of themselves, offered their tribute of respect and veneration to the Catholic cause, and tacitly acknowledged the respectability, the majesty, and the divinity of that institute which they affect to despise. The blaze of evidence shone so bright in favor of the Catholic doctrine that clouds of dust had to be kicked up to blind your eyes. The voice of truth spoke so plain, through the mouth of the ministry of Christ in the Catholic church, that thundering vociferations had to be raised to deafen your ears. The proofs of its divinity were so convincing, that your attention had to be diverted from those proofs, by drawing the same on the seeming contradictions and absurdities which corrupted reason may readily find in mysteries which it is not able to understand.

In truth, it requires very little learning to be able to ridicule transubstantiation and other mysteries of the Christian religion. The puny reason of a bad reasoner is sufficient for the task; and where the defect or lameness of his argument might expose him to censure or to a discovery of the cheat, the defect may be supplied by a little exertion of his wit. A few sarcastic remarks, a few tales to excite a roar of laughter, such as the tale of the tub, from Dean Swift, (p. 33 of the *Vindication*), will answer the purpose very well.

My protestant brethren! The following *Letter to a Protestant Friend*, I offer for your perusal. The main subject of it is the holy scripture, which the Catholic church venerates as the word of God, and from which we draw the doctrine of salvation. By reading that part of the letter, you will be surprised to find how ill-grounded the charge is, which your minister makes against Catholic priests, of concealing scripture, etc.

In the latter part of the letter, you will find several more points of Catholic doctrine explained, which are not mentioned in the *Defense of Catholic Principles,* and also an answer to several objections of your minister. If I did not answer all his objections, or refute all his arguments or assertions, it was for the following reasons:

One: To answer them all minutely, would take more time than I have to spare.

Two: Most of his assertions are destitute of proof and therefore do not require an answer.

Three: Some of his arguments were either too sublime or too obscure for my weak understanding. I really could not comprehend them. I read page 27, on transubstantiation, over and over again; I paused; I meditated; I read again; I put my brains to the rack. All in vain. I found myself obliged to pass on, without understanding the minister's meaning. I then recollected the following words of Dryden, which put an end to my perplexity:

> The literal sense is hard to flesh and blood,
> But nonsense never can be understood.

Four: Some of the minister's assertions are so evidently false, that it would be time lost to refute them. For instance (p. 115), where he asserts that the numbers of those of the Romish church are now small, in comparison of those who have protested against its tyranny, etc.. Again (pp. 48, 49), where he (upon the authority of his very inaccurate theologian, Buck) attempts to deny that the Greeks believe in transubstantiation, the seven sacraments, confession, purgatory. Never did any differences exist between the Latin and the Greek churches on those essential articles of faith.

Five: Many of his arguments are only sarcasm and therefore no arguments at all.

Six: Many more of his arguments consist in abuse, unbecoming epithets, and those I should be very sorry to notice.

These are some of my reasons for passing over a great part of the protestant minister's *Vindication*, in perfect silence. Some particular points, nevertheless, that would require a refutation, may have escaped my notice. If I shall discover any such, I may probably make them the subject of some future publications; for I feel very anxious to conceal no part of the truth from you, that I may have nothing to answer for at the day of judgment, if you should be found out of the pale of Christ's church.

I know, my protestant brethren, that it is very difficult to divest one's self of prejudice, especially of prejudice contracted in one's infancy. I therefore venture to give you an advice which, at any rate, can do you no harm. I know that, from the prejudices in which you have been raised, the very words Roman Catholic convey to your mind ideas of absurdity, nonsense, bigotry, superstition, etc., therefore I advise you (before you begin to read this or any other Catholic book) to try to divest yourself of all your old prejudices, to forget that you ever heard a word against the Catholic church to remember that *truth* always was, and always will be, hateful to this sinful world, that Jesus Christ was hated and persecuted because he was a preacher of the truth; that his church cannot expect better treatment than himself, because His church is also a constant preacher of the truth, and according to Christ's promise, will have the Spirit of Truth forever (Jn. 14:16-17). Well then, before you begin to read, pray your heavenly father who is infinitely merciful and both able and willing to save you, that he may discard prejudice from your mind, that he may give you grace to read and to examine without partiality, that he may enlighten your weak understanding, give you faith to believe, and courage (in spite of all difficulties) to embrace that faith which alone can convey you to everlasting happiness.

My Dear Friend,

In reading the *Vindication of The Doctrines of the Reformation,* lately published by one of your ministers, you must have taken notice of one particular point of accusation, which he repeatedly urges against us, *viz.* that we (the Roman Catholic priests) have taken away the key of knowledge, by keeping the sacred scripture from the eyes of the people. The more serious the accusation is, the more it is deserving of an impartial and dispassionate investigation; and to you in particular, my dear friend, you who are seriously engaged in search of the true religion, it is a matter of great importance to know whether the above accusation be founded on truth or not; for, if you believe it true, you will at once make up your mind not to listen to me, or to any other of the impostors who withhold from the knowledge of mankind the sacred writings of their God and savior, published for the salvation of their souls.

I confess I am much surprised at the accusation so repeatedly brought against the Catholic clergy by men who are not remote from correct sources of information.

I lived, during fifteen years, in a Catholic country, under a Catholic government, where both the spiritual and temporal power were united in the same person — the reigning prince of that country was our archbishop. In that country, you may be sure, the Catholic rules and principles were strictly observed; and in that very country I saw the Catholic bible, in the German language, in all the bookseller's shops, printed, and reprinted, and sold, without exception, to any person that wished to purchase. During a great part of that time I was not a member of the Catholic church. An intimacy, which existed between our family and a certain celebrated French philosopher, had produced a contempt for revealed religion. Raised in prejudices against revelation, I felt every disposition to ridicule those very principles and practices, which I have adopted since. I only mention that circumstance in order to convince you that my observations at that time being those of an enemy, and not of a bigoted member of the Catholic church, are, in the eyes a protestant, the more entitled to credit; and from the same motive, I shall also add, that during those unfortunate years of my infidelity, particular care was taken not to permit any clergyman to come near me. Thanks be to the God of infinite mercy, the clouds of infidelity were dispersed, and revelation adopted in our family. I soon felt convinced of the necessity of investigating the different religious systems, in order to find the true one. Although I was born a member of the Greek church, and although all my male relations, without any exception, were either Greeks or protestants, yet did I resolve to embrace that religion only, which upon impartial inquiry, should appear to me to be the pure religion of Jesus Christ. My choice fell upon the Catholic church, and at the age of about seventeen I became a member of that church. I read the bible, and saw my neighbors, rich and poor, reading it, without any objection on the part of the clergy. I frequented numbers of Catholic churches and in all of them heard numberless quotations from the bible, as from the written word of God. I was acquainted with hundreds of the Catholic clergy; and do assert, nay, am willing to swear, if called upon by legal authority, that I never knew any Catholic bishop or parish priest to withhold the scripture from the knowledge of the people committed to their care. I am intimately acquainted with numbers of German, French, Italian, English, Irish, and American priests, and never could hear from any of them that the reading of the holy scriptures was prohibited in their respective countries. I have seen many Catholic bibles printed in France, England, Ireland, Scotland, etc.. In this country the English Catholic bible has been printed and reprinted in several cities of the Union. The Catholic priests, scattered in the different provinces of the United States, are generally subscribers to a great amount and encourage the sale of that sacred volume with the utmost zeal. I myself, on my last return from Baltimore, brought several English Catholic bibles with me; one of them at the particular request, and for the use of, the protestant minister's townsman, Mr. Henry Dopp, of Huntingdon, who will have no objection to show it to the protestant minister, in order to undeceive him.

As long as I live, I intend to encourage the reading of the bible, and am not in the least afraid of incurring thereby the blame of my bishop, or the censures of the Catholic church. Is it not surprising my dear friend, that I should be, during thirty years, a member of the Catholic church, that I should live so many years near the center of Catholicity, that I should be, during twenty-three years, an acting, though unworthy, minister of the Catholic church, and during all that time was not clear-sighted enough to find out that the Catholic clergy were in the habit of withholding from their people the key of knowledge, the sacred scriptures? You will ask me, probably, what then can be the reason that the accusation of concealing the scriptures is so generally brought against the Catholic clergy by all protestant ministers of every denomination? Is it possible that so many respectable characters would unite in propagating a palpable lie? Charity, my dear friend, forbids such a supposition. I am far from accusing the protestant minister or his colleagues of propagating a willful lie. I am sensible that a lie bawled out with an impudent assurance, by any person of weight and influence, is often received as an undoubted truth, and as such propagated by thousands, without the least suspicion of its falsehood. The first broachers of the accusation were guilty of a willful lie. Rebelling against the lawful authority of the church, they had to give satisfactory reasons for their rebellion. Thus, they contrived numberless accusations against that church; charging the church with all the crimes and abuses of which many of its ignorant and corrupted members were guilty, and affecting to attribute these crimes and abuses to the ignorance in which they were kept by the church, which, however, was to be attributed to their own neglect and corruption, or perhaps in many instances, to the negligence, corruption, and bad example of some of their teachers.

You are sensible, my friend, that the act or the neglect of one or more of the clergy is not the act or neglect of his church. I have acknowledged, in my *Defense Of Catholic Principles*, and I do acknowledge again that many of the clergy, as well as of the lay people, in the Catholic church, have been guilty of most culpable negligence, and even of very great crimes, which was particularly the case at the time of the pretended reformation; in consequence of which the curse of God fell upon the earth and caused many, struck with blindness, to forsake the church, in the bosom of which they would have found a remedy for all their spiritual maladies, and to follow the smoother and broader roads of the pretended reformation. The standard of rebellion being raised by the hand of pride, it was easy to persuade lust and luxury that eating is more pleasant than fasting; that a change of wives is more pleasant than being confined to one; that a confession made in general terms to God alone is less restraining than a detailed one made to God's minister; that self interpretation of God's word affords a greater chance to the unruly passions of a corrupted heart than the submitting to the interpretation of the church; and that liberty and independence is more sweet than obedience and submission. Well might the reformers proclaim to the world to be ruled by the bible when they granted to every individual liberty to interpret and to judge for himself.

What would be the consequence if every individual in this country was permitted to interpret the law of the land for himself; and if the criminal, guilty of the most flagrant breach of these laws, enacted for the safety and protection of its citizens, was not obliged to submit to the interpretation and application of that law upon his particular case, made by the authority of the court and jury. The murderer would never find the law against the crime of murder to apply to his peculiar case; the thief or robber would find his case entitled to an exception from the law against thieving or robbing; the blasphemer would find, in his interpretation, security against the punishment inflicted by the laws against blasphemy. The laws then, although good and sufficient in themselves, would prove nugatory. The holy scriptures are the Christian's code of law. The church does not say "you shall not read it"; but the church says, "you shall not interpret it as you please." Scripture itself gives us this caution, "No prophecy of scripture is made by private interpretation" (2Pet. 1:20).

The general council of Trent, session five, chapter one, has given strict orders for establishing lectures and expositions of holy writ, in churches, monasteries, and colleges; and the reason it gives is that so that heavenly treasure of holy scripture, with which the Holy Ghost, in his infinite bounty, has provided us, may not be neglected. But the same council knew that as the law misinterpreted, is not the law, so also, scripture misinterpreted, is not the scripture — not the word of God. The holy council knew that, according to St. Peter (2Pet. 3:16), many wrest the scriptures to their own perdition. Therefore, the council made a decree in session four: "That nobody, relying on their own private judgment, presume to wrest the holy scriptures, in matters of faith or manners, to their own private sense, contrary to that sense which the holy church has held, and does hold, to whom it belongs, to judge of the true sense of scripture, or contrary to the unanimous consent of the holy fathers."

In addition to this we find a rule laid down by Pope Pius IV, but not a law enacted by the general council, laying an obligation on the bishops and parish priests to restrain those only from reading the bible in the vulgar tongue, whom they see so self-conceited or rash as to be in danger of wresting it to their own destruction.

Read the letter of Pope Pius VI to the archbishop of Florence, which is prefixed to our Catholic bible, and you will see how far he is from condemning the practice of reading the bible.

If, my dear friend, you blame the Catholic church for opposing and condemning private interpretation of the bible, you certainly suffer your reason to be obscured and overruled by prejudice. Liberty, no doubt, is a blessing, but it should be confined to its own province, and within proper limits. Although we enjoy that blessing in this country, and that to the utmost degree consistent with safety, yet I do not find our government disposed to leave the interpretation of the laws to every individual; everyone is compelled to submit in practice to the interpretation and judgment of the judiciary, no matter how much his own private opinion and judgment differs from that of the honorable court. Why then will you not allow the same dispensation, the same principles in church government, as the misunderstanding and misinterpreting of the laws intended for the salvation of man would be attended with worse consequences than the misunderstanding and misinterpreting of the laws of the country.

The first reformers could not expect to succeed in making proselytes unless by pleasing. They could not please, except by flattering the passions; and as the main passion of man is the love of liberty and independence, they took care to flatter that particular passion by declaring their intention to emancipate nations from the yoke and tyranny which the pope had imposed and exercised over them, contrary to the written word of God, which alone ought to be their guide. Their assertion was easily proved to the ignorant and the corrupt, especially at a time when real abuses practiced by many clergymen (though not authorized by the church), furnished ample matter for declamation, and therefore a good opportunity for the reformers of exhibiting themselves, as burning with zeal for the glory of God.

At the period of the pretended reformation, the bible in the vulgar language was in but very few persons' hands; not in consequence of a prohibition from the church, but in consequence of the art of printing being but lately discovered. The first book that ever was printed was David's Psalter; printed in 1457, by Faust and Schoeffer, of the city of Metz, about sixty years before the beginning of the reformation. It required many years to bring the art of printing to that degree of perfection which it has now acquired. Before printing was known, and generally introduced, books of any kind must have been very scarce, and in the hands of very few; no wonder, then, if, during the first fifteen centuries of the church, the bible could not be in everybody's hands.

You would do well, my friend, to ask the protestant minister from whom the first reformer received that bible, from which they took occasion to blaspheme the holy church of Christ, and on which they and their successors have bottomed all their manifold contradictory systems. Did that sacred volume rain down from heaven into their hands? No. Did the almighty send the Archangel Gabriel, the former messenger of happy tidings, to deliver the sacred volume into the hands of the reformers? No. Did they, through divine inspiration, discover it among the ruins of the holy city? No. Where then did they find it? In the Catholic church which, during fifteen hundred years, had always carefully preserved this precious deposit of divine revelation. From it all the holy fathers of the church, all the pastors, lawful successors of the apostles, had derived that heavenly doctrine, recorded in many of their writings, for the instruction of their flocks, for the conversion of nations, and the edification of the church.

If the popes had become antichrists, the church a sink of idolatry and superstition, in short, the whore of Babylon, why did the clergy not destroy those pure sources of divine revelation, which in the course of time would have obliterated the very remembrance of their existence, and thus prevented a discovery of the changes and novelties which they introduced, and by which they totally perverted the holy religion of Jesus Christ?

The protestant minister will be compelled to own, then, that it was in the very bosom of the Catholic church the first reformers found the sacred volume of scripture, which he says the Catholic clergy have carefully kept from the eyes of the people. The grand reason for admitting the books of scripture as divine and canonical is the constant and unvarying testimony and tradition of the Catholic church.

I hope, my dear friend you are convinced by this time that we are innocent of that particular charge brought against us, of concealing the scriptures.

However, I am not done yet; I wish to be very particular on this important subject, and point out to you, as clearly as possible, the dangerous principles of the pretended reformation and, in opposition to them, the doctrine of the Catholic church concerning the bible or the written word of God.

There is nothing the protestant gentleman can say in praise of the sacred volume in which we do not heartily coincide. Call it a most beautiful flower in the garden of heaven, and we say, it is; but remember, that whilst the bee sucks from it the pure honey of life, the spider draws from it the poison of death. Call it the precious pearl (Mt. 13:46) for the acquiring of which man should sacrifice even the whole of his property, and we say, it is. But at the same time we shall tell you not to suffer it to be trampled by swine. Call it the treasure of God's revelations, and we again say, yes. But we shall pray you to remember in whose hands was left the key of that precious treasure (Mt. 16:19; 18:18). Call it the bread of life, and we shall remind you that the most wholesome bread may occasion a surfeit, and even death.

From all I could find in protestant authors, I cannot discover any fixed rule by which protestant ministers enable their hearers to find out infallibly the true sense of scripture, the sense of the Holy Ghost. Some tell us that scripture is sufficiently plain to convey its true meaning, at least by conferring one text with another. Others tell us that common sense and reason are adequate to the task of discovering the true sense of scripture. Others again, that by sincere and fervent prayer, any person may obtain grace to understand the scriptures. I have no doubt that these several means have been used by protestants to ascertain the meaning of scripture. What has been the result? Confusion and contradiction. The first reformers already quarreled, foamed, and raged, cursed and excommunicated one another, on account of their different and contradictory explanation of the same scripture texts.

Men emancipated from the government of the church, divided and subdivided into numberless sects, which have increased and multiplied to the present day, their differences are not about trifling matters only; no they differ about matters essential to salvation; such as, baptism, the Lord's supper. Now contradiction in such essential points is an evident sign of falsehood in cases where truth alone can save.

The protestant rules, then, are altogether insufficient to give us the true interpretation of scripture, and to give us perfect security that we have infallibly found the true meaning of the Holy Ghost. I must confess, my dear friend, that I am astonished to see how easy it is to satisfy protestants on the all-important subject of religion. Running from one meeting house to another, they hear the sacred text expounded in different ways, often in contradictory ways; no matter, to them it is still the word of God; although contradiction proves it to be, in many instances, the word of Satan, or the word of death. I cannot conceive how I could, with any degree of devotion, nay even with patience, listen to such arbitrary explanations, unless the preacher could satisfy me, that by some means he has found the key of that precious treasure, and is himself an infallible interpreter of scripture. Read the *Vindication of the Doctrines of the Reformation* with the utmost attention, and you will not find anything satisfactory on this all-important subject.

After what I had advanced on the subject of holy scriptures in my *Defense of Catholic Principles* (pp. 14, 20-22) it became the protestant minister's duty, if he thought that I was wrong, to confute my arguments, and to prove that I was mistaken when I stated:

One: that the divine books cannot be interpreted unless by a divine authority; and, two: that the written word could not have been intended as the supreme judge to fix our belief in matters of faith; which I proved by four arguments.

Instead of confuting those arguments (which indeed all the protestant synods of the whole protestant world are not able to do), what does the protestant minister do? Read his *Vindication* (pp. 9-12), and you will find that by a kind of pious fraud, he misrepresents my very plain words, and attempts to make his readers believe that I condemn the reading of scripture.

I wish to be plain, very plain, so plain as to be understood by the meanest capacity. So plain as to leave no chance to sophistry; and I should be happy to see the combined wisdom of the protestant world, guided by the love of truth, and fired with the heavenly fire of charity, arrayed against the arguments that are brought in support of our principles.

I say again: the sacred volume, although it is the word of God, is not the supreme judge to fix our belief in matters of faith. The letter we see, the sense we cannot see.

Christianity subsisted during many years without the gospels or epistles. It was established not by reading, but by hearing (Rom. 10:17). During fifteen centuries (printing not being invented) the sacred volume was in very few hands. The golden age of the church, the age of martyrs, the age of saints, the age of pure and unshaken faith, was the age when the written gospel did not exist at all, or existed in very few hands.

To this day there are many thousands that cannot read, and yet their faith is strong, their morals pure; and I do not know whether I would be wrong in asserting that the most humble, the most obedient, the most edifying Christians, the most firm believers in the gospel, are generally found among those that cannot read.

Who are those who, separating from the Catholic church, and running in different directions, have established so many contradictory systems of religion? Protestant bible readers. Who are those who, foaming and raging continually against the Catholic church, and telling the most unwarrantable lies against her, are continually sinning against truth and charity, the main duties of religion? Protestant bible readers.

Who are those thousands and thousands who, forsaking the very fundamentals of the Christian religion, and rejecting all its mysteries, are erecting in Baltimore and in many other cities very large and costly churches for the worship of the Socinian divinity? Protestant bible readers.

Who are those, and not few in number, who, pretending a great regard for the gospel deny the divinity of Christ and the eternity of punishments; men high in office, great in learning (Remember, I can prove what I say.)? Protestant bible readers.

Who are those who, contrary to the precept of St. Peter (2Pt. 1:20), are continually calling the divine books before the judgment seat of their own limited and corrupted reason? Protestant bible readers.

Who are those, who, measuring the profound mysteries of God by the narrow and limited measure of their understanding, make void those very mysteries, thus pronouncing that "this is my body," means, it is not my body; and also that "whose sins you forgive they are forgiven," could not mean what it says, because where is that power given to a sinful creature, and one who has to answer for his own sins (*Vindication*, p. 19). I ask, who are those men? Protestant bible readers.

I expect, my dear friend, you begin to perceive that the reading of the sacred volume alone, is not sufficient to fix the religious principles of any person; nay, that a person might have the whole bible by heart, and yet be at a loss what religious principles to adopt.

We respect the bible at least as much as you do. We believe it to be divinely inspired. We read it with fear and trembling. We kiss the sacred text every time we read the gospel of the day, in the Mass. But we do not presume to interpret it: we do not throw that precious pearl before the swine. We caution our hearers against the danger of self-interpretation; and do publicly acknowledge that we are not able, by the utmost exertion of our mental powers, to fathom its profound mysteries.

We do preach from scripture, it is true; but far from presuming to put our own interpretation on the sacred text, we deliver to our hearers that interpretation which the Catholic church gives us, believing the church to be guided by the Spirit of Truth forever (Jn. 14:6). Believing Christ the fountain of truth and salvation to be with his ministers until the consummation of the world (Mt. 28:20). Believing the church to be the pillar and ground of truth (1Tim. 3:15). Thus all our interpretations of all essential parts of scripture, are exactly alike, and were you to listen to the Catholic minister in Peking China, or at Loretto in Cambria County, Pennsylvania, you would find everywhere the same interpretation, the very same doctrine. The strong food of scripture digested by our holy mother the Catholic church, the sacred spouse of Jesus Christ (Eph. 5:25), we suck at her breasts, reduced to pure and wholesome milk.

Ask your protestant minister what objection he can have against this our practice? He tells us in his *Vindication*, that the bible alone is infallible. What does he mean by that? Does he mean that the dead letter of scripture carries with it its own interpretation? If it does, why then so many quarrels between the first reformers; and much more so between the numerous tribes of their offspring, Lutherans, Calvinists, Zuinglians, Wicliffites, Anabaptists, Quakers, Arminians and Gomarists, etc., and many more differing in most essential matters, necessary for salvation?

Although this fact stares the protestant minister in the face, as a most stubborn proof that the protestant rule of faith is very deficient, and that the letter of scripture alone is not a sufficient guide to salvation, yet he attempts to establish his principle by an argument *a priori.* "If the scripture is not plain," says he (p. 9), "then we must either say that the Holy Ghost could not dictate clearly, or that he would not. To say the former of which, would be blasphemy; and to affirm the latter, is, in effect, to say that the scriptures are no revelation of the will of God to men."

The answer to this argument is obvious. The Holy Ghost could express himself sufficiently plain; and he also did speak plain enough to be understood by applying to the proper interpreter, which the Holy Ghost himself points out, when he commands us to "Hear the church" (Mt. 18:17); also, when he tells the apostles, by the mouth of Christ, "He that hears you hears me" (Lk. 10:16); again, when he tells us, by the mouth of St. Paul (Eph. 4: 11-15) that "He gave some apostles, and some prophets, and other some evangelists, and other some pastors and doctors, for the perfecting of the saints, for the work of the ministry, for the edifying of the body of Christ, till we all meet in the unity of faith that henceforth we be no more children tossed to and fro, and carried about with every wind of doctrine" etc.

In consequence of the protestant principle of private interpretation, the wind of doctrine blows every way; the members of the different protestant sects are tossed to and fro; and instead of that unity of faith of which St. Paul speaks, there is nothing but contradictions, fluctuations, uncertainties, and perplexities. To return then to your minister's argument, we say (without incurring the guilt of blasphemy) that the Holy Ghost would not express himself sufficiently plain, to be understood by every individual, guided by the faint light of his limited and corrupted reason only. The Holy Ghost, who has declared by the mouth of Christ, that unless we become as little children, we shall not enter into the kingdom of heaven (Mt. 18:3), would have us bow down in the dust and acknowledge our dependence on the power and mercy of God; would have us be indebted to God alone for all we know; would have us make a generous sacrifice of our mental faculties, of our self-will, of our pride, etc., to the dictates of the supreme being, would have us "glory in nothing," as St. Paul says (2Cor. 12:5), "but in our infirmities," "for power" (says he again, verse 9) "is made perfect in infirmity."

If the old man, according to Adam, sinned by preferring his own will, at the instigation of Satan, to the will of God, and thus falling under the curse of God, became a prey to all kinds of evils, temporal and eternal, the new man according to Christ, treading in the steps of his divine savior, the most perfect pattern of humility and obedience, sees no surer way to recover the blessings lost, than by renouncing the treacherous light of his understanding, and the corrupt inclinations of his will.

My dear friend, ask the protestant minister what he means when he tells us that "he will take no guide as infallible but what is written in the Old and New Testaments?" (*Vindication*, p. 9).

From what has been stated already, you must plainly perceive that the minister's principle is very defective. I say defective; and in order to convince yourself of it, go to him and ask him to tell you, in the name of God, whose minister he considers himself to be? What security he can give you that he understands, and does not misunderstand, the many texts of scripture? What security, that in expounding scripture, he never gives poison instead of wholesome food? As he lays no claim to infallibility, your question may possibly puzzle him. Here are a few more questions which will puzzle him no less. As all the reformers have adopted the same principle, of following no guide as infallible but what is written in the Old and New Testament, ask him by what rule you are to find out infallibly which of the many hundreds of interpretations, made at different times, and by different reformers, is the right one? Ask him to tell you what St. Paul meant (2 Thess. 2:14) when he desired the

Thessalonians to hold the traditions received by word, as well as those received by his epistle?

Ask your minister to point out to you those unwritten traditions. Ask him also to point out to you the instructions which our blessed savior gave his apostles during "forty days appearing to them, and speaking of the kingdom of God" (Acts 1:3). Ask the protestant minister next to point out to you the text of scripture which commands to keep holy the Sunday or first day of the week, and which does away the Sabbath or seventh day? The next question you may ask your minister is to show you the text of scripture which repeals the prohibition made by the apostles against the use of blood? (Acts 15:29). Protestants eat blood puddings, and yet protestants pretend to follow no guide as infallible, only what is written in the Old and New Testaments. Ask your minister why protestant elders do not, according to the command of St. James (5:14), anoint their sick with oil? And also, why protestants do not, according to the positive command of Christ, wash one another's feet? "You also ought to wash one another's feet. For I have given you an example, that as I have done to you, so do you also" (Jn. 13:14-15).

I wish to be consistent, and I wish every person to be consistent, or to act according to those principles which each one lays down for a guide and a rule of his conduct. If your minister is sincere when he tells you that he will take no guide as infallible, but "what is written in the Old and New Testaments," then we must conclude that whatever is written in the Old and New Testaments is, in all cases, the minister's infallible guide, *i.e.*, that the minister thinks himself in duty bound to comply with all the positive injunctions of that sacred volume, and as a minister of Christ, also enforces the same injunctions on his hearers. Consequently, (as there is not a word to be found from Genesis to the Apocalypse repealing the command of keeping the Sabbath or Saturday), the minister must think himself in duty bound to keep the Saturday, and to check and reprimand his hearers for keeping the Sunday instead of the day clearly appointed in scripture.

From the same principle of admitting no guide as infallible but what is written in scripture, it is evident that he ought, both by word and example, to discountenance the practice of eating blood puddings (Acts 15:29). That he is in conscience bound, to admonish his elders to anoint their sick with oil (Jas. 5:14); and to instruct his hearers to wash one another's feet (Jn. 13:14-15).

How your protestant minister will extricate himself I do not know, but I sincerely believe, nay, I am certain, that the above questions, which I have taken the liberty to suggest to you, cannot be satisfactorily answered but by the ministers of the Catholic church. Their principle is that the Holy Ghost, the Spirit of Truth, alone can be the true and infallible interpreter of his own words. Now if Christ did not deceive us, that holy Spirit of Truth is forever in the church (Jn. 14:16-17), the church then, "the pillar and ground of truth" (1Tim. 3:15), is the grand tribunal which explains and expounds the sense of scripture; which discriminates between those commandments of scripture that continue in full force and those that have been abrogated or changed in some of their circumstances. In consequence of that principle, and consistent with himself, the Catholic keeps holy the Sunday, although he finds clearly written in the sacred volume the commandment of keeping holy the Sabbath or seventh day; because in the authority of the church which is inspired by the Holy Spirit of truth forever, and which has received the jurisdiction of Christ (Mt. 28:19 and Jn. 20:21), he finds a sufficient warrant for altering or transferring the obligation from Saturday to Sunday. The protestant, on the contrary, admitting only the letter of scripture as his infallible rule, and rejecting the authority of the church, has no other alternative but to conform to every plain injunction of scripture, and therefore to keep holy the

Sabbath or Saturday, or to acknowledge the insufficiency of the letter of scripture to be his guide. This acknowledgment is actually made in practice by nearly all protestants who in many instances, deviate from plain instructions of scripture, and yet do not consider themselves guilty of any breach of the law; and the same acknowledgment is made in plain words by some eminent protestant divines.

"There are hundreds of particulars" (says the protestant Bishop Montague, p. 396), "which have been instituted by God in the point of religion, commanded and used by the church, of which, we own, that the scripture delivers or teaches no such things."

It must be plain to you, my dear friend, that whatever God has instituted in the point of religion is of divine authority, let it be written or not written, let it be found in scripture or not; and that our divine savior has instituted very many things that never were written, is evident from the above quoted texts (2Thess. 2:14; Acts 1:3; Jn. 21:25).

From the protestant minister's principle it would evidently follow:

One: That the instructions which St. Paul delivered to the Thessalonians by word only, and not in writing, are of no account whatever, because not found in the scriptures.

Two: That the heavenly instructions given by our divine savior to his apostles during forty days after his resurrection are also to be despised and disregarded, because not written. From the protestant principle of following no guide but the written word, those heavenly instructions are entirely lost to them, although they must have been very important, as being the last ones, and as being delivered to the apostles when on the point of commencing their ecclesiastical career, and delivered to them after the resurrection of their master had fully confirmed their belief in his divinity, and of course enabled them to bear and to digest stronger food than before that glorious event.

Three: From the same protestant principle it follows that the instructions given by St. Philip, St. Bartholomew, etc., are altogether lost, and indeed very unimportant, because not transmitted in writing.

Four: It also follows from the same principle, that the Apostles' Creed, "I believe in God the Father almighty," etc., is not at all entitled to credit, and by no means the word of God, because not found in scripture.

You will plainly perceive my dear friend, that the Catholic principle levels all those difficulties, and banishes all doubts on these different subjects. Convinced that the Catholic church is the holy spouse of Christ, we believe with a firm faith, which all the quibbles of your protestant minister cannot shake, that this holy spouse of Christ has received the precious deposit of the divine word, whether written or unwritten; that by the light of the Spirit of Truth infused into that church (Jn. 14:16-17); she is always, and always will be, able to retain and to transmit that precious deposit of divine revelation, pure and undefiled, to the most remote ages. On the word of that church we receive the holy scripture as the word of God; on her word we receive the Apostles' Creed as the word of God; on her word we also receive as divine whatever we know of the sacraments, of the government and hierarchy of the church, of the celebration of Sundays and holy days, etc. from her we receive the true sense and interpretation of the written word; from her we know what books are canonical, and which of the many translations of scripture is faithful and genuine. You are sensible, my dear friend, that nothing less than an infallible authority is required, in order to satisfy us on all those different heads so as to leave no doubt on our minds. With regard to the written word or the holy scripture, we must be certain: 1) that the original scripture, in other words, the Old Testament in Hebrew, and the New Testament in Greek, is really the pure word of God, dictated by the Holy Ghost. 2) We must be certain which books belong to the canon of scripture, that is to say, which books are canonical, or of divine authority. 3) As the original scriptures have been translated into nearly all the different languages of the globe, we must be certain that the translation which is put into our hands is a faithful translation that does not deviate from the original, or from the sense of the Holy Ghost; for it does not require any arguments to prove that a false translation of any sentence of scripture is not the word of God. 4) Finally, as many sentences in scripture are hard to be understood, and admit of various interpretations, and as a false interpretation is not the word of God, we must have a certainty whether we understand or misunderstand scripture.

In order to acquire a perfect certainty on all those different heads, and to banish even the possibility of a doubt, we must derive our knowledge on all those different heads from an infallible authority; from an authority that is not subject to error: and where shall we find this unerring authority? Not in the wisdom of man, nor in the collected wisdom of all mankind. For as St. Paul says (1Cor. 3:19), "The wisdom of this world is foolishness with God. For it is written: I will catch the wise in their own craftiness." And again, "I will destroy the wisdom of the wise: and the prudence of the prudent I will reject" (1Cor. 1:19).

In truth, my dear friend, the greatest wisdom you can attain to in this world is the knowledge of your own ignorance, of your insignificancy, of your dependence on the great God in every case, in every instance, and every moment.

I ask again, where shall we find this unerring authority, to establish the canon of scripture, to point out the faithful translation, and to determine the true sense of scripture? Nowhere, my friend, but in the Catholic church; which has the promise of the Spirit of Truth forever (Jn. 14:16).

I think it necessary to dwell on each of those particular subjects. The canon of scripture must be determined by an

infallible authority. Your protestant minister thinks himself
able to establish the canon of scripture by the powers
of reason, and he gives us a specimen of his ingenuity
(*Vindication*, p. 48) in the following words:

> We reject the apocryphal books which were never
> received by the Jews, to whom the oracles of God were
> committed. Of these, some are only abridgments, etc.
> Others have very much the resemblance of a romance,
> as the pretended histories of Judith and Susanna; and
> lastly, who would believe the history of Tobit and his
> dog except a Roman Catholic, who can swallow any
> absurdity.

My dear friend, all the ancient fathers of the church
agree that Esdras was the compiler of the Jewish canon,
which contained twenty-two books. This compilation took
place after the Babylonian captivity, and did not comprehend
any books but those that had been written before the said
captivity; and it does not appear that any other book was
afterwards added to that canon. But remember that our
savior Jesus Christ does not send us to the Jews, but to
his church, for instructions, and that he invests the church
with the Spirit of Truth forever, in order to make her a
fit instructor in the ways of truth and salvation. Now,
that holy church, in the third Council of Carthage, Anno
Domini 397, declares the Machabees, Tobias, Judith, etc.,
to be divine books, as well as those contained in the Jewish
canon; and the same declaration is made about 1,200 years
afterwards by the Council of Trent. Nearly all protestants
agree that the church of Christ was pure yet at the above
period, Anno Domini 397, and of course that credit is due
to her declaration made at that time.

Is not the unanimous consent of the Catholic or
universal church of all ages a safer rule to establish the
canon of scripture than the private and contradictory

opinions of innovators? I say contradictory, for the different reformers did not agree about the different parts of scripture. Martin Luther tells us plainly (vol. 3, pp. 40-41), "We will neither hear nor see Moses, for he was given only to the Jews; neither does he belong anything to us."

Again in his *Table Discourses*, chapter of the laws and the gospel, Luther tells us, "I will not receive Moses with his law, for he is the enemy of Christ (p. 118); Moses is the master of all hangmen." And in his sermon of Moses, he says "The ten commandments belong not to Christians; let the ten commandments be altogether rejected, and all heresies will presently cease, for the ten commandments are, as it were the fountain from whence all his heresies spring."

Islebius, Luther's scholar, taught the same doctrine. From him came the sect of Antinomans, who taught publicly, "if thou be a wh—e, if an adulterer, or otherwise a sinner, believe, and thou walkest in the way of salvation. . . . All that busy themselves about Moses, that is the ten commandments, belong to the devil; to the gallows with Moses" (See *Confession of the Manfield Ministers*, in Latin. Tit. de Antinomi, p. 89, 90).

Castalio commanded the canticles of Solomon to be thrust out of the canon (See Beza in *Vita Calvini*).

Calvin rejects these words of St. Matthew, "Many are called but few chosen" (*Sermon on Mt. 20:16*).

Zuinglius and other protestants affirm that all things in St. Paul's epistles are not sacred, and that in sundry things he erred.

Rogers makes mention of sundry protestants who reject as apocryphal the epistle to the Hebrews, of St. James, the first and second of Sts. John and Jude, and the Apocalypse (*Defense of the Articles*, art. 6, p. 32).

Calvin charges St. Peter to have erred in faith and morals (See Calvin in Gal. 2, p. 510-511). There are other protestant divines who admit the very books as canonical which the Jews rejected, and which are admitted by the Catholic church.

The Calvinists of Geneva, in their preface to a bible published *anno* 1551, by John Tornesius, have the following instruction to the reader: "We are not to stand to the censure of the Jews, in regard of this maiming of the canon of scripture: and in these books (rejected by the Jews) there are true prophecies and hidden mysteries, which could not be spoken but by the Holy Ghost," etc..

Dr. Bancroft, in his Conference Before the King (p. 60), rejects the objections of the Jews, calling them, "the old cavils of the Jews," etc.

Conradus Pellican, protestant divine at Tigure, says in his dedicatory epistle, that

> those books were always counted ecclesiastical and biblical; that even from the apostles' times they were read in the Catholic church with much reverence, although they were not produced in authority against the Jews, who received not these books into their sacred canon. ... for the most part they clearly carry the right style of the Holy Ghost etc.

It is evident, then, that the very first reformers did not agree among themselves on the canon of scripture, and that your protestant minister is much mistaken when he says (p. 48), that "the reformed church receives no other books but those which are acknowledged canonical by all Christians, etc. and reject the apocryphal books which were never received by the Jews," etc. In fact, there are so many reformed churches, so many different opinions and variations even among protestants of the same denomination, and so many changes in the faith and principles of the same reformed church from time to time, that it would be more correct to say that the principle of the reformed churches (not church) is to have no fixed principle, but to be guided by mere opinions.

It is your minister's opinion that the histories of Judith and Susanna have very much the resemblance of a romance, and that the history of Tobit and his dog is an absurdity.

Ask your minister what he thinks of Balaam and his ass, and also of Samson and his foxes? Ask him also how he will ever succeed in establishing a firm unshaken belief in his canon of scripture, when he cannot bottom it upon an infallible unerring authority?

The true and faithful translation of scripture ought also to be pointed out by an infallible or unerring authority, as nothing short of an infallible authority can give a perfect certainty to the readers of scripture in the vulgar language that what they read is the pure word of God.

The protestant minister tells you that "the Roman church, or it's rulers, in order to hide the absurdities they taught, were obliged to make a bible for themselves, so unlike the true translation of that sacred book, that they who can read it in the original, would scarce know it to be the same" (*Vindication*, p. 133).

Those that live in the neighborhood of the protestant minister have a very good opportunity of reading the English Catholic bible, if they chose so to do; and anyone clear–sighted enough to discover the priest's spittle and the live coal in the holy water (*Vindication*, p. 75), will also be able to discover the enormous difference between the Catholic and the protestant bibles.

The truth is, my dear friend, the two bibles are not quite so different as the minister would persuade you; but still there are some differences, even in some essential points, which may escape the notice of the reader, unless he reads very attentively. The question is then (and a very important question), which translation is the genuine one?

The minister will tell you at once that it is the protestant bible. If he does, ask him which of all the protestant translations he means? For you must know, my friend, that there are many protestant translations, differing from one another, as well as from the original; and you must know that the translations made by some protestants are most bitterly condemned by other protestants.

Zuinglius, writing to Luther about his German translation, has the following words: "Thou dost corrupt the word of God; thou art seen to be a manifest and common corrupter and perverted of the holy scripture: how much are we ashamed of thee" etc. (vol. 2, of *The Sacrament*, pp. 412-413).

Keckman, another protestant divine, affirms, that "Luther's German translation of the Old Testament, etc. has its blemishes, and those no small ones" (See Keckman's *System of Divinity*, book 1, p. 188).

I shall only mention two of Luther's willful corruptions.

Where St. Paul (Rom. 3:28) says, "We account a man to be justified by faith, without the works of the law," Luther translates, "justified by faith alone," etc., to support his aversion to good works; and when admonished of this foul corruption, his answer was: *Sic volo, sic jubeo, sit pro ratione voluntas*, etc., that is, "so I will, so I command, let my will be for a reason"; Luther will have it so. "The word, *alone*, must remain in my New Testament, although all the papists go mad. If thy papist show himself angry for the word alone, forthwith tell him a papist and an ass are the same thing" etc. (See *Luther's German Writings*, vol. 5, pp. 141-144).

Also where it is said, (2Pet. 1:10) "Wherefore, brethren, labor the more, that by good works you may make sure your vocation and election," Luther here omitteth these words, "by good works," which are also omitted in most of the English protestant translations.

On the other hand we find Luther rejecting the translation of the Zuinglians, and calling them "fools, asses, antichrists, deceivers," etc. (See Zuinglius, vol. 2. *ad. Luth. of the Sacram.* p. 388).

The Tigurine translation was condemned by other protestant divines and, as Hospinian writes in his book called *The Concord of Discord* (p. 238), it was rejected with great anger by the elector of Saxony.

The translation set forth by Oecolampadius and the protestant divines of Basil is reproved by Beza as "wicked in many places, and altogether differing from the sense of the Holy Ghost."

The translation of Castalio, another protestant, which Dr. Humfrey affirms to be "thoroughly conferred, examined and polished," (see Humfrey *De Rat. Interpret.*, Vol. 2, pp. 62-63, etc.) is also condemned by Beza as "sacrilegious and wicked," etc., (See Beza in *Test.* 1556, in *Præf.* and in *Annot.* in Mt. 3, in 1Cor. and in Mt. 4, etc.).

Concerning Calvin's translation, the famous protestant, Charles Molinæus, affirms that "Calvin makes the text of the gospel to leap up and down; he uses violence to the letter of the gospel; and besides this, adds to the text," (See Molinæus in his *Translation of the New Testament*, part 11, p. 110).

The same Molinæus also charges Beza "to change the text in his translation." King James thinks the protestant translation of Geneva to be "the worst of all" (*Conference Before His Majesty*, p. 46).

Thus you see, that the very first reformers already quarreled about their different translations of scripture. Now to speak more particularly of the English protestant translations, we find great complaints made against them by protestants themselves.

In the petition presented to King James by numbers of the protestant clergy (p. 75), they complain, "The book of Psalms alone differs from the Hebrew in at least two hundred places."

Mr. Carlisle, a protestant divine, asserts that the "English translators have depraved the sense of scripture, obscured the truth, and deceived the ignorant: that they show themselves to love darkness more than light, falsehood more than truth" (See pp. 116, 117, etc., of *Christ's descending into Hell*).

The protestant ministers of the diocese of Lincoln affirm that "The English translation takes away from, and adds to, the text, and that, sometimes to the changing or obscuring the meaning of the Holy Ghost; a translation which is absurd and senseless" (See the *Abridgment* which the ministers of Lincoln delivered to his majesty, p. 11).

Mr. Burges, another protestant, in his *Apology* (sect. 6), excuses himself for not subscribing to that protestant translation. "How shall I approve," says he, "under my hand, a translation which has many omissions, many additions, which sometimes obscureth, sometimes perverteth the sense, being sometimes senseless, sometimes contrary."

Mr. Broughton, a protestant divine of great learning, wrote an epistle to the lords of the council, desiring them to procure a new translation of the scripture, and assures the protestant bishops that "The English translation perverts the text of the old testament in eight hundred and forty-eight places; and causes millions of souls to run to eternal flames."

Had not King James then just cause to complain, "that he could never yet see a bible well translated into English?" (See *Conference Before His Majesty*, p. 46).

Take notice, my dear friend, that the reformation had already existed about one hundred years when these complaints were made; and remember here your minister's assertion, that nothing is to be taken as infallible but what is written in the Old or New Testament, which, however, according to the protestant doctor Whitaker, "is not the word of God, unless it faithfully expresses the meaning of the authentic (or original) text," (See *Whitaker's Answer to Rein*, p. 235).

From the testimonies of protestants themselves then, you plainly see upon what foundation the edifice of the reformation was raised; to wit, upon the dead letter of scripture, corruptly translated, curtailed, and perverted, which of course was not the word of God, and which besides, everyone was to interpret for himself.

The English protestant bible, they pretend, is a faithful translation from the Hebrew and Greek originals.

This I declare to be impossible. Why so? Because the Hebrew and Greek originals are no longer in existence. Time, that demolishes the strongest monuments raised by the hands of men, has also destroyed the originals of scripture. The present Hebrew and Greek texts are only copies, which in many places deviate from the original; of which I shall give you a few instances.

First, in the present Hebrew Old Testament we read, "he shall call wonderful," (Isa. 9:6), whereas it is evident from the context, and Calvin owns to it, that it must be "he shall be called wonderful." Again, in Psalm 21:17, where all Christians read "they have dug my hands," the Hebrew text says, "like a lion," which has no sense at all. In Psalm 18:5, where we read "their sound hath gone forth into all the earth," which is quoted by St. Paul in the very same words, Romans 10:18, the Hebrew text says, "their line of perpendicular went forth into all the earth," which the protestant minister is perhaps more capable of explaining than I am.

Again, Genesis 8:7, where we read the raven "went forth and did not return," etc. the Hebrew text says, "did return." From the translation of the Septuagint, and from all the ancient fathers who have quoted that text, it must be "did not return."

There are besides, whole sentences omitted in the present Hebrew text; for instance, in Exodus 2:22: "And she bore another whom he called Eliezer, saying: for the God of my father, my helper, hath delivered me out of the hand of Pharao." These words must have been in the Hebrew original, as they are found in the Septuagint, which is a Greek translation from the Hebrew original, and also in St. Jerome's translation.

The present Greek text is not pure either, which I shall prove by a few instances: 1Corinthians 15:47, where we read, "the first man was of the earth, earthly: the second man from heaven, heavenly," which Calvin confesses to be the true way of reading. The Greek text says, "the second man, the Lord from heaven."

Romans 12:11, where the *Vulgate*, as well as the protestant testament, says "serving the Lord," many Greek copies say "serving time"; which is evidently wrong, as appears from all the Greek fathers who have quoted the above text.

Moreover, it is evident that in many Greek copies, words are added to the sacred text, as, for instance, to the Lord's prayer (Mt. 6:9-13) the words "for thine is the kingdom, power and glory," etc., which words are not to be found in any of the ancient fathers that have quoted and explained the Lord's prayer from the holy scripture.

In most of the Greek copies, considerable parts of holy writ are omitted; for instance, the last chapter of St. Mark, as well as the history of the woman apprehended in adultery (Jn. 8:3-11).

The present Hebrew and Greek, then, of which the protestant bible is said to be a translation, is not pure; of course the translation cannot be pure, admitting it to be a faithful translation; which, however, is not the case, as I have proved by many protestant authorities.

It is true that upon so many complaints being brought before King James, the bible was revised; but the most of its errors remained untouched, and continue in it to this day.

The Catholic church makes use of the Latin bible, called the *Vulgate*, which was published by St. Jerome, under the pontificate of Pope Damasus, sometime about the year 370. This is the bible which, the protestant minister says, "the Roman church or its rulers, made for themselves, in order to hide the absurdities they taught, and which is so unlike the true translation, that they who can read it in the original, would scarce know it to be the same."

Many learned protestant ministers are of a different opinion. Hear what Beza says, in his preface to the New Testament: "I do embrace, for the most part, the *Vulgate* edition, and prefer it before all others." And in his *Annotations on Luke 1* "The old interpreter seems to have interpreted the holy books with greatest religion."

Dr. Humphrey, a protestant minister, confesses that "The old interpreter was much addicted to the propriety of words, and that over scrupulously, which yet (says he) I interpret him to have done upon religion, and not upon ignorance" (Humphrey *de Ratione Interpret*, book 1 p. 74).

Molinæus, another protestant, declares that he can hardly depart from the *Vulgate* and accustomed reading, which also (says he) "I am accustomed earnestly to defend: yea I prefer the *Vulgate* edition before Erasmus, Bucer, Butlinger, etc., also before John Calvin, and all others." (See Molinæus on the New Test. part 30, and on Lk. 17).

Conradus Pellican, another protestant minister, finds "the *Vulgate* edition of the Psalter to agree for the sense with such dexterity, learning and fidelity of the Hebrew, that I doubt not (says he), but the Greek and Latin interpreter was a man most learned, most godly, and of a prophetic spirit" (See part 2 of *the Def. of the Minister*, p. 136).

"We grant it fit," says Dr. Dove, in his *Persuasion to Recusants* (p. 10), "that for uniformity in quotations of places, in schools and pulpits, one Latin text should be used. And we can be contented for the antiquity thereof with the *Vulgate* before all other Latin books."

In confirmation of this antiquity, Dr. Covell, in his *Answer to Burges* (p. 94), tells you that "It was used in the church thirteen hundred years ago"; that is at present more than fourteen hundred years, or more than eleven hundred years before the pretended reformation; and he himself doubts not "to prefer that translation before others"; and he adds, that "whereas there are many protestant translations that disagree among themselves, the approved translation authorized by the church of England is that which cometh nearest to the *Vulgate*, and is commonly called the bishop's bible" (Covell to Burges, p. 91).

You see then, my dear friend, that all protestants do not agree with your minister in condemning our Catholic bible; and I do not think that he is able to give any other proofs for his assertion, that the Roman Catholic rulers made that bible to hide the absurdities of their doctrine, except his hatred against the Catholic church.

Hatred and spite, my friend, are dangerous passions that blind the sight and obscure the understanding. Persons actuated by those passions lose sight of the very first principles of logic, and of all the rules of sound criticism, and condemn merely because they are determined to condemn.

According to the rules of sound criticism, the *Vulgate* bible used by the Catholic church deserves the preference before all the translations of the reformers.

First, because it was translated from the Hebrew and the Greek nearly 1,400 years before the pretended reformation, at a time that those original sources were much purer than they are at present.

Second, because St. Jerome, the translator and reviser of that divine book, was, not only a man of very great learning, but in particular a most complete master of the three languages, Hebrew, Greek, and Latin.

Third, because, after being appointed by Pope Damasus to revise and translate the holy scriptures, he transported himself from Rome to Jerusalem, and spent several years in perfecting himself in the knowledge of Hebrew, and in examining and comparing all the ancient manuscripts of the bible which he was able to procure.

Fourth, because said bible thus translated and revised by St. Jerome was received by the whole Catholic church at a time when even our adversaries confess it to have been the true church. The most of them suppose the whole world to have been buried in superstition and idolatry during the space of about eight hundred years before the pretended reformation, *i.e.*, from about the year 700 to 1500; but the above translation adopted by the Catholic church was made about the year 370.

Judge then, my dear friend, whether the *Vulgate* translation, which the Catholic church has adopted as her standard of scripture, is not far more to be depended upon, as being the genuine, pure word of God, than any of those modern translations made by reformers, and made from a spirit of spite and opposition to the Catholic church? Made at a time when the original Hebrew and Greek did no longer exist in their purity, and made without the help of that infallible and unerring Spirit of Truth, which undoubtedly guided the holy Catholic church in approving and adopting the translation of St. Jerome: for Christ had promised (Jn. 14:16-17 and 16:13) that the Spirit of Truth, the Paraclete, should guide his church into all truth, and should guide her forever. Certainly never was the fulfilling of that promise more necessary than on the solemn occasion of determining the important question, "Which is the pure and genuine translation of the original written word of God?"

The reformed translators of scripture were left to the light of their own limited and corrupted reason only when they undertook, out of corrupted and polluted sources, to draw the pure and heavenly doctrine of salvation. No wonder then, if those translations deviate in many instances from the pure word of God, as has been proved by the testimonies of numbers of protestants.

You will now understand the several positions contained in the pope's *Brief Against Bible Societies*, which the protestant minister publishes in a tone of triumph (pp. 136-138), because in it he finds it completely proved that the Roman Catholic church opposes the reading of scripture. The leading positions in that brief are:

One: That the bible printed by heretics is to be numbered among prohibited books.

Two: That the holy scriptures, when circulated in the vulgar tongue have, through the temerity of men, produced more harm than benefit.

Three: As a consequence of one and two, that no versions of the bible in the vulgar tongue be permitted except such as are approved by the Apostolic See, or published with annotations extracted from the writings of the holy fathers of the church.

I do not find in the whole of the pope's brief any expressions more forcibly, more energetically, expressing the danger of false translations than those above quoted expressions of the protestant minister Broughton, in his epistle to the lords of the council, "that the English translation [used in his time] perverts the text of the Old Testament, etc., and causes millions of souls to run to eternal flames."

The pope calls the circulating false translations of scripture, and scattering the same by millions among the nations of the globe, "a defilement of the faith imminently dangerous to souls." This is certainly correct.

If adding to, or taking away from, the words of God's revelation will, according to the Apocalypse (22:18-19), accumulate on the person guilty of that sacrilege all the woes announced in the sacred volume, what else but curses and the most dreadful punishments have those to expect who overflow the world with false translations of the word of God, and thus practice the most criminal deception on millions of souls.

But even admitting the translation to be genuine, it is not by throwing the sacred volume by millions among the nations that they will be converted to Christianity. Throwing the pearl before the swine (which is expressly forbidden) will never turn those swine into rational beings, and teach them to esteem that pearl.

The Catholic missionaries, who in all ages have preached the gospel, and converted many nations in every part of the globe, found it necessary to adopt a far different method in order to bring under the yoke of Christ millions of savages that had of human nature nothing but the outward form; that were more brutal than the tigers of the forest. With the most ardent charity, with the most heroic courage, and the most persevering patience, they hunted them up in their almost impenetrable forests and, renouncing all the commodities of life, they adopted the same mode of living, the same nourishment, had nothing but the cold earth for their beds, in short they became savage with the savages, in order to gain them to Christ (1Cor. 9:20, 22). Many of those missionaries were massacred before ever they had any chance of announcing to them the tidings of salvation. Their persevering endeavors were crowned with success. About three hundred thousand families in South America alone were persuaded to leave their forests and their vagabond way of living, to form settlements and to range themselves under the cross, the standard of Christianity; and it is proved by the testimonies of the Spanish governors under whose jurisdiction those Indian settlements were, and also by the testimonies of numbers of travelers, that those Indians were examples of Christian virtue and perfection, and that those vices which are so very common among the Christian nations were entirely unknown to them.

Take notice, my friend, that those nations were not converted by reading the bible, but, as St. Paul says, by hearing (Rom. 10:17), for none of them had any idea of a letter; and even after their conversion very few of them ever learned to read. Their days were spent in praying and laboring. Without ever diving into the profound mysteries of scripture, they listened and submitted with the docility of children to their fathers in Christ, and received from the church the doctrine of salvation. In short they were not bible readers, but practicers of its commandments.

They were not improved enough to measure the immeasurable abyss of omnipotence, but they had a sufficient share of learning to know that nothing is impossible to omnipotence.

They were not wise enough to comprehend the profound mysteries of revelation, but had humility and grace enough to believe them. They were not philosophers enough to pronounce on the possibility or impossibility of the mysteries, but had common sense enough to know that the God of truth could not be the author of lies and deception.

They had not pride enough to sit in judgment over the divine revelations, and to determine their sense and meaning by the feeble light of their reason, but they had sense enough to know that a church guided forever by the Spirit of Truth and being the pillar and ground of truth could never deceive them.

They could not read the bible, but they received the heavenly doctrine therein contained, digested and accommodated to their limited understanding, from their spiritual fathers; in hearing them they heard Christ himself, (Lk. 10:16), and not being ingenious enough to know the wonderful power and virtue belonging to the words, "it means", which changes flesh into bread, life into death, power into weakness, substance into shadow; they simply believed, without scrutinizing. They were all united in the bonds of faith and charity. Thus, what the mere reading of the bible never was able to produce was accomplished by humility and obedience.

Put the bible into the hands of the proud, luxurious, and corrupt man and, guided by the corrupt inclinations of flesh and blood, he will find in it what will authorize his criminal practices; especially when he is told to interpret for himself. Thus the most abominable heresies, the most impious systems, and the most immoral practices have been deduced from the sacred volume.

It is not the reading of the bible itself, then, that the pope condemns in his brief, but reading with a bad disposition; reading with pride and self-conceit; reading without deference to the interpretation of the church; and especially reading false translations condemned by the church.

Before I close this subject I shall point out to you a few instances of false translations in your protestant testament:

Roman Catholic Testament

Luke 2:14
1. Glory be to God in the highest: and on earth peace to men of good will.

Matthew 19:11
2. Who [He] said to them: All men receive not this word, but they to whom it is given.

John 2:4
3. And Jesus saith to her: Woman, what is it to me and to thee? My hour is not yet come.

Acts 19:35
4. And when the town clerk had appeased the multitudes, he said: Ye men of Ephesus, what man is there, that knoweth not that the city of

Protestant Testament

Luke 2:14
1. Glory to God in the highest, and on earth peace, good will towards men.

Matthew 19:11
2. He said unto them: All men cannot receive this saying, save they to whom it is given.

John 2:4
3. Jesus said unto her: Woman, what have I to do with thee? Mine hour is not yet come.

Acts 19:35
4. And when the town clerk had appeased the people, he said: 'Ye men of Ephesus, what man is there that knoweth not how that the city

the Ephesians is a worshipper of the great Diana and of Jupiter's offspring?

of Ephesians is a worshipper of the great goddess Diana, and of the image which fell down from Jupiter?'

Romans 11:4.
5. I have left me seven thousand men that have not bowed their knees to Baal.

Romans 11:4
5. I have reserved to myself seven thousand men, who have not bowed the knee to the image of Baal.

1 Corinthians 9:5.
6. Have we not power to carry about a woman, a sister, as well as the rest of the apostles . . . .?

1 Corinthians 9:5
6. Have we not power to lead about a sister, a wife, as well as other apostles . . .?

1 Corinthians 11:27.
7. Whosoever shall eat this bread, or drink the chalice of the Lord unworthily shall be guilty of the body and of the blood of the Lord.

1 Corinthians 11:27
7. Whosoever shall eat this bread and drink this cup of the Lord unworthily, ...

Galatians 5:17
8. For the flesh lusteth against the spirit: and the spirit against the flesh. For these are contrary one to another so that you do not the things that you would.

Galatians 5:17.
8. The flesh lusteth against the spirit, etc.,. so that ye cannot do the things that ye would.

Philippians 4:3
9. And I entreat thee also, my sincere companion, help those women who have labored with me in the gospel
. . .

Philippians 4:3
9. And I entreat thee also, true yoke fellow, help those women . . ..

Hebrews 11:21

10. By faith Jacob, [when he was] dying, blessed each of the sons of Joseph, and adored the top of his rod.

Hebrews 11:21

10. By faith Jacob, when he was dying, blessed both of the sons of Joseph, and worshipped, leaning upon the top of his staff.

Hebrews 13:4

11. Marriage honorable in all, and the bed undefiled. . . . For fornicators and adulterers God will judge.

Hebrews 13:4.

11. Marriage is honorable in all, and the bed undefiled

2 Peter 1:10.

12. Brethren labor the more, that by good works, you may make your calling and election sure.

2 Peter 1:10.

12. The rather, brethren, give diligence to make your calling and election sure.

I have given you here a few instances of the corruptions of the protestant testament. The Catholic texts quoted are a faithful translation from the Latin *Vulgate*, which was translated from the Greek about the year 370, and adopted by the church, at a time when most protestants acknowledge it to have been pure yet. The protestant texts are not a faithful translation from the Greek, but seem to be willfully corrupted to condemn the Catholic doctrine.

Numbers two and eight: "cannot receive" instead of "receive not," also "cannot do, instead of "do not," seems to establish the favorite doctrine of the first reformers, that it is impossible to keep the commandments. This was plainly asserted by Martin Luther. "Let this be your rule," says Luther, "where the scripture commands the doing a good work, understand it in this sense, that it forbids thee to do a good work, because thou canst not do it" (Vol. 3, p. 171). Again: "As it is not in my power not to be a man, so it is not in my choice to be without a woman. And as it is not in my power not to be a woman, so it is not in my choice to live without a man" (*Serm. ad Matrim.* vol. 5, p. 119).

This is saying plainly that it is impossible to live chaste, although God commands it.

Number three: "Woman, what have I to do with thee?" seems to authorize the contempt which reformers have ever shown to the mother of Christ.

Numbers four and five: The word "image" added to both texts must have been foisted in, perhaps with the view of condemning Catholic images.

The addition in text four turns sense into nonsense. The Catholic text, "worshipper of the great Diana and of Jupiter's offspring," is very intelligible; for it is known from the mythology of the ancients that Jupiter was considered the father of the gods, and that the other pretended divinities were, of course, Jupiter's offspring. But I am much at a loss how to understand the protestant text, "the image which fell down from Jupiter."

In number six, where St. Paul only speaks of such devout women, as — according to the custom of the Jews — waited on the preachers of the gospel and supplied them with necessaries of which we see many instances in the gospel, the reformers say "a sister, a wife," instead of "a woman, a sister": in condemnation of the single life of the Catholic clergy.

From 1 Corinthians 7:7-8, it appears plainly that St. Paul was not married.

Number seven: The reformers, that they may prove the necessity of receiving the holy sacrament in both kinds, have falsely translated "eat and drink" instead of "eat or drink," as is acknowledged by the protestant minister Steel, in his sermon on the Lord's supper (See *Morning Exercise Against Popery*, p. 768).

Number nine: "true yoke fellow" instead of "sincere companion," must have been adopted by reformers in order to intimate that St. Paul was married.

Number ten: The sense here is entirely changed by the addition of two words, "leaning upon." The Catholic text represents the patriarch Jacob on his death bed, worshipping, in the spirit of prophecy, the savior in which alone he confided for salvation; whose power was prefigured by Joseph, the savior of Egypt, in whose rod, or scepter, Jacob, by faith, beheld the future scepter or power of the Messiah. But the reformers, not relishing this relative honor which savored too much of popery, took the liberty to accommodate the text to their own weak ideas and opinions. We would fain wish to know how the leaning on the top of a staff could be an argument of Jacob's faith?

Number eleven: Here the word *is* is foisted in, probably to excuse the sacrilegious marriages of the first reformers, who had most solemnly consecrated themselves to the service of God in a single life, by a vow of perpetual virginity.

The Catholic text, "Marriage honorable in all, and the bed undefiled," is a caution to those that are lawfully married. Let marriage be honorable, and no liberties or irregularities admitted that would be contrary to the sanctity to the state of matrimony.

Number twelve: The willful omission of the words, "by good works," encourages the abominable doctrine of Luther and other arch heretics that faith alone is sufficient for salvation.

You see then, my dear friend, how strangely lay people are imposed upon by false translations of scripture which are given them as the pure word of God, upon which they are to build their faith, and from which they are to draw their religious principles.

You perceive also how necessary it is that there should be an infallible, unerring authority to point out the true translation of scripture. It is no less necessary to determine THE TRUE SENSE OF SCRIPTURE.

That the letter of scripture is not a sufficient guide to salvation is self-evident. "The letter killeth: but the spirit giveth life" (2Cor. 3:6).

And the minister's repeated assertions, that he will take nothing as infallible but what is contained in the Old and New Testaments, is only an imposition on common sense.

In my *Defense of Catholic Principles*, I laid down as a self-evident principle the fact that the written word may be misunderstood, even in matters essential to salvation, therefore it could not have been intended as the supreme judge to fix our belief in matters of faith, but that Christ must have provided, and actually has provided, a living, visible, and supreme authority, to decide infallibly, and without appeal, the true sense of scripture etc. (*See Defense of Catholic Principles*, pp. 21-25).

Now sir, look at your minister's answer (pp. 9-12), and you will find it to be no answer at all.

To be sure, I do not blame him for not answering what he, and the collected wisdom of all protestant ministers never could answer, but I must censure him for his want of candor and willful misrepresentation of my argument, which he represents to be, against reading the scripture, whereas it is only against making the scripture the supreme judge of controversies.

All the woes and curses which he denounces against the Catholic priests (pp. 9, 10) will not deter me from asserting the above principle; and if I had not made up my mind not to address your minister any more, for the reasons stated in my *Appeal to the Protestant Public*, I should certainly press him very hard to give me a rule by which controversies about the sense of scripture are to be infallibly settled, settled without appeal, settled in such a manner as to leave no doubt on the minds of scripture readers.

Was I to become one of your minister's hearers, I am certain that I should not be satisfied with his interpretations of scripture, unless he would prove himself infallible. Any protestant sincerely desirous of salvation must feel very uneasy, when he, on the one hand, reads, in the scripture, "unless you believe or do such and such things, you shall not enter the kingdom of heaven," and on the other hand, from his own ignorance, from the fallibility, and the perpetual contradictions of his ministers, can never promise himself that he has obtained the true sense of those essential passages of scripture. Your minister tries to supply this want of infallibility in himself by the boldness of his own decisions: "It is evident", "it is absurd", "it is contrary to reason", "we defy the world to show a notion so absurd", "it is unscriptural," etc., and also by quotations from certain celebrated characters, whose names sanction as truth the most palpable lies, such as Tillotson, Hume, Buck, etc. However, we shall have opportunities to notice some of their lies in some future publication; suffice it to say that in Britain where the Catholics have been persecuted ever since the reformation, and persecuted in the most cruel manner, deprived of all the privileges of citizens, their priests hanged and quartered for saying Mass, or even for coming into the kingdom, their schoolmasters transported for teaching, and hanged for a second offence etc., that in that country, I say, the only way for a clergyman or a historian to acquire popularity and to be promoted, was, as the English poet says, "Like a tall bully to lift his head and lie." It was by vomiting their bold and impudent lies against Catholics, from their pulpits and printing presses, that the hatred against popery was kept up, and the vengeance of the law brought down upon the heads of an unoffending loyal people. I cannot help noticing here the assertion of your minister (p. 126). "We who are protestants have certainly a great advantage over papists in that divine grace of charity. We have never persecuted, and put to death, with the most cruel torture, millions of our fellow creatures, because they could not believe impossibilities."

After this assertion of your minister, who will believe anything he will say? The fact is my dear friend, and I shall make it appear in some future publication, that (notwithstanding your minister's clamors about popish cruelty and persecutions) ever since the beginning of the reformation, the most cruel persecutions have been carried on without exception, against Catholics in every country where protestants had the power in their hands, and I engage to make it appear that the balance of toleration is not in favor of your minister's church.

But let us return to our subject.

Your minister ridicules the idea of an infallible authority to interpret scripture, and tells us repeatedly, in his *Vindication*, that there is no infallible authority upon earth.

Ask him what security he can give you that his interpretations of scripture are correct?

He tells you in his *Vindication*, and I suppose preaches the same from the pulpit, that "the gates of hell shall not prevail against the church," MEANS, that death shall not prevail against the genuine members of the church. (p. 14). "Unless you eat the flesh of the Son of Man and drink his blood," MEANS, that we must believe in Christ (p. 24). "This is my body etc., this is my blood etc.," MEANS, this is not my body, this is not my blood (pp. 27, 28). "Receive ye the Holy Ghost, whose sins you shall forgive, they are forgiven," and "I will give to thee the keys of the kingdom of heaven, and whatsoever you shall bind upon earth, it shall be bound also in heaven," MEANS nothing at all, for where is that power (of forgiving sins) given to a sinful creature, and one who has to answer for his own sins? (p. 19).

"Faith is the substance of things to be hoped for, the evidence of things *not seen*" (Heb. 11:1), and "blessed are they that have *not seen*, and have believed" (Jn. 20:29), means nothing, for the foundation of our faith must rely on the truth of our senses (p. 29). "Yet so as by fire," means, "yet so as out of the fire etc." (p. 47).

Now, giving such explanations of scripture, in print, or from his pulpit to his congregation, is what your minister would call preaching the word of God. Pray, my dear friend, does this satisfy you or does it not leave a certain uneasiness on your mind, lest perhaps your minister be mistaken in his interpretations; and lest perhaps what he gives you for the word of God, turns out to be the word of Satan? But you will tell me that the minister gives you arguments, and quotes authorities for his interpretations. Aye, true enough? He fairly overwhelms us with the number of his arguments; and he also quotes the learned Archbishop Tillotson, the pious Bishop White, the great Arabian philosopher Averroes, the great historian Flume, and the famous author of *The Theological Dictionary*, Buck. Admitting all those men to be men of candor, as well as men of learning, what weight can their authority, joined to all your minister's arguments, have in matters of revelation, in matters far more remote from the reach of the human understanding than Saturn is from the earth?

He attempts by arguments to prove the meaning of the Holy Ghost, but this is the very thing he has forbidden: "No prophecy of scripture is made by private interpretation" (2Pet. 1:20).

He attempts, by the force of arguments, to explain the thoughts and the ways of God; but the spirit of God condemns the attempt. "As the heavens are exalted above the earth, so are my ways exalted above your ways, and my thoughts above your thoughts" (Isa. 55:9).

He attempts, by the calculations of human wisdom, to establish the sense and meaning of divine revelation, but he forgets that God "will destroy the wisdom of the wise," and that God hath "made foolish the wisdom of this world" (1Cor. 1:19, 20).

He is not ashamed to bring forward the testimony of Averroes, a pagan philosopher, and a man noted for his irreligion, in order, as he says, to put the Catholic church to the blush (p. 32), and in order to overthrow the interpretations which the said church makes of the written word of God. Averroes lived more than three hundred years before the reformation, at the time when almost the only known Christian religion was the Roman Catholic. His attacks on the church were not confined to those tenets which now distinguish it from the protestant sects, but were directed also against the very tenets adopted by protestants of all denominations. He called the Christian religion a religion impossible; the Jewish, the religion of children; and the Mahometan, the religion of hogs.

It is remarkable, although not surprising, that protestants and philosophers, those educated in the schools of infidelity, have generally agreed in their opinions of Catholic mysteries. I say it is not surprising because, from the same principles as causes, the same effects must necessarily flow. Both protestants and philosophers place reason on the judgment seat; both form their opinions on religious subjects from the dictates of that judge; both reject what they do not comprehend; both only admit what is conformable to their limited notions. The protestant, it is true, admits the letter of scripture but as he takes the liberty to call it before the tribunal of his reason, and gives his reason full jurisdiction to decree without appeal, not what scripture says, but what it means to say; the protestant belief is of course, a system, the offspring of reason, and only nominally deduced from scripture. The philosopher, perhaps more consistent, and more candid, applies to reason at once, without the farce of consulting scripture, which he declares to be, together with all the mysteries of revelation, absurd and ridiculous.

What the protestant professor Robison says, in his book called *Proofs of a Conspiracy*, is much to the purpose here.

"The spirit of free inquiry was the great boast of the protestants, and their only support against the Roman Catholics; securing them both in their religious and their civil rights. It was therefore encouraged by their governments, and sometimes indulged to excess. In the progress of this contest, their own confessions did not escape censure; and it was asserted that the reformation, which these confessions expressed, was not complete. Further reformations were proposed. The scriptures, the foundation of our faith, were examined, by clergymen of different capacities, dispositions, and views; till by explaining, correcting, allegorizing, and otherwise twisting the bible, men's minds had hardly anything left to rest on as a doctrine of revealed religion. This encouraged others to go further, and to say that revelation was a solecism, as plainly appeared by the irreconcilable differences amongst the enlighteners of the public, and that men had nothing to trust to, but the dictates of natural reason. Another set of writers, proceeding from this as a point already settled, proscribed all religion whatever, and openly taught materialism and atheism. Most of these innovations were the work of protestant divines, from the causes I have mentioned."

Here is a candid acknowledgment made by a protestant well acquainted with protestant principles and their consequences. The liberty of self-interpretation is the destruction of all religious principles; all must necessarily lead to infidelity. You must be blind, my dear friend, if you do not see infidelity gaining ground in the ranks of protestantism, and especially among those that have received the most liberal education. What is more common than to hear them deny the divinity of Jesus Christ and the eternity of punishments? What more common than a total neglect and even a contempt of religious exercises, a contempt of the sacraments, and even of those sacraments which Christ declares to be absolutely necessary for salvation? The progress of infidelity among protestants in this country, as well as in Great Britain (which a great orator in congress emphatically calls the palladium or bulwark of protestantism), is truly alarming.

It is a matter of fact that the learned in this country, especially in the eastern states, are crowding the ranks of Socinianism, and having rejected the mysteries of the trinity, and divinity of Christ, express their creed in four words, "I believe in God."

It is a matter of great scandal and alarm to the truly pious to see a very large and most magnificent temple erected in the city of Baltimore, by those that believe Christ to be a mere man. The progress of infidelity is far more alarming in Great Britain, where the very ministers of the church of England, the dignitaries of said church, nay the very lord bishops, that have solemnly declared their belief of the thirty-nine articles, are openly preaching and printing against the fundamental mysteries of the Christian religion. Among those who are conspicuous, Dr. Hoadly, lord bishop of Bangor, shows a decided opposition to the doctrines of the blessed Trinity and the divinity of Jesus Christ, also, and more plainly so, Dr. Balguy and Dr. Sturges, prebendaries of the cathedral church of Winchester, Dr. Clarke, etc., etc.

I am alarmed, but I am not surprised. The leading principle of protestants (I mean the principle of self-interpretation of the scriptures) has been sapping the foundation of religion ever since the pretended reformation, and must, at no distant period, overthrow the whole fabric.

Poor, silly, blind reason, biased and led by passion and prejudice, is a false and treacherous guide, and never more so than when presuming to dive into the arcana of revelation, and with Satanic pride, to explain, without appeal, the meaning of the Holy Ghost. The wise man has said it, "The searcher of majesty shall be overwhelmed by glory" (Prov. 25:27).

Those that search into the incomprehensible ways of God, those that shall presumptuously look into the ark of God's sanctuary, their weak eyes will be blinded with the excess of light and glory. Being thus blinded, they shall not even see what they used to see, and what they still would have been permitted to see, had they not made the rash and presumptuous attempt. Thus it is that thousands, relying on their reason to explain the mysteries of revelation, have lost sight of the very fundamentals of Christianity, and have become real infidels.

The following remarks from the pen of the Rev. Mr. Thayer, formerly a Presbyterian minister in Boston, but since a Catholic priest, confirms the above remarks:

This uniformity which had subsisted among Catholics through all ages, made a lively impression on me, because I had never discovered it among protestants. I had been connected with the heads of our sects; I had often conversed with them; I knew their sentiments; there were not two among them who agreed in the most essential articles. What is more, there was not one who had not varied in his doctrine. I recollect that one of our most celebrated preachers once made the same declaration to me. *When I preached in such a place,* said he, *I passed for heterodox; I was eighty at that time, for I had very erroneous sentiments; but I have changed since; and were I to preach there at present, my doctrine would be judged pure and orthodox; but this is common to all our preachers, I do not know one who has not, like myself, varied in his doctrine.* This declaration made no impression on me at the time he was speaking; but it has occurred since, and has given rise to many reflections," . . . "This instability of our leading men in their doctrine caused me much pain. I saw that it was an inevitable consequence of the fundamental principles of protestants, which constitutes each one the judge of his own belief. By this principle there can be no fixed rule of faith. It is this which causes the eternal contradiction of ministers among themselves, and the frequent variations of each of them in their doctrine. I had endeavored to conciliate their systems together, but could find no other way than by supposing it sufficed to believe in Jesus Christ, and to intend to honor God; but I soon found that this method, with which I was much pleased, tended equally to reconcile the most opposite and monstrous sects; I consequently, from day to day, gave myself greater scope, and fixed no bounds to the liberty of thinking, and in a short time I should have adopted a system of toleration in its greatest extent. Protestants vainly pretend that they admit scripture for the rule of their faith. Since they acknowledge no living authority to determine its sense; since each one is suffered to give it a private interpretation, it is impossible to convince them of error; and when the Socinian, for instance, says, that he cannot find in scripture a demonstrative proof of the divinity of Jesus Christ, no one has a right to require that he should believe this dogma, or to condemn him because he rejects it. This principle goes farther, and leads the man who reasons justly to an indifference to all religion, and saps the very foundation of Christianity, by establishing the private judgment of each individual the supreme arbiter of his creed. (See *An Account of the Conversion of the Rev. John Thayer, lately a Protestant Minister.* London edition, p. 15-18).

Your protestant minister then will not be surprised if all his arguments, his assertions, his decisions, *"it is certain,"* *"it is evident,"* etc., will never make the least impression on the mind of any Roman Catholic that knows his religion, and has been taught to view all the attempts of human reason in fathoming and explaining divine mysteries and revelations in the same light as he would the attempt to penetrate into the third heaven. This is not said through any disrespect or contempt for your minister. Admitting him to be the wisest among the wise, and the best among the good, it is a fundamental principle among Catholics, grounded on their idea of the infinite being that is the author of revelation, and grounded on his own plain words, that all human wisdom is inadequate to the task of explaining divine revelation, and that none but God can explain the words of God.

Our faith does not "stand on the wisdom of men, but on the power of God" (1Cor. 2:5).

It is then in vain for the protestant minister to tell us that the learned and pious Archbishop Tillotson says, that the pious Bishop White beautifully explains, that the Arabian philosopher scornfully laughs, that the sleight-of-hand man blasphemously mocks the words of Christ by saying 'hocus-pocus.' You are all welcome, gentlemen, we say, heartily welcome, to take your way; you may say and unsay as you have done ever since the beginning of your reformation; you may laugh till you split your sides at our folly; you may 'hocus-pocus' the scriptures into whatever shape you please; you may 'beautifully explain' the words of Christ, till you explain all the substance into empty figures; but permit us to take our own way. We are fools, you say; we sincerely believe it; and it is because we believe ourselves to be fools that we do not wish to undertake to explain the divine word, but apply to the church to know how we are to understand the several texts of scripture. We are such fools that we are not able to conceive how a church built upon a rock by the hands of omnipotence can ever fall, especially when the sacred promise of eternal truth is pledged for its everlasting duration. We are so stupid that we cannot conceive how the ministry of Christ, which has the promise of the Spirit of Truth (Jn. 14:16), ever could have become teachers of falsehood, and false interpreters of scripture. We are so blinded by prejudice that we cannot understand how the apostles or their successors, to the very end of time, can ever deviate from the primitive doctrine, whilst Christ fulfils his promise to be with them all days until the consummation of time.

Such is our folly, my friend; and take notice, that this our folly has kept us these eighteen centuries in perfect unity of faith, whilst the wisdom of reformers has caused them to divide and subdivide into numberless sects, differing from one another even in the most essential and fundamental points of religion. Yes, we may defy the whole world to point out one single instance of variation in any article of our faith, or one single instance of difference in matters of faith between different parts of the Catholic world. Your minister, jealous of this unity, which distinguishes the Catholic church from all the sects, fills two pages (101-102) with arguments to prove that we are divided and distracted with dissentions and contests of various kinds, of which he quotes many instances; vain attempt, my friend. As men, we have been divided, and will be divided on many points of doctrine, which have been derived from mere human knowledge, or are deduced by human arguments, but are by no means necessary for salvation, or have not been, as yet, determined by the church, thus: whilst the whole Catholic world is agreed in the belief of the infallibility of the whole body or a majority of pastors united with their head, great disputes have been carried on between some divines on the question, "whether the pope was infallible or not?" Thus again, whilst the whole Catholic world is agreed in believing the Blessed Virgin a powerful intercessor in heaven with her divine son, Jesus Christ, great disputes are carried on between the divines of the Catholic church on the question, "whether she was conceived in original sin or not?"

In the third century a great dispute took place between St. Cyprian, Bishop of Carthage, and Pope St. Stephen, on the question, "whether baptism administered by heretics was to be considered valid or not?" The whole church having decided the question in the affirmative, it has never been a matter of dispute since.

What your minister adds (p. 102) about the pretended Catholic sects called Georgians, Mingrelians, Copts, Abyssinians, etc., is only intended for a joke, for he well knows that those are the names of nations, not of sects, and nations that are schismatic, not belonging to the Catholic church at all.

I repeat it, my dear friend, Catholics who constitute about three-fourths of the Christian world are perfectly united in the belief of all articles of faith necessary for salvation.

All agree that out of the Catholic church there is no ordinary possibility of salvation.

All agree that baptism remits original sin, and is necessary for salvation.

All agree that there are seven sacraments instituted by Christ.

All agree that the keys of the kingdom of heaven, the power to forgive and retain sins, were given to the apostles and their successors to the end of time.

All agree that Christ is really present in the Eucharist and, therein is both our victim of propitiation and the spiritual food of our souls.

All agree that the pope is the successor of St. Peter, and the visible head of the church.

All agree that the scripture, which we use, is the pure word of God.

All agree that the church is the living and infallible tribunal appointed by Christ to determine the sense of scripture, and to hand down divine and apostolic traditions from age to age.

All agree that Christ is our only mediator, and that from his merits alone all blessings flow.

All agree that it is good and wholesome to apply to the intercession of the saints in heaven.

All agree that there is a place of temporary punishment after this life, for those who were not in this life perfectly purified from the dross of sin.

All agree that it is good and wholesome to pray for the dead.

All agree that it is useful and commendable to keep and to honor (not to worship) religious pictures, crucifixes, etc., etc.

And why are they all agreed? Because they do not presume to interpret scriptures, which would soon create as many different sects among them as there are among the protestants. They all apply to the church for the sense of scripture. From the church they learn what texts of scripture are to be understood in the literal sense, and what texts in a spiritual sense; also which of the many spiritual senses of which a text may be susceptible is the true one; for there are different kinds of spiritual senses noticed by divines, to which, for the full understanding of scripture, attention must be paid, namely:

The allegoric sense, which relates to faith.

The anagogic sense, which relates to eternal life.

The tropologic sense, which relates to morals.

Although it is admitted, as a fundamental principle of religion, that each and every text of scripture is most true, as being the word of God, yet each and every text is not always true in every one of the above-mentioned senses. It is of course necessary for the right understanding of scripture, to know, by the direction of the church, in which of the above senses the several texts are to be taken;

otherwise we will often be tempted to believe many of those texts to be false and contradictory, of which we have a most curious instance in page fifteen of your minister's *Vindication*, where he attempts to sweep off, like so many cobwebs, no less than four of Christ's solemn promises, by opposing to them corresponding promises made to the Jewish church, which latter promises (if I understand him right) he intimates not to have been fulfilled.

To give his argument a logical form, it runs thus: almighty God had made solemn promises to the Jewish church, to "dwell among the children of Israel," etc., "To reign over them in Zion from henceforth and forever," etc., etc. Now almighty God did not fulfill his promises, for the church of Judah has failed; therefore the promises made by the same God, Christ Jesus, "to be forever with the church," "to send the Spirit of Truth," etc., etc., ought to be disregarded.

Here is logic, here is wisdom, but wisdom, merely human; such wisdom as the foolishness of God confounds (1 Cor. 1:25).

The very idea of a God the fountain of truth, forbids the supposition of promises made and not fulfilled. All promises made by almighty God to the Jews, or by our blessed savior to the church, were undoubtedly fulfilled. We are not always able to discern in what way they have been fulfilled, because the feeble light of our reason is not always able to distinguish in what sense the promises are to be understood; but the Spirit of Truth infused into the church is very able to unravel the mystery and to level all difficulties. By this authority we are told that Jerusalem or Zion, which literally is a city of Juda, allegorically means the church of Christ on earth; anagogically, means the kingdom of heaven; tropologically, means the faithful soul. If we take the promise of God to the children of Israel in the literal sense, it will not be found true, but if we take it in the allegorical sense, it is certainly most true.

Had your minister made those distinctions, he certainly would not have made use of God's promises under the old law in order to invalidate the promises of Christ in the new. On the contrary, he would have seen the connection of both, and would have been convinced that the promises in both cases relate to the same object, and are of great support to each other. To understand this better, let us take a general view of revealed religion, and we will soon perceive that the Old and the New Testaments only form one system of religion; the rites, ceremonies, sacrifices, and precepts of which entirely relate to Jesus Christ the Messias. Before his coming, that is, under the old law, to Jesus Christ to come; and after his coming, specifically, under the new law, to Jesus Christ already come.

Jesus Christ himself shows this connection and continuation, when he tells us, "I am not come to destroy, but to fulfill" (Mt. 5:17). And the promises which he makes with regard to the indefectibility, perpetual visibility, infallibility, or unerring authority of his church, are only a repetition and a confirmation of those promises made repeatedly by his servants the prophets, some of which the protestant minister has quoted (p. 1). He promises to "reign over them in Mount Sion, from this time now and forever" (Mich. 4:7). "This is my rest forever: here will I dwell." (Ps. 131:13-14). Here are some more: "This is my covenant with them, saith the Lord: My spirit that is in thee, and my words that I have put in thy mouth shall not depart out of thy mouth, nor out of the mouth of thy seed, nor out of the mouth of thy seed's seed, saith the Lord, from henceforth now and forever" (Isa. 59:21). "And I will make a covenant of peace with them; it shall be an everlasting covenant with them. And I will establish them, and will multiply them, and will set my sanctuary in the midst of them forever. And my tabernacle shall be with them: and I will be their God, and they shall be my people" (Ezec. 37:26-27). Jesus Christ confirms those very promises when he tells his apostles, "Behold I am with you all days," etc., and when he promises them the Spirit of Truth forever.

You see, my friend, how Catholic unity in explaining scripture, and in all matters of faith, necessarily flows from Catholic principles, and how divisions among Catholics never can take place, only concerning such matters as have never been in any way determined by the church. Protestant divisions necessarily flow from the protestant principle of self-interpretation; as it always has, it always will prevent that unity which is a main characteristic of truth, and the reverse of which is a sure sign of falsehood. I do not know whether the protestant minister is in earnest when he talks of a unity made up of the aggregate of contradictions, which in the language of theology might be styled *Concordia Ecclesiarum Discordantium.*

I will give you his very words (*Vindication,* p.117), which purport to be an answer to mine (*Defense of Catholic Principles,* pp. 129-130). The question which I proposed was, "Comparing together those many hundred religious systems, which your fruitful reformation has produced, contradicting one another in the whole or in part, is it uncharitable to say that but one of them (if any at all) can originate in the fountain of truth etc."?

Here is your minister's answer: "No reason can be assigned why churches of different communions may, notwithstanding, be true parts of the true church, so long as they adhere to and hold the essentials of a true church". Indeed, so long as divisions and separations remain, there is a criminal schism lying somewhere. But still those schismatical churches are parts of the true church? Their schism does not cut them off from being members of Christ's kingdom. It is certain there were separations and schisms, and different communions, even in the earliest times of Christianity, even in the church of Corinth when one would say, "I am of Paul, and I of Apollo, and I of Cephas, and I of Christ," etc.

Here is something very curious, "the true church of Christ composed of schismatical churches"; that is to say in plain English, the true church composed of parts not belonging to it; the kingdom of Christ made up of materials belonging to the kingdom of Satan; and truth composed of an aggregate of falsehoods and contradictions. *Risum teneatis amici.*

St. Paul had a different idea of the church of Christ when he wrote to the Ephesians, that being sanctified by Christ it became a glorious church, "having neither spot nor wrinkle, holy and without blemish" (Eph. 5:26, 27). Also when he calls the church "the pillar and ground of truth" (1 Tim. 3:15).

There is a criminal schism somewhere says your minister, but in the church of Christ there is a criminal schism nowhere, for there is no spot, no wrinkle, no blemish at all; nothing but truth, holiness, and perfection. And when St. Paul blames the Corinthians for contending and boasting about their teachers, he does not even intimate that there were schisms or different communions among them; on the contrary, he plainly tells them, that those teachers were laborers in the same vineyard of the Lord. "I have planted, Apollo watered: but God gave the increase" (1 Cor. 3:6).

They all taught the same doctrine, were teachers of the same church, and perfectly united in the same faith. You plainly see, then, that your minister's answer is no answer to my question, the amount of which was whether an aggregate of contradictions could form unity? I asked, and I now ask again, whether the necessity of baptism for salvation, and the non-necessity of baptism, can both be admitted as articles of faith in the same church of Christ?

Whether in the same church of Christ one minister can be sent by the God of truth to preach up the real presence of Christ in the sacrament, as Luther did, and another minister sent by the same God of truth, to tell you that the former is a liar, and that there is nothing in the sacrament but bread and wine?

Whether Christ can send one set of ministers to preach up the insufficiency of communion in one kind, which is the doctrine of your protestant minister and others, and also ministers to preach up the sufficiency of one kind, the doctrine of the Calvinist Synod of Poitiers and La Rochelle.

In short, whether Luther, Calvin, Zuinglius, Gomar, Arminius, Fox, etc., who contradict one another in the most essential points of doctrine, in those very matters which Christ declares essential for salvation, whether all those can be considered ministers of the same God of truth and whether their churches or communions are to be considered as parts of the holy church of Christ? Your minister says, yes. Hear, my friend, what the celebrated English poet Dryden says:

> In short, in doctrine or in discipline,
> Not one reform'd can with another join;
> But all from each, as from damnation, fly;
> Nor union they pretend, but in non-popery.
> Nor, should their numbers in a synod meet,
> Could any church presume to take the seat,
> Above the rest, their discords to decide,
> None would obey, but each would be the guide;
> And face to face dissentions would increase;
> For only distance now preserves the peace:
> All, in their turns, accusers and accus'd,
> Babel was never half so much confus'd.
> What one can plead, the rest can plead as well,
> For amongst equals lies no last appeal,
> And all confess, themselves are fallible.
> Now since you grant some necessary guide,
> All who can err are justly laid aside:
> Because a trust so sacred to confer

Shows want of such a sure interpreter,
And how can he be needful who can err.
Then granting that unerring guide we want,
That such there is, you stand obliged to grant;
Our savior else were wanting to supply
Our needs, and obviate that necessity;
It then remains that church can only be
The guide, which owns unfailing certainty.

It would surprise you much, my dear friend, were you to know the wonderful contradictions in most essential points of doctrine not only between protestant ministers of different denominations, not only between ministers of the same denomination, but even between the doctrine of the same minister at one time and his doctrine at another time.

We will begin with Martin Luther, the father of the reformation, whom the learned Bishop Tillotson styles a bold or a rough wedge, fit to split the knotty block of popery which, however, is not split yet.

Luther says, in the seventh volume of his works (Wittenberg edition, A.D. 1551, page 32), that there are seven sacraments, but in the 12th article on confession (p. 74), and again in the 13th article on the sacraments, he asserts "there are only three sacraments." Again, he says there are five sacraments (*Sermon of the New Testament*, vol. 7, p. 34). In the seventh volume, page 350, Luther teaches that the holy sacrament of the Eucharist ought to be revered and adored, but in the thirty-second article against Henry, King of England, he teaches the reverse.

In his writings against Zuinglius and Oecolampadius, Luther requires (article 16), that we submit to the decisions of church councils; but in his writings against the King of England (volume seven, chapter fifteen, page 262), he teaches that there is no obligation to submit to the decisions of any councils.

In his sermon on the first commandment, Luther maintains the merits and intercession of saints, but in his *Sermon de Mammona* he flatly denies the same.

In vol. 8, pg. 27, on the 122nd psalm, he maintains that baptism confers grace: also in chapter six, Genesis vol. 5, pg. 53, that it blots out original sin, and in his second sermon for Trinity Sunday on John three, that it is necessary for salvation. But in vol. 3, pg. 349, on good works, and again, in vol. 7, pg. 6, Baptism does not blot out original sin, and is not necessary for salvation etc.

These are only a few instances among many, which I could quote, to prove that the very father of the reformation contradicted himself in most essential parts of doctrine.

Now hear what the first reformers say of one another, and there you will be surprised to find them tearing one another like wild boars, instead of joining hand in hand in their spiritual campaign against what they called Antichrist and the whore of Babylon: "We censure in earnest as heretics and aliens from the church of God, all Zuinglians and sacramentarians who deny Christ's body by the carnal mouth in the venerable Eucharist" (*Luther Cont. Art. Luvan. Theo.* pg. 27).

Conrad Schluoselburg, a Lutheran divine, speaking of the Calvinists says, "Satan speaks by the Calvinists as by his own organs and instruments" (*Orig Lib.* 3. art. 8). John Modestus, another Lutheran divine, says, "they are no Christians, but baptized Turks and Jews."

Shutre, in his preface to the *Fifty Causes*, tells us that the "Calvinian profession is a sink whereunto many heresies flow, and the very last anger of Satan, which he, stirred up with fury, exercises against Christ and his church."

"Let any holy or friendly reader" (says Osiander in *Enchiridion Contra Calvin*, p. 267), think what deadly poison Satan pours into men under the Calvinian doctrine, by which all Christianity is almost overthrown."

Now hear what other protestant divines say about the church of England.

"Ministers of the church of England are Egyptian enchanters, limbs of the devil, sycophants, angels of hell in whom are the uttermost deceits and effectual delusions of Satan" (Bernard in his *Book of Separatists, Schism*, p. 72).

The protestant author of the *Dangerous Positions* says, "The church of England's ministers put no difference between truth and falsehood, betwixt Christ and Antichrist, between God and the devil. They are an antichristian swinish rabble enemies of the gospel" etc., (*lib.* 2. c. 9).

"They are all infidels" (says Allison) "that go to the late church of England, it shall be easier for Sodom and Gomorrah in the day of judgment than for the court of parliament by which the protestant religion was confirmed. The English congregation consists of all sorts of unclean spirits, and is no member of Christ. Their sacraments are no sacraments; it is a very Babylon" (*Reply to Usher*, pp. 24–5).

Hear what Castalio, another protestant, says, in speaking of Geneva, the very center of the Calvinian reformation.

"They name their Geneva the holy city, and their assembly Jerusalem; but in truth we should call it, 'O Babylon, Babylon! O infamous Sodom and Gomorrah!'" (*Castalio apud Recium*, p. 54).

Sir Edward Sands affirms that "the contentions of protestants tend mainly to the increase of Atheism within, and Mahometism abroad." (Edward Sands' *Relation of Religion*, pp. 4, 5, 6). And Zanchius, another protestant, affirms, "Atheism has been brought out of hell by the ministers of Satan in some of the reformed churches" (Zanch. *in his Epistle Before His Conf.*, p. 7).

Mr. Perks in his *Dedicatory Epistle* before his *Apology*, speaking of the contention in England concerning religion, complains that, by it settled minds are distracted, the parts of the same body dismembered, and religion itself brought to be a matter of mere dispute and altercation, not without fear, that it befall unto us as it did to the builders of Babel. These contentions are no small preparatives to atheism, so that we may say "that there are as many faiths as wills, and as many doctrines as names of men in so much that many are brought to their wit's end, not knowing what to do."

The protestant Bishop Bilson, of Winchester (*On Church Government*, ch. 16), and the above quoted Edward Sands both complain of these contentions and lament that "they are past all hopes of remedy." And so they are; for I have proved that these multiplied differences and contradictions, even in matters of the first importance, necessarily flow from the protestant principle of self-interpretation; of course they must continue, and even increase and multiply, by forming more and more sects, whilst it shall continue to be a fundamental principle that everyone must draw his religious system from scripture interpreted by himself.

You would be much surprised, my dear friend, were you to read the creeds or professions of faith formed by the first reformers, by those who are said to have been inspired, and sent by the almighty to reform the church; and were you to compare them with the professions of faith of modern protestants. Supposing the assertion true, supposing the reformers to have been like the first apostles, inspired with the holy Spirit of Truth, what must be the consequence? The necessary consequence is that their professions of faith, formed by inspiration of that Holy Spirit, must be perfectly true in all its parts. The further consequence is that the same professions of faith ought to be, at the present day, the standard of all protestants in every part of the world, for what is true and genuine divine doctrine in 1500 must be true and genuine divine doctrine in 1600, and what is true divine doctrine in Germany, must be true divine doctrine in England or America. How much would you be surprised then to read in the *Confession of Augsburg*, which is the first standard of faith, formed by the reformers themselves:

Article three: "Mass is retained by us, and celebrated with utmost reverence. The usual ceremonies are likewise mostly all preserved," and, Article nine: "Private absolution is to be retained in the churches."

Now take up the thirty-nine Articles of the church of England, and their book of common prayer, which may be called the first standard of faith of English reformers, and you find, in article eight, the three creeds admitted: the Apostles' Creed, the Nicene Creed, and the Creed of St. Athanasius, which positively asserts that "he that does not hold the Catholic faith whole and entire, shall, without doubt, perish forever." In article twenty you find a declaration that the church has authority in controversies of faith.

You also find, in the order of visitation of the sick, confession recommended to be made to the minister and absolution by him pronounced in almost the very same words used by the Catholic church.

In the ordination of ministers you find the following words: "Receive the Holy Ghost, whose sins thou dost forgive, they are forgiven; and whose sins thou dost retain, they are retained."

In consequence of this you also find numbers of primitive protestant bishops and ministers maintaining those doctrines, such as Cranmer, Ridley, Jewel, Parker, Hooker, Alison, Andrews, Parson, Land, Gunning, Ken.

By the fifth Canon of the Convocation, A.D. 1603, it is decreed, "Whoever shall affirm that any of the thirty-nine Articles are in any part superstitions or erroneous, let him be excommunicated."

After reading these solemn professions of faith made (it is said) by inspired reformers, and adopted in so solemn a manner, who would not exclaim, "Thank God, the grand work of the reformation is accomplished, the standard of faith is planted, the colors of Christianity are living, the dark clouds of popish superstition and idolatry are scattered, and the sun of divine revelation is illuminating the globe." No such a thing, my friend.

The first reformers proved themselves to be quacks; they did not understand the scriptures. Their reformation must be reformed again. It will be found, under King Edward VI that Christ is not present in the sacrament, and the words expressing his real presence will be expunged, as Dr. Heylin informs us; and it will be declared in the twenty-ninth article that, "the body of Christ being now in heaven, cannot be also in the sacrament."

Under Queen Elizabeth this article is put out again, and the old belief re-adopted.

After some time, numbers of reforming quacks start up and reform the reformed church of England, having got a better understanding of scripture than the first reformers. The church of England ministers are by them declared to be ministers of Satan, a swinish rabble, etc., and they set up a new reformation. The farce is not ended yet. George Fox, the cobbler, declares they are all fools, and shaking his head, he groans out the operations of the spirit that spiritualize the whole of the scriptures. From England transport yourself over to America, and here you will see the church of England reformed over again, accommodated to the genius of a free and independent people, dividing and subdividing into numberless branches, and degenerating into deism and even atheism. The thirty-nine articles, which in England are divine truths, are falsehoods in America.

Christ, who is present in the holy sacrament in England, has nothing to do with the sacrament in America.

The power of absolution given to the reformation of England is denied to the reformation of America — what is divine truth in England is heresy in America — and the interpretation of scripture, which is correct in England, is false in America.

The reformation, then (pretended to be the work of God wrought by inspired men) is not the same thing in every place and in every age, as it ought to be to prove itself the work of God.

The reformation of Germany is not the reformation of England; that of England not the same as that of America.

The reformation of Luther is not the reformation of Calvin.

The reformation of Zuinglius [is] not that of Wesley and the reformation of Wesley [is] not that of Fox.

The reformation of 1517 is not the reformation of 1800, and nobody living at present is able to foretell what the reformation of 1900 will be.

If it be permitted to form a conjecture, I think that your protestant minister is going to introduce a new reformation, for he has discovered (p. 69) that kissing a crucifix is an act of idolatry. Now I recollect seeing numbers of protestants kissing the calfskin cover of the bible. Ask your minister whether kissing leather is not as much idolatry as kissing wood or brass? If so, then it becomes necessary to reform that practice.

The truth is, my dear friend, by misinterpretation and rash judgments, many of the most innocent and even edifying practices of religion may be construed into acts of idolatry and no wonder if those who, from hatred against the Catholic church, squeeze and screw the scripture into senses the most congenial to their feelings and prejudices, should also, from the same disposition, put most hateful constructions on the most innocent Catholic practices.

Thus your minister, who is determined that Catholics shall be idolaters, willfully shuts his eyes against the doctrine of the Catholic church, which in her profession of faith, in all her catechisms, in all her general councils, founded on the word of God, plainly declares her belief in one only God, the only fountain of all blessings, and plainly condemns any confidence in the power of the blessed saints and angels, only that, which as mere creatures, they have obtained from the great creator, "to rule over nations" (Apoc. 2:26-27); "to minister for them who shall receive the inheritance of salvation" (Heb. 1:14. and Acts 5:19) "to pray or intercede for us sinners" (Zach. 1:12; Apoc 5:8). Your minister, I say, determined that we shall be idolaters, shuts his eyes against the very words of scripture, which he pretends to revere, and thus perverts our praying to the saints into an unscriptural act of idolatry.

The scripture says, "judge not" etc. (Mt. 7:1), but your minister says, "I will judge the papist; and in their confessing to God and to the whole court of heaven, and in their prayers to the saints, I am determined to find them guilty of idolatry."

The scripture gives us several instances of miracles wrought by the almighty by means of the bones, of the clothes, and even of the shadow of saints (4Kings 13:21; Acts 5:15, 19:12), but your minister is determined that we shall be guilty of idolatry whenever we show any respect for the relics of saints, or any confidence that the almighty, who makes use of the most weak and despicable means and timings to bring about great ends, will still make use of those relics as instruments to convey certain blessings, of which there are thousands of instances in the Catholic church. It was a miracle of that kind which accelerated the conversion of Mr. Thayer, a Presbyterian minister of Boston, who had been as loud and clamorous against praying to the saints and venerating their relics as your minister (See *The History of Mr. Thayer's Conversion* written by himself).

When we pray to the saints for certain blessings, or to be delivered from certain evils, your minister (by an evil interpretation of our words) finds us guilty of idolatry, although we protest that we do not expect anything from them on our behalf but their intercession, and the exercise of that subordinate power, which as creatures, but as glorified creatures and as friends of God, they have received from the great creator. "He that shall overcome, and keep my works unto the end" (says the almighty) "I will give him power over the nations" (Apoc. 2:26).

It is no wonder, indeed, that your minister, who is willing to screw and squeeze the sacred text of scripture into what sense he pleases, should be willing to misinterpret our prayers, and even our intentions, to make them appear idolatrous.

The protestant minister has filled a great number of pages with irrelevant matter, as so many auxiliaries in his ecclesiastical campaign against the Catholic church. As my time is very limited, I shall embrace the opportunity which the present letter affords me, in order, by a few additional lines, to supercede the necessity of a confutation in form.

The protestant minister has ransacked some old libraries, and shaken off the dust of many an old book, that lay forgotten and neglected, in order to furnish himself with arms against popery, and behold the happy discovery he has made.

He has found some authors that say God gave the Virgin Mary the half of his kingdom that the prayers made to her are better than those made to Christ; that the mother's milk is equally to be esteemed with the son's blood!" etc. (*Vindication*, p. 55).

My friend you certainly will not be deceived by such tricks. If all the nonsense, all the blasphemies, all the impieties, written by individual Catholics, laymen or clergymen, together with all the nonsense and absurdities falsely attributed to them by their enemies, and published under forged Catholic names, where put up in one heap, an acre of ground would not be sufficient to contain them. But remember that I have only undertaken to defend the doctrine of the Catholic church, not the absurdities and blasphemies of individuals. Your minister says (after quoting the above absurdities), this is "a part of the service the church of Rome puts up to the Virgin Mary" etc. (p.55).

Tell your minister to remember the commandment, "Thou shalt not bear false witness," etc. and to remember also the priest's spittle in the holy water! I pray that none of his slanderous assertions may rise against him on the awful day of God's eternal vengeance.

What he calls (*Vindication*, p. 55) abundance not only of superstition but also of idolatry, *viz.* our confiding in the merits and prayers of the saints, is also founded on his misconception or misrepresentation. Listen to his reasons: "It is the will of God," says he, "and the express command of scripture, that we should regard Jesus Christ as the only cause of our salvation."

The Catholic church never acknowledged any other but her divine spouse Jesus Christ, as the fountain of salvation. But ask your minister, my friend, whether he believes the declaration made by God himself, that he would spare a whole city for the sake of ten just men (Gen. 18:32).

That he will accept the face of Job (his prayers and intercession) in behalf of his three friends (Job 42:8).

That he will forgive the people of Israel for the sake of Moses (Num. 14:20).

It is truly ludicrous to see with what degree of tenacity your minister is determined to carry his point, and to prove its idolaters.

He is not aware of the consequences of his assertions. Jesus Christ, says he, is the only cause of salvation, and therefore Catholics are idolaters for applying to the friends of Jesus Christ for help, for that help which they can only grant in virtue of the power of Jesus Christ. Retorting his own argument, I shall now prove that all protestants, with their clergy, are idolaters; for it is evident that Jesus Christ alone is the fountain of all knowledge, of all wisdom. Now it is also evident that protestants, instead of applying immediately to that fountain, address themselves to their ministers (who are but weak mortals) for instruction. It is also evident that the ministers themselves are idolaters, for although they know Jesus Christ alone to be the sole author of all spiritual power, yet instead of going straight away to him for knowledge in divinity and for ordination, they go to a college conducted by mere men in order to obtain both learning and ordination.

I expect, my friend, you will acknowledge my argument to be as good as that of your minister. If applying for help of any kind to subordinate beings in heaven be an injury to Christ and an act of idolatry, it is a greater injury to Christ, and a more gross act of idolatry, to apply for help of any kind to subordinate beings on earth, and as Christ God is the fountain of all blessings, the king, and only rightful owner and ruler of the whole universe, everybody is guilty of idolatry who in any case whatever applies to man for any favor instead of applying to Christ.

Such are the absurd consequences of your minister's doctrine; what then is the conclusion? If it be no sin, no idolatry, to apply to weak mortals for many favors or blessings, for bread, for money, for instruction, for offices for prayers, etc., provided we acknowledge God alone to be the author of all those blessings, neither is it idolatry to ask blessings, favors, prayers, etc., of the blessed saints, provided we acknowledge God alone to be the fountain of those blessings, which by God's own appointment are often distributed through the ministry, and at the intercession of those blessed spirits, as I have proved (Apoc. 2:26, 27; Acts 5:19, 23,27; Heb. 1:2; Zach. 1:12. etc.).

Your minister peremptorily decides (p. 54), "It is certain the saints cannot hear us."

Ask him, my friend, at what time he was by the almighty admitted, like St. Paul, into the third heavens? Unless he was, I do not understand how he is able to make that bold decision, especially when he has to make it in contradiction to scripture, which declares the angels capable of knowing our very thoughts, as I prove in my *Defense* (p. 97) from Luke, 15:10 etc.

I shall say nothing here about his charge concerning our using charms and conjurations in blessing water, salt, oil, etc., which in plain English means that we invoke the devil in blessing those things. The minister has read the Roman Mass-book, ritual, pontifical, etc., as plainly appears from page 110 of his *Vindication*, and therefore he knows himself guilty of bearing false witness.

A few words more on the following six subjects (*Vindication*, p. 8,) and I shall close the present letter, which I am afraid begins to tire you.

One: Celibacy of the Clergy

The celibacy or single life of the clergy is founded on the declaration of St. Paul (1Cor. 7:34–35, 38, 40), by which it is plain that virginity, is by the spirit of God, preferred to marriage, and the reason given "that you may attend upon the Lord, without distraction." No man is compelled by the church to remain single but the church declares herself unwilling to admit to ordination any but those who after mature deliberation and many years' trial are willing to promise continence, that being undivided (1Cor. 7:34), they may the better attend to the things of the Lord.

Against this holy doctrine of St. Paul's, embraced by the Catholic church, if one should object the dangers arising from the corruptions of human nature, my answer is, that the grace of God, which by proper means can be obtained, is sufficient to overcome that corruption, and that without the grace of God, marriage itself offers no sufficient security, as woeful experience proves.

How great an obstacle the encumbrance of a family must be to zealous clergymen, in the discharge of their duties under many particular circumstances, must be obvious (says Bishop Milner, letter 3, p. 60, Baltimore edition), such as in times of persecution, when religion is to be propagated amongst infidel and barbarous nations, and when persons dying of infectious diseases require the consolation and help of religion to support them.

Some years ago, when that dreadful contagion raged amongst the prisoners of war confined in the king's house, London, which carried off so many hundreds, numbers of them, who were French protestants, called upon protestant ministers for that attendance which they saw administered to the Catholic prisoners by one or two priests. They called in vain; which caused those protestant prisoners to apply to the priests and to die Catholics. What was the excuse of the protestant ministers for not attending? It was what might be expected: "We are not more afraid," said they, as individuals, "to face death in the discharge of our professional duties, than the priests are, but we must not carry a contagion into the bosom of our families."

Another advantage which a continent clergy has over a married clergy is in the case of missions for the conversion of infidels.

An expedition of missionaries was sent from London, at all immense expense, for the conversion of the people of Otaheite and the neighboring islands. The married missionaries took their wives with them. The consequence was that jealousy and quarrels concerning the women soon took place between the savages and their preachers, the latter being obliged to take up arms, and to learn the manual exercise, in order to restrain the lustful passion of the former, which they were unable to quell by the sword of the spirit (See their letter, dated March 6, 1798, published in the London Courier, Dec. 18, 1799. See also *Memoirs of a Missionary Voyage in the Ship Duff*, pp. 81, 85).

It has been partly owing to this disadvantage in their ministry that the protestants have hardly yet succeeded in converting any but very few infidels to Christianity, whilst the Catholics have made converts by thousands and millions among the infidel nations of the globe.

Two: The Holy Office of the Inquisition

If it had been established (as your minister would fain wish to make you believe) in order by tortures, etc., to force the consciences of men, I should no more attempt to advocate it than your minister will attempt to advocate the proceedings of the court of high commission against the Catholics under Queen Elizabeth; both then would be monuments of barbarism and of the infernal spirit of religious fanaticism and bigotry. Of this I shall say more in some future publication. Remember, meanwhile, that the said institution and the nature of its proceedings, have been very much misrepresented by protestant writers.

Three: Works of Superogation

Praying, fasting, alms deeds, and other good works recommended in many texts of holy writ, and by almighty God [are] recompensed with great blessings.

Moses fasted forty days without eating or drinking (Exod. 34:28).

"Achab put haircloth upon his flesh, and fasted, and slept in sack cloth" etc., and the Lord said, "because Achab has humbled himself for my sake, I will not bring the evil in his days" (3Kings 21:27-29).

The angel Raphael said to Tobias, "Prayer is good with fasting and alms etc., for alms delivereth from death:

and the same is that which purgeth away sins, and maketh to find mercy and life everlasting" (Tob. 12:8, 9).

By fasting and prayer the people of Bethulia obtained the grace of God to be delivered from Holofernes (Jud. 4:7). By fasting and prayer, the Ninevites, doomed to destruction, appeased the anger of God, and obtained their pardon (Jonas 3:5-10).

Christ himself fasted forty days before entering on his ministry, etc. Besides many things commanded by holy writ, there are many other things counseled, and great rewards promised, to those who follow those counsels, for instance: "If thou wilt be perfect, go sell what thou hast, and give to the poor and thou shalt have treasure in heaven. And come follow me" (Mt. 19:21).

Again, St. Paul advises to a single life and perfect continence, as [he] himself followed (1Cor. 7:7).

When a Christian, with the view of pleasing God, of punishing himself for his sins, of obtaining mercy from the Lord, of being admitted to a greater degree of glory hereafter, performs those things which are not absolutely commanded but counseled, he is said to do works of supererogation.

Four: Persecution of Protestants, that is, Burning the Body for the Good of the Soul

I am much at a loss to know why your minister has introduced this article, which he well knows is no article of the Catholic creed. Does not this look like wishing to kindle up a flame? (See preface to *Dr. Johnson's Vindication*). Would he think it fair if I was to attack his religion, by bringing forward the bloody statutes of England against Catholics, the confiscations of property that reduced millions to poverty, the hangings, burnings, disemboweling, etc., inflicted on Catholic priests and schoolmasters, for saying Mass or teaching?

The Catholic church so much abhors persecutions for the sake of religion that the clergymen of that church have upon all occasions exerted their zeal to prevent it and to oppose it.

Read the letters of the celebrated Bishop Bartholomew de Las Casas, and you will see with how much zeal he opposed, during fifty years, the detestable cruelties exercised by the Spaniards against the Indians, which gave the latter an insurmountable hatred against the Christian religion.

When the celebrated Fenelon, Archbishop of Cambray, was appointed to bring back to the church so many Calvinists of France, and was informed that Louis XIV had determined to back his mission with a military force, Fenelon absolutely opposed the measure, obtained its repeal, and having undertaken their conversion, by his zeal tempered with mildness and charity, brought many of those strayed sheep back to the pale of the church.

So did also the celebrated St. Francis de Sales, Bishop of Geneva, whose mission among the Calvinists of his diocese was to be protected by an armed force sent by the French king. Armed only with the cross and with confidence in the protection of God, he succeeded in converting about seventy thousand of them.

At the time of the execrable massacre of the French Calvinists, under Charles IX, thousands of those poor devoted victims found shelter in the houses of Catholic bishops and priests, upon which many of them embraced the Catholic faith.

I am happy to have it in my power to state that an illustrious example of that kind is found in the late generous reception and protection granted by the protestant clergy of England to thousands of the persecuted Catholic clergymen of France.

Times are altered, my friend. The faggot [bundle of sticks] (as O'Leary says), which formerly roasted the man at the stake, is now confined to the kitchen, and destined to feed him. Catholic or protestant potentates who abused their power, in order to force the consciences of men, and by tortures to oblige them to embrace their own creed, were monsters and not Christians; and the Catholic church so much abhors the shedding of blood, or any acts of cruelty, that by a law of said church, all those are excluded from ordination, and are declared irregular, who either directly or indirectly have any hand in the effusion of blood, even although no crime is thereby committed; thus, any person cooperating towards bringing a malefactor to capital punishment, as accuser, lawyer, witness, notary to write the sentence, or as judge, becomes irregular, and inadmissible to holy orders.

Five: Miracles Wrought by the Priests and Monks of the Church of Rome

This article, of which your minister demands an explanation, is no article of our creed. But to gratify his curiosity, I shall only observe that miracles are some of those extraordinary means which God uses, when he pleases, for the promotion of his glory and the salvation of souls, and in the performing of which he may use not only priest and monks but also lay people as his instruments. The apostles of Christ had the gift of miracles, by which they proved their mission and convinced nations of the necessity of embracing the law of Christ.

St. Patrick, the apostle of Ireland, St. Augustine who converted England, and many other clergymen who converted pagan nations of Europe (in later times St. Francis Xavier, the apostle of the East Indies, and others in different parts of the new world) had the gift of miracles, which established the divinity of their mission, and converted millions. God is master of his gifts, he communicates them to whom he pleases, and his arm is not shortened, his power not curtailed, but there are persons who, contrary to the advice of Christ to Thomas (Jn. 20:29), will not believe unless they have seen.

Six: Mass Celebrated in an Unknown Tongue

For example, in the Latin tongue. This custom is founded upon very good reasons:

First: The Latin is a dead language, not subject to changes, therefore, better adapted than a living language to prevent changes creeping into the liturgy of the church.

Second: The use of the Latin establishes an uniformity in the service throughout the whole world.

Third: There are priests of all nations. Mass, which is the principal part of the Catholic worship, being everywhere celebrated in Latin, a priest from any country whatever may go to any country under the globe, and the very day he arrives he is fit to step before the altar and celebrate Mass.

Fourth: The Mass contains awful and tremendous mysteries, therefore, although celebrated in public, the sacred words therein used and pronounced ought not to be exposed to profanation, therefore they are pronounced in a language only known to the more improved classes of society. An instance of such profanation your minister has recorded in his *Vindication*, with his own hand (p. 43), where he has attempted to intimate that 'hocus-pocus' is derived from the sacred words of Christ *hoc est [enim] Corpus meum* (this is my body). He meant to throw a slur on Catholic priests, but as the words originate with Christ himself, and not with the priest, it is upon Christ that the aspersion falls. Any blasphemy, any sacrilegious scurrility, will pass with certain persons if it only militates against the Catholic church.

Catholics assisting at Mass suffer no detriment by not understanding the Latin language, as they have the Mass prayers in the vernacular language in almost all their prayer books.

Your minister thinks (*Vindication*, p. 149) that greater service could not be done the reformation that by translating into English the missal or Mass-book, breviary, etc.. You may tell him that this has been done long since in the city of London, where Catholics are nevertheless increasing from year to year.

What your minister states of the wickedness of popes is nothing to the purpose. It no more disproves the divinity and holiness of the Catholic church, than the prevarication of Judas or the fall of St. Peter. Nor does it disprove the validity of the pope's supremacy (*Defense of Catholic Principles*, pp. 116-130.) Ask him whether bad conduct, extravagant claims, or usurpation of power by a president would prove the constitution of the United States to be bad? His account of the corruption of popes is much exaggerated, and no wonder, when he draws his information on that subject from such sources as David Hume, Buck, Father Paul, etc., the two former of whom were as eminent for their inaccuracies and misrepresentations, as the latter was for his hypocrisy and treachery, as is proved by the protestant Bishop Burnet, and others. However, let this pass with all the other misrepresentations contained in your minister's *Vindication*. It unfortunately requires more time to confute calumnies than to advance them. It would take volumes to confute very minutely every falsehood advanced to the few pages of said publication, which would require more time than I have to spare, nor in fact is it necessary, as much of that matter is altogether irrelevant. I mean to confine myself to what is really important, as belonging to the substance of religion. I shall, therefore, for this time, only notice one more passage in your minister's *Vindication*, which indeed is too curious to be omitted.

After spending 133 pages, in order, by scurrility, abuses, misrepresentations, etc. to prove the Catholic church to be the whore of Babylon; the pope Antichrist; the priests magicians, sorcerers, bloodhounds; the lay people silly, ignorant, stupid, etc.; in short, the whole church a sink of corruption, superstition, and idolatry, he tells us very gravely (p. 134), "It has been, and yet is, the opinion of the protestants, that an ignorant and unlearned people, who have been brought up and educated in such or such religious principles, though never so absurd, should adhere to them, as the prejudice of education will go a great length" etc.

Accordingly, if some of our Roman Catholics, after reading your minister's *Vindication*, should begin to open their eyes and finding that they have been imposed upon and led astray by their priests, should apply to your protestant minister for instruction, here is what he would tell them:

My dear popish brethren:

When meditating seriously, in the silence of retirement, on the sublime truths of revelation, I am struck with awe and terror at the dreadful remembrance of the judgments denounced against idolaters. My heart melts within me, and my eyes flow with tears of compassion and sorrow, seeing so many millions of you embracing the wh—e of Babylon and riding the seven-headed beast, which is bringing you along the broad road to eternal flames. Ah, my friends! My brethren! Why do you suffer yourselves to be imposed upon by your priests? Why are you so simple as to believe what they tell you about the promises of Christ, that the Spirit of Truth should never leave his ministers, that himself will be with them to the consummation of the world, etc.? Cannot you see with your own eyes, that Christ has broken his promises long since, and that the church, the grand work of Christ, was going to destruction fast, had not we (the reformers) risen in our might, to mend it, and restore it again? Ah, my brethren! As a pastor of souls, as a minister of Christ, I feel myself consumed with the fire of divine love, and with zeal for the salvation of your souls. Forsake then, my friends forsake the road of idolatry, the road of damnation. Search the scriptures. Interpret for yourselves. The scriptures alone are infallible. If you should be at a loss about the sense of scripture, or if you should be staggered by our contradictory interpretations, never mind that; at all events fly, my brethren, fly from the wh——e of Babylon. Behold the ark of salvation, the holy reformation, the concord of discordant doctrines, the most perfect unity made up of all manner of contradictions! But no, my friends: Stop, I was mistaken, stop, be comforted! You are ignorant and un-learned, therefore continue as you have begun. You began the career of idolatry; continue to the end. You have been riding the seven-headed beast, do not forsake that beast; and may the broad road to hell and damnation bring you to the kingdom of heaven. Amen".

How do you like the above advice? I shall now give you the advice of a Catholic clergyman to his protestant brethren, and then leave it to your judgment to determine which of the two advices is the most rational and the most safe, and which of the two you will adopt.

My dear protestant brethren:
Do not be deceived; there is only ONE LORD, ONE FAITH, AND ONE BAPTISM (Eph. 4). Only ONE church, raised by the hands of Jesus Christ, against which all the powers of hell shall never prevail (Mt. 16:18). Only ONE church in which the Spirit of Truth abides

forever (Jn. 14:16). Only ONE ark of salvation, of which Jesus Christ is the pilot, until the consummation of the world (Mt. 28:20). Whoever is not in that one only vessel shall suffer shipwreck; whoever will not hear that church will meet the fate of heathens and publicans (Mt. 18:17).

Search the scriptures, my friends; they loudly proclaim the divinity of Jesus Christ, and of course bear testimony to the truth of his words.

Search the scriptures; they clearly point out to you the church as your only guide in the ways of salvation. It is to her, and not to their own dead letters, they send you for instruction.

Search the scriptures; but do not erect yourselves judges of their contents. Search them in the spirit of humility, and you will discover an abyss of divine wisdom that will baffle all the efforts of human reason; a splendor of light, which your weak eyes will not be able to bear; a food too rich, too strong for your weak stomach. Be not dismayed. Like a little child, apply to your mother the holy church of Christ, and you will find that strong food, by her digested, and adapted to the weakness of your stomach.

Do not be imposed upon by the assertion of your ministers. All their learning (and some of them are men of great learning), all their ingenuity (and some of them are very ingenious), all their bible quotations (and some of them have almost the whole bible by heart), will never be able to invalidate the promises of Christ.

Remember that the combined wisdom, learning, and ingenuity of ALL protestant bishops will never be able to hurl the Catholic church from the rock on which it was raised, to deprive the said church of the Spirit of Truth, which is to guide it forever, or to tear Jesus Christ from the helm of that vessel of salvation, which he has promised to conduct until the consummation of the world.

Do not be imposed upon by great names. The true greatness of man depends on the depth of his humility, and the perfection of his obedience. Learning and talents are useful when applied to their proper objects; to those, I mean, that are within the grasp of the human understanding. When applied to objects which are of their own nature impervious or impenetrable to human reason they are very dangerous; they turn wisdom into folly, and make of the greatest divines mere quacks and empirics.

When you are told then, that the celebrated Bishop Tillotson, the most learned Bishop White, the great philosopher Averroes, have by their powers of reasoning, by the ingenuity of their sarcastic remarks, or by their thundering vociferations, etc., overturned transubstantiation, confession of sins, etc., admire the height of human folly, in attempting to measure immeasurable abysses, and to compass with the senses or with a limited reason, what is transcendently above the nature of human things.

Do not be imposed upon by a pretended respect for the bible. By the magic powers of the words IT MEANS, the reformed ministers make the bible say what they please. With all the dignity of power, with all the self-importance of a ridiculous pride, with the most impudent assurance, they determine the sense of the Holy Ghost; and they always take care to make their interpretations militate against the Catholic doctrine. They are very fond of quoting from the most difficult and obscure parts of scripture, such as the book of the Apocalypse and the epistles of St. Paul, which being mysterious, and hard to be understood (2 Pet. 3:3-5), afford a great chance to self-conceited and prejudiced interpreters.

Do not be deceived by your minister's long tales (some true and some false), about the wickedness of some popes and other Catholic clergyman. Christ did not promise impeccability or exemption from sin to any clergymen. He promised the Spirit of Truth to teach all truth to the body of the pastors and when he enjoins obedience to their commands he in the same breath cautions us against their bad examples (Mt. 23:2-3). He foretells that until the harvest day, good and bad shall be mixed in his church; and he suffered two of his apostles to fall into very great crimes. Your ministers are very fond of blending together those two distinct subjects, impeccability and infallibility, in order to create a confusion, and to impose on the ignorant and the simple, many of whom honestly believe that by infallibility we mean exemption from sin, whereas we mean nothing but what your own scripture plainly teaches you, that from the foundation of the church until its consummation, the divine Spirit of Truth shall be always with the apostles and their successors in the ministry (Jn. 14: 16), to enable them to teach all truth and no falsehood (Mt. 28: 20), to enable them to know the true meaning of the different scripture texts, to discern the trite from so many false translations, to know the canonical or divine books, and also to distinguish divine from human traditions; in short, to preserve the whole deposit of faith in its original purity. To know all these things, my brethren, is so essentially necessary for salvation, and to know them is so completely impossible, without a divine infallible or unerring authority, that, to deny this infallible authority, so clearly and pointedly established by Christ, is to subvert the religion of Jesus Christ, and to establish in its place the fluctuating opinions of men.

Pray then, my friends, pray sincerely that your eyes may be opened; pray for humility to submit your understanding in all matters of religion to the dictates of the ancient church of Jesus Christ, which alone is guided by the Spirit of Truth forever, which alone is Catholic or universal, spread among all nations and embracing about three-fourths of Christendom, which alone is perfectly one in all matters of faith and salvation, which alone is the immaculate spouse of Christ, without spot or wrinkle (Eph. 5:27). I again pledge my salvation, that in it (provided you will submit to its precepts) you will find salvation, which (as sure as Jesus Christ is God) cannot be obtained in any of those churches that have separated from that only spouse of Christ.

My dear friend, if the above advice appears to you rational, and conformable to what you already know of the word of God, you will take it. After meditating seriously on the subject, you will let me know your sentiments: and you may expect to hear more on the subject, from

Your humble servant and friend,

Demetrius A. Gallitzin
March 29, 1819

Postscript

Before sending off this letter, I think it necessary to add a few lines, in order to explain the words which your minister quotes from page 143 of my *Defense*, and which he calls a strong imprecation. The words which I there made use of, and which I shall be willing to repeat in my dying hour, if, by the mercy of God, I die in my senses and in the state of God's grace, are as follow:

"May the day of judgment be for me the day of God's ETERNAL VENGEANCE, if the holy Roman Catholic church is not the only one, true, and immaculate spouse of Christ. May my soul be doomed to suffer for you eternally all those torments which you would deserve, by following all the pretended superstitions of the church of Rome!"

"I have never met with a stronger imprecation," says the protestant minister, "one excepted, which was, when the Jews crucified the savior of the world, etc. they cried out, 'His blood be on us and on our children, etc.,'" (*Vindication*, p. 126).

My dear friend, you may tell your minister that all the Catholic clergy, together with all the well-informed lay members of our church, will, with the greatest pleasure, join with me in this pretended imprecation.

Words to the same amount, in the mouth of a protestant, would be extremely rash and presumptuous, because, the protestant having no guide but his blind reason in the interpretation of the divine word, can never acquire a certainty sufficient to justify the above expressions. The utmost influence that any protestant creed can possibly have over a protestant mind is a mere hope or presumption that it may be true; which from the acknowledged fallibility of that guide (blind, puny reason) must leave a fear on the protestant mind that he is perhaps mistaken, nay, a certainty that thousands are actually mistaken, as the different protestant creeds do contradict one another in most essential points, even in the very fundamentals of Christianity.

The case of a Roman Catholic is far different. He believes that Jesus Christ is God and, as a necessary consequence, that every word spoken by Jesus Christ is a divine truth.

He therefore believes that the church of Christ stands on a rock ever since the time it was by the divine architect raised on that rock (Mt. 16:18). He also believes that on the same rock it will stand until the end of time, and that the gates of hell (the powers of darkness) will never prevail over it.

He believes that the Spirit of Truth has never departed from the ministers of that church, of which Christ is the founder; and that the same Spirit of Truth will continue to teach them all truth, forever (Jn. 14:16:17, 26; 16:13).

He believes that Christ himself has been, ever since the foundation of the church, and will be to the consummation of the world, the guide of his ministers, when they teach all nations, and administer to them baptism and the other sacraments (Mt. 28:18-20). These truths, my friend, cannot be disbelieved, only by those that impiously deny the divinity of Jesus Christ they cannot be misunderstood, as they are expressed in as plain words as ever proceeded from the mouth of eternal truth.

Founded on these divine truths, which may be called the axioms of religion, and which are much more certain than the axioms of Euclid, the Catholic can say without any rashness or presumption:

As sure as God is God, the Catholic church of Christ, founded by Christ on a rock, has these 1,800 years been, and will be to the end of time, a teacher of the truth, without the least mixture of error.

As sure as God is in heaven, the Catholic church never stood in need of being reformed, being always holy, without spot or wrinkle (Eph. 5:27).

As sure as Jesus Christ is God, the protesting against that church (and much more so, the attempt made by sinful man, a miserable worm of the earth) to reform the church, the most noble of all works of God is a most horrible, most detestable act of impiety.

As sure as Jesus Christ is truth itself, the churches raised in opposition to the Catholic church, called protestant churches, are not part of the church of Christ; [but] are churches of Satan, ways to perdition.

As sure as Jesus Christ is not an impostor, every point of doctrine taught by the Catholic church is divine, and as true as if taught by the mouth of Jesus Christ himself, although the puny reason of a protestant minister can not comprehend, nor the pride of the philosopher submit to its doctrine.

Without any rashness then, without any presumption, the Catholic can offer you his soul and salvation in security for the truth and divinity of his holy religion.

The protestant is not able to offer you the same security, because he has no certainty. All he can venture to say, when he preaches or expounds the scripture is, "IT IS MY OPINION" or, "IF I AM NOT MISTAKEN." This, my dear friend, proves to you at once that he is not a minister of Christ, for a minister of Christ is appointed to teach you in the place of Christ, and under the authority of Christ; he that hears him, hears Christ himself (Lk. 10:16). He does not hesitate, he does not waver; he has no opinions of his own to deliver unto you; but under the guidance of the church, which is the Spirit of Truth forever, he (without any hesitation, without any doubt or uncertainty in his mind) tells you, in the name of Christ, plainly and distinctly what you must believe, and what you must do in order to obtain salvation; and he runs no risk in pledging his salvation for the truth of his doctrine. Why so? Because he has the veracity of Jesus Christ pledged for the continuance of the Spirit of Truth in the church forever, for the continual guidance of the church by Jesus Christ, until the consummation of the world (Mt. 28:18-20). In short, for the perpetual infallibility, indefectibility, and holiness of the church.

Observe, my friend! No Catholic priest will pledge his salvation that every Catholic will be saved or that everything done or said by Catholics, or even by their clergyman, is correct; far from it. We very willingly acknowledge that (while our doctrine, as ministers of Christ, dictated by the church, is divine) our own example and our words as men are often, too often, scandalous.

We do not say that the Son of divine truth shall never be obscured by clouds, or by fogs raised by the corruption and wickedness of men, even of clergymen, but we pledge our salvation that the sun itself behind these clouds shall always be bright, and shall never cease emitting the purest rays of light, which shall, even through those clouds, penetrate unto the earth.

We do not say, that the vessel shall never be beaten by tempests, by howling winds and raging waves, so as to appear to the eyes of man to be in danger of sinking, but we pledge our salvation that Jesus Christ will be and remain at the helm, consequently, that the vessel will ride out the storm, and in safety reach the harbor.

We do not say that the house which Christ raised on the rock will never have its floors or walls overspread with cobwebs, or sullied with the dirt flung against it by its enemies, but we pledge salvation that the house itself will stand firm and unshaken until the consummation of time.

One more passage of the minister's *Vindication* I shall notice, and then I mean to dismiss the subject for this time (p. 135). The protestant minister affects to express the greatest astonishment that I should really believe the tenets of the Catholic faith, which he calls absurd and contradictory, and that I should even pledge my salvation for the truth of them. "This" says he, "we could not have believed unless we had seen it from under his hand."

How much more astonished will he be to hear that the late Archbishop Carroll, one of the most learned men, one of the most amiable characters, one of the most accomplished gentlemen in the United States, lived and died in the firm belief of all those several tenets, of which he made an open profession on his deathbed, and that in the presence of a numerous circle of both

Catholic and protestant friends that surrounded his bed on that mournful occasion.

How much more astonished will he be to hear that numbers of well-informed gentlemen, even clergymen, both in Europe and in America are continually leaving the reformation and crowding the ranks of Catholicity. Although my information on that subject is very limited, yet I know of eight protestant and Methodist preachers in this country, that have become Roman Catholics, and some of them Roman Catholic priests.

His astonishment must he inexpressible, if he is in the least acquainted with history, and especially with the history of the late times.

So firm was the belief of thousands of the clergy and millions of the lay people of France in those very tenets, which the puny reason of your minister very rashly decides to be absurd and contradictory, that they cheerfully submitted, in defense of these tenets, to the loss of all their property, of all that was dear to them on this side of the grave, and even to the loss of their lives; and met death, inflicted in the most cruel manner which the infuriated Jacobins could devise, with the most intrepid courage. Of one hundred and thirty-odd archbishops and bishops (and those were generally men of the most profound learning), only four or five renounced their belief in order to save their lives and property. The number of priests that renounced their religion was also comparatively small. When one word would have saved the whole of them, must it not appear astonishing beyond conception to your minister, that so many thousand of learned men could persevere to their last breath in the belief of those absurd and contradictory tenets, which their temporal interests certainly required them not to believe.

Whilst those pastors, renowned for their learning and piety, and millions of their flocks, were laying down their lives for their faith, and whilst the streams of Catholic blood that fattened the soil of France and reddened its rivers was a more than convincing testimony that those men really and sincerely believed in these tenets called absurd and contradictory, many of your protestant ministers (behold here a proof of their great charity) were exulting at the downfall of popery, and prophesying its utter destruction.

Your minister, whose ingenuity is never at a loss for evasive answers, will probably attribute the sufferings of the French clergy, etc., in the cause of religion to the enthusiasm of the moment. Let him in turn his eyes to Great Britain, and especially to Ireland; there he will see what will raise his astonishment to the highest pitch — the sword of persecution hanging, during two hundred years, over four or five millions of Catholics, for believing the very tenets which he calls absurd and contradictory.

Transportation to Botany Bay, hanging, whipping, tortures, etc., inflicted for saying Mass, for hearing Mass, for teaching the Catholic catechism; nearly the whole population of Ireland deprived of every foot of their real property, ground down by enormous taxes, treated like aliens, nay, like slaves in their own country: compelled to pay the tenth of all their produce to the protestant ministers, every moment at the mercy of vile informers and protestant spies, who are encouraged by the greatest rewards, to accuse them of complying with the duties of Catholics. See the very laws of nature overturned by a protestant government, and the son, (by the laws of that country) authorized to turn his Catholic father into the street, and himself (by becoming a protestant, and informing against the father) stepping into the whole of his father's property. In short, my friend, behold a system of the most cruel persecution, written in letters of blood, dictated by a protestant government — out of pure charity, I suppose (*Vindication*, p. 1, lines 5-10; p. 115, lines 18-21) — and persevering in its cruel operations, during two hundred years, against four or five millions of Catholics on account of remaining faithful to those tenets which they had received from their apostle St. Patrick, such as transubstantiation, confession of sins, purgatory, etc.

To secure themselves from the sword of persecution, and from the bloody statutes enacted against them, they had nothing to do but go to the next meeting house and renounce the absurd and contradictory tenets of the Catholic faith; this they would not do, but preferred all the punishments the law could inflict, and even death, to renouncing any one of these tenets. Your minister will not deny, but among those several generations of Catholics, and in so extensive a population, there must have been (and especially among their prelates and other clergymen) many thousands endowed with at least as great a share of learning and talents as he himself possesses, and yet it is proved by the above facts, that they sincerely believed in the divinity of the very tenets which your minister, relying on the dictates of his fallible reason, decrees to be absurd and contradictory. If your minister would seriously meditate on the above matters of fact, his astonishment at my stupidity for believing the tenets of the Catholic creed, would cease, or would be turned against himself. He would be, or ought to be, surprised to find himself astonished at the belief of tenets adopted by the sages and the most brilliant geniuses of all ages, such as the Alfreds, the Bedes, the Fenelons, the Bossuets, the Popes, the Drydens, the Stolbergs, etc., who have astonished the world by their profound erudition and the brilliancy of their genius, and some of whom (being born protestants), after the most mature deliberation and many years close study, did embrace the Roman Catholic faith.

In truth, my friend, that a Christian believing Christ Jesus to be God, to be omnipotent, should be willing to believe the most incomprehensible mysteries plainly revealed by Christ, is by no means astonishing.

It is not astonishing that a Christian, really believing Christ to be the incarnate wisdom, the fountain of all knowledge, and himself blind and corrupted, should read the sacred book of Revelation [the Apocalypse] with fear and trembling, should acknowledge that he is not able to understand its contents.

It is not astonishing that he should, in that state of perplexity, apply to that very authority (the authority of the church) which Christ himself points out; nor is it astonishing that he should listen to that authority as to the voice of God, when he hears Christ God declare, "He that hears you, hears me," and when he hears the positive promise from the mouth of Christ, that the Spirit of Truth shall be with his ministers forever, and that he himself will be their guide, their pilot, their teacher, until the consummation of the world.

It is not astonishing that a believer in the divinity of Christ should expect to hold the keys of the kingdom of heaven, the power of forgiving sins, in that place and with those persons where Christ declares he left those keys and that power.

It is not astonishing that a believer in the divinity of Christ should also believe that Christ, who commands us repeatedly to eat and drink his flesh and blood, must have left that flesh and blood, in order to enable us to fulfill his commandment.

It is not astonishing that Catholics, who believe God to be incomprehensible, should believe the incomprehensible mysteries by him revealed.

On the other hand, it is truly astonishing that a believer in the bible should disbelieve many parts of its contents.

It is truly astonishing that a believer in the divinity of Christ should be a disbeliever in all the different and most essential powers granted by Christ to his church.

It is exceedingly astonishing that a learned man, and a man calling himself a minister of Christ, should read in his testament, "Receive ye the Holy Ghost, whose sins you shall forgive they are forgiven" etc. and after reading these words of his divine Master, should ask the question, "Where is that power given to a sinful creature, and one who has to answer for his own sins?" (*Vindication*, p. 19).

It is, beyond expression, astonishing that a believer in the sacred records, who tells us repeatedly that he will believe nothing but what is contained in the Old and New Testaments, at the same time proclaims to the world that he, even in most essential matters, believes the very reverse.

Whereas the sacred record, dictated by the Holy Ghost, tells him that the church is the spouse of Christ, holy, glorious, without spot or wrinkle, and without blemish (Eph. 5:25-27), "No, no," says the minister, "it is not so; for the church proved an adulteress, a wh——e, a sink of corruption, idolatry, and superstition."

Whereas the sacred record plainly exhibits Christ as promising to his ministers the Spirit of Truth, not for three or four hundred years only, but forever (Jn. 14:16-17); "No, no," says the minister, "not forever; for after a few hundred years the church became the teacher of errors and not of truth."

In short, whereas every word in the sacred record proceeds from the infinite abyss of eternal wisdom, and cannot be fully understood and explained, except by the holy Spirit of Truth; "No, no," says the minister (substituting his own puny reason to that guide which Christ left his church forever), "No, no; I can explain all myself." And then assuming an authority which I never knew an earthly judge to assume in explaining the laws of man, he goes on to decree what Jesus Christ evidently MEANT; he goes on to discard the most essential powers that Christ left his church; he goes on to level down all the difficulties and mysteries of revelation to the level of his contracted understanding.

This is truly astonishing, and more astonishing than transubstantiation and all the other mysteries of the Catholic church; for it certainly is not surprising that out of the abyss of infinite power and infinite wisdom incomprehensible mysteries should proceed.

It is not surprising that the very authority should be found in the church which Jesus Christ left with the church, when he declares, "As the father has sent me, I also send you. Receive ye the Holy Ghost" etc., (Jn. 20:21-23).

With power and authority the Father sent Jesus Christ; with power and authority then Jesus Christ sent his ministers.

According to your protestant minister, there is not an atom of power left in the church, and the ministers themselves are the most useless beings on earth.

They have not the power of forgiving your sins.

They have not the power, by consecration, to procure for you the flesh and blood of Christ, which Christ declares (Jn. 6) to be the spiritual food of your souls.

They have not the power to bless water, salt, or any of God's creatures. Your minister laughs at the very idea (*Vindication*, p. 15).

They have not the power of banishing evil spirits.

They have not the power of explaining to you the true sense of scripture. By the minister's acknowledgment, their church or churches are fallible, subject to errors and mistakes.

You know then, my friend, from your minister's *Vindication* what powers he has not. It would be worth your while to go to him and to ask him what power he has? I cannot imagine what his answer would be; for after having discarded all the different powers essentially necessary to enable the ministry of Christ to be of service to their flock, I do not see any power left for him to claim, but a power that any lay person may claim as well, in other words, the power of saying some prayers and the power of reading a text of scripture, and putting on it some sort of construction, either true or false, which even Satan is able to do (Mt. 4:6).

I am acquainted with a very respectable man, formerly a protestant, whom this acknowledged want of power in his minister, caused to forsake the pretended reformation, and with his whole family, to embrace the Catholic faith. For a considerable length of time he was persecuted, and his property destroyed by the agency of evil spirits; the clothes belonging to him and his family were seen (by invisible hands) a cutting to pieces, stones were seen moving across the room held by invisible hands, fire bursted repeatedly from out of their beds at broad day light, strange and frightful apparitions and strange noises terrified them very often at night.[1]

The good man, reading in his bible that Christ had given to his ministers power over evil spirits, started from home to Winchester in Virginia, and having, with tears in his eyes, related to his minister (parson S-t) the history of his distress, losses, and stirrings, begged of him to come to his house and to exercise in his favor the power which he had received from Jesus Christ. The parson candidly confessed that he had no such power. The good old man insisted that he must have that power, for he had found it in his bible. The parson replied that that power only existed in old times, but was done away now (*Vindication*, p. 125, lines 1-15). The old man, although living in this 'enlightened age,' had not sagacity enough to understand the distinction between old times and new times, but according to your minister's rule, believed nothing but what he found contained in his bible. He therefore rationally concluded that parson S-t could not be a minister of Christ;

---

1. *The Mystery of the Wizard Clip*, Raphael Brown. Loreto Publications, 2009

and having left him, he applied to other persons calling themselves ministers of Christ, some of whom promised relief. They came, prayed, and read; but they prayed and read in vain. Finally, the old man having (through the means of a respectable Catholic neighbor) obtained the assistance of a real minister of Christ, found the relief for which he had prayed so fervently; and soon afterwards became a most edifying member of the Catholic church.

Your minister would laugh heartily if you should relate to him the above facts; for with wise turn of our enlightened age he has peremptorily decided that miracles, etc., are no longer necessary, and of course they have ceased. Since when I did not learn; nor did I ever find any passage in scripture which authorizes the belief that miracles should ever cease altogether, or that evil spirits should never have it any more in their power to molest the bodies and property of men, as they used to do during the life time of our savior, and even after his resurrection (Acts 5:16).

Thousands of the most respectable, the most learned, the most holy of our missionaries, in all the different parts of the globe, met with numberless instances of the kind, especially among the infidels, and had as many opportunities of exercising in their favor the power which Jesus Christ granted his apostles over evil spirits (Mt. 10:1), which power has descended to their successors.

The same missionaries acknowledge that with many of those poor infidels all their arguments would have been lost, had not an eager desire to free themselves from the molestations of the infernal enemy almost forced them to fly for help to the cross of Jesus Christ, and to apply to those means (so very despicable and ridiculous in the eyes of your minister, yet) so powerful and efficacious in the hands of the ministry of Jesus Christ, who, in order to confound human pride and human wisdom, makes use of the most weak things of this world that he may confound the strong (1Cor. 1:23); who in order to baffle all the calculations of the wise men of our enlightened age, makes use of poor weak sinful men, with no other help but that of [the] weak elements of the sign of the cross, and of a few words, to break down the stratagems of the infernal spirit.

Facts, my dear friend, even the best authenticated facts, are no proofs, for those who are determined to disbelieve them; and the protestant minister is determined not to believe any facts that would tend, ever so remotely, to establish the authority of the Catholic church.

General principles, in order to be correct, ought to be the result of logical reasoning, the first link in the chain of which ought to be a fact or an axiom, a self-evident truth that needs no proof. To our enlightened age it was reserved to frame general principles not the result of reasoning, not deduced from any facts or from any axiom, and to establish them by the boldness of the assertion and by the ridicule thrown on those that would undertake to dispute those principles; in short, by making them fashionable. Thus it is that the general principle has obtained among protestants "that miracles have ceased, that nothing miraculous or supernatural ought to be believed, etc., and that anyone asserting as fact anything of the kind, is a fool or an impostor."

A fox having lost his tail in a trap, gathered all the foxes in the neighborhood, and having placed himself against a tree, so as to hide his defect, he railed out against their long tails as a worse than useless encumbrance, and tried to convince them of the advantage they would reap by parting with them, etc.

The above fable accounts for the clamors generally raised by protestant ministers not only against miracles, but against all the powers which the ministry of Christ very justly claim, in consequence of the grant of their divine master, and which the first reformers lost in the trap of Satan, by leaving the only church which Jesus Christ had invested with all spiritual power and authority.

Judge then, my dear friend, from the acknowledgments made by your protestant minister, whether you can consider him to be a minister of Jesus Christ who declares that he sends his ministers as his heavenly father sent him; who plainly specifies the several powers which he grants to his ministers, specifically: the power over evil spirits (Mt. 10:8), the power of reconciliation, or of forgiving sins in baptism and penance (Mt. 28:18-19; Jn. 20:22-23), the power of consecration to procure the spiritual food of our souls, the flesh and blood of Christ (Lk. 22:19-20; 1Cor. 11:24-25), and the power of preaching the true, genuine doctrine, without any mixture of error (Mt. 28:19-20; Jn. 14:16-17, 16:13; Eph. 4:11-14 etc.).

My dear friend, meditate seriously on the above subjects and let me know the result.

You shall probably hear more on the subject from
Your humble servant,

Demetrius A. Gallitzin

Biographical Sketches

Brother Francis, M.I.C.M.,

(Fakhri Boutros Maluf) was born July 19th, 1913, in the town of Mashrah, Lebanon, thirty miles from Beirut. He was the oldest child of Boutros (Peter) and Nazeera Maluf; three brothers and two sisters would follow. Boutros died August 15th, 1924, and Fakhri, at the age of eleven, became the "man" of the house. He taught in the school his father had founded (which was located in the Maluf house) and would later attend the American University of Beirut where he earned a Bachelors Degree in mathematics June 26th, 1934. He taught mathematics and physics at that same university for five years before moving to the United States to attend the University of Michigan, Ann Arbor, where he received an M.A. and Ph.D. in philosophy.

It was at Ann Arbor that Dr. Maluf was brought into the church on the feast of St. Andrew the Apostle November 30th, 1940. His conversion was complete. He was on fire with the Faith and he maintained his love and enthusiasm for all things Catholic until the end of his life.

Dr. Maluf relocated to New England in 1942 where he taught mathematics at Holy Cross College in Worcester, Massachusetts, and philosophy, theology, and mathematics at Boston College. (He also pursued post-graduate work at Harvard University and St. Bonaventure University.) These appointments and pursuits were the means by which God brought together three of the most talented, well educated, and deeply committed Catholics in America, and used them as the foundation stones of what was to become a school, a doctrinal crusade, and a religious order. Dr. Maluf, Catherine Clarke, a lay-woman operating St. Benedict Center in Cambridge, Massachusetts, and Fr. Leonard Feeney, S.J., one of the most celebrated priests in America, became the three principal leaders and teachers at the core of a group of Catholics whose work was to precipitate one of the most important doctrinal controversies of the 20th century.

The efforts and labors of these zealous Catholics at St. Benedict Center produced in a few years over 200 converts—many were young Harvard students from prominent families—and over 100 religious vocations to the priesthood and religious life. The primary goal of the Center was to convert America to the Catholic religion. Their methods seemed to be working. Yet, Fr. Feeney hoped for more. He felt that the entire structure of the church in America was weak and was not producing the conversions that it should, and he was convinced that it was because the church in general seemed to lack one of its marks—apostolic vigor. He ultimately concluded that one of the most fundamental doctrines of the church, "Outside the church there is no salvation," was either being played down or totally denied by many Catholics and especially by most of the hierarchy.

In September 1947, Professor Maluf wrote *Sentimental Theology*, an article clearly defending that dogma in the

Center's magazine *From the Housetops*. He wrote, "A great deal of what is being said by Catholics today sounds in very sharp contrast with the accent of the authentic voice of the church, teaching, warning, and defining. The sharp weapons of Christ are being blunted, and the strong, virile doctrines of the church are being put aside in a conspiracy of silence..."

It was this article more than anything else that appears to have sparked the controversy that would ultimately culminate with Dr. Maluf's dismissal from Boston College on April 13, 1949, and the news of the reason for this dismissal exploding in the organs of the worldwide press. Two other professors and a teacher at Boston College High School, all of whom were associated with the Center, were also terminated. "No salvation outside of the church" was at the heart of it all.

The school of Catholic thought that had coalesced around the three brilliant and charismatic teachers had produced its initial fruits of conversion and sanctification. Now, once their strenuous defense of this dogma brought upon them a vicious persecution by fellow Catholics, and when a series of public statements by various church officials appeared to cast some doubt upon the status of this thrice defined dogma, they determined to crusade in its defense. In order to fight that crusade more effectively they bound themselves together by vows, and so, on January 17th, 1949, Fahkri Maluf, along with Catherine Clarke, Father Leonard Feeney, and 53 others became Slaves of the Immaculate Heart of Mary.

Fakhri was one of the founding members who eventually became a fully professed religious, and as such he continued the fight to convert America and to defend the dogma *Extra Ecclesiam Nulla Salus* for over sixty years. He took the name Brother Francis (Xavier) in honor of the incomparable Jesuit missionary who believed and taught the same dogma for which they were being attacked and vilified. He spent the rest of his life in intense apostolic activity, teaching, lecturing, writing, and traveling throughout the United States distributing Catholic literature.

He died September 5th, 2009, in Richmond, New Hampshire and is buried in the cemetery on the grounds of the St. Benedict Center monastery where he spent the last twenty years of his life.

Demetrius Augustin Gallitzin

was born December 22nd, 1770, at The Hague, Netherlands. His father, Prince Dimitri Alexeievitch Gallitzin, was an ambassador of Empress Catherine the Great of Russia and his mother, Countess Amalia von Schmettau, was the daughter of Field Marshal von Schmettau of Prussia. They had one other child, Marianne, who was a year older than Demetrius.

Prince Gallitzin (Fr. Gallitzin's father), nominally Russian Orthodox, was a Freemason, Grand Master of the Oriental Lodge in Paris, and his social circle included such notables as Voltaire, Diderot, Goethe, and Rousseau. Amalia was baptized Catholic for it had been agreed upon by her parents at their marriage that any boys born to the union would be raised Lutheran; any girls would be brought up Catholic. Amalia was educated at a convent boarding school in Breslau, Silesia, where she was noted for her piety. But in those days of The Enlightenment piety was not in vogue and, once out of school, she fell into worldly ways.

But upon the birth of her children, Amalia underwent a sudden and dramatic change. She began to feel empty amidst all the glitter of court life and, after intense study and searching, she returned to her Catholic roots. Ever full of true Christian zeal, she never lost an opportunity to speak to those outside of the church about the Faith.

Concerned for the education of her children, she eventually established a school in Munster, Germany. It was an immensely successful endeavor. She was able to fill teaching positions with qualified and able instructors in a variety of fields and many prominent families chose to send their children to her. It was here that Demetrius received a personal, wholesome, religious, and well-rounded education. His mother's efforts were not in vain—he converted to Roman Catholicism in 1787. He said: "I soon felt the necessity of investigating religious systems, in order to find the true one. Although I was born a member of the Greek church, and although all my male relations, without any exception, were either Greeks or protestants, yet did I resolve to embrace that religion only, which upon impartial inquiry, should appear to me to be the pure religion of Jesus Christ. My choice fell upon the Catholic church…" (*Letter to a Protestant Friend*).

Five years later he was on his way to America and entered the Sulpician Seminary in Baltimore under the assumed name Augustine Smith. He was ordained March 18, 1795, and four years later was appointed pastor of McGuire's Settlement in Pennsylvania. At the time of this assignment, he established the community of Loretto, Pennsylvania, on 300 acres of land he had previously purchased. This was to be the center of his apostolic and missionary activities for the remainder of his life.

He proved a true father to his little flock "… comport(ing) himself among his own like a solicitous, resolute father of a family; and because he was recognized as such and everyone was convinced that he meant only well and sought for nothing but the temporal and the eternal welfare of others, the people submitted to many things which many others in the land of freedom and equality could scarcely have made bold to do…In his church Gallitzin maintained edifying discipline and order...Many an old man in the parish recalls how as a boy...his ears (were) boxed for unbecoming behavior during the services" *(The Life and Work of Prince Demetrius Augustine Gallitzin*, p. 204).

But his fatherly concern was not limited to the spiritual realm. His "...spiritual and temporal duties flowed together, so that any attempt to separate them under different heads must always fail" *(Life of D. A. Gallitzin*, p. 172). Fr. Peter Lemcke, who was appointed his assistant in 1834, tells this story:

> On a cold morning, as the first snow put in its appearance, he happened to pass a house in which the father of the family had died but shortly before. The widow hailed him, making many excuses for being in arrears still with their contribution to the church for the preceding years and because the funeral expenses had not yet been paid. She stated that only now had she succeeded in obtaining the money and that she wished to turn it over to him.
>
> 'But how about the children?' Gallitzin asked. 'I see that they are still scamping around barefooted, and winter is definitely approaching. Therefore, good Lady, first see that you have shoes for them'; and with a friendly smile he refused the hand offering the money" *(The Life and Work of Prince Demetrius Augustine Gallitzin*, p. 205).

Always at the forefront of his mind was the salvation of souls. "Unrelenting in his austerities, ever cheerful with his people, he pointed every word and act towards the one great aim he had in view: to make every life within his reach loyally, practically, fervently Catholic" *(Life of D. A. Gallitzin*, p. 128). He embraced St. Paul's Epistle to Timothy as though written personally to him: *"Take heed to thyself and to doctrine: be earnest in them. For in doing this thou shalt both save thyself and them that hear thee"* (1 Tim. 4:16). His published works are a testimony to how seriously he took this admonition.

Perhaps one of the most painful crosses he bore was his father's death outside of the church. Credible witnesses attested to the voluntary penances he undertook for his father's soul. *"...when the tidings of his father's death reached him in 1803, he slept on the bare floor, his head resting on a large book... this and other practices were undertaken in fulfillment of a vow: his father had departed from this world in a dubious state—and this he told weeping bitterly" (The Life and Work of Prince Demetrius Augustin Gallitzin, p. 82).*

Forty years of missionary work, fasting and traversing through the wilderness caring for his flock, eventually took their toll. Moreover, he had been declining steadily since 1834 when he had been injured when thrown from his horse; he never fully recovered and suffered the rest of his life from the consequences of that fall. The winter of 1839-1840 found him looking sickly, walking with a stoop, and speaking with a weakened voice. Friends were alarmed but he brushed it off *"...remarking that since there was not much opportunity anymore for a missionary to render praise to God through bloody martyrdom, he should at least desire to be permitted to collapse like an old worn-out carthorse" (The Life and Work of Prince Demetrius Augustin Gallitzin, p. 237).*

On Easter Sunday, April 19th, 1840, Fr. Gallitzin offered his last Mass. His condition rapidly deteriorated, and he underwent surgery to alleviate his suffering, but the attending physician knew there was no chance of recovery. He died peacefully on the evening of May 6th, 1840, surrounded by his faithful and sorrowing flock.

Prayer for the Conversion of America

O Mary, Mother of mercy and Refuge of sinners, we beseech thee, be pleased to look with pitiful eyes upon poor heretics and schismatics. Thou who art the Seat of Wisdom, enlighten the minds that are miserably enfolded in the darkness of ignorance and sin, *that they may clearly know that the Holy Catholic and Apostolic Roman Church is the one true Church of Jesus Christ, outside of which neither holiness nor salvation can be found.* Finish the work of their conversion by obtaining for them the grace to accept all the truths of our Holy Faith, and to submit themselves to the supreme Roman Pontiff, the Vicar of Jesus Christ on earth; that so, being united with us in the sweet chains of divine charity, there may soon be only one fold under the same one shepherd; and may we all, O glorious Virgin, sing forever with exultation: Rejoice, O Virgin Mary, thou only hast destroyed all heresies in the whole world. Amen.

Hail Mary, three times.

An Indulgence of 500 days. (S.C. Prop. of the Faith, Dec. 30, 1868; S.P. Ap., March 18, 1936. *Raccolta* RaNo. 579).

Other Loreto Books

DIVINE ALCHEMY
BROTHER FRANCIS MALUF, M.I.C.M.

Brother Francis Maluf, who has a gift for impressing with similitudes, wrote these fifty-nine poems for leisure. Those of us who know him would have a hard time imagining him sweating for too long over a verse. When he was deeply moved, whether it be by a devotional grace, by wonder at something beautiful to behold, by a gospel story or character, or even by astonishment over some mystery of iniquity, his contemplative heart would seek a means of expression. These poems are the expression of Brother Francis' contemplative heart.

Sewn-hardbound, 96 pages, $12.95

THE CHALLENGE OF FAITH
BROTHER FRANCIS MALUF, M.I.C.M.

This is a book of seventy-two concise meditations with each one pondering a different subject. Whether it is an event, as the Day, or a virtue, Gratitude, or a ravaging infidelity, as Islam, or a person, Our Lady, our author zeroes in on the topic and, with an amazing depth of understanding, simplifies it in relation to time and eternity. The salient theme throughout Brother Maluf's daily reflections is that every challenge one experiences in this wayfaring state has the capacity to elevate our human frailty to supernatural heights if we engage it with the magnanimous attitude of confident sons of God.

Sewn-hardbound 96 pages $14.95

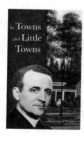

IN TOWNS AND LITTLE TOWNS
FATHER LEONARD FEENEY, S.J.

So you do not like poetry. Too many flowers and angels and stars and clouds. And too many adjectives ending in "Y". Besides, the better the poem the less you can understand it, right? You are an ordinary Joe who prefers more solid food for his mind and you do not really care if the words rhyme anyway. Well, Joe, lighten up! Let your mind get a taste of Father Feeney's verse. Your whole family will enjoy the new turf. It will warm the heart. In fact, everyone of Father's poems comes with that guarantee.

Sewn-softbound 96 pages, $12.95

www.loretopubs.org

Other Loreto Books

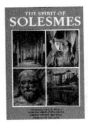

THE SPIRIT OF SOLESMES

An Anthology

This book contains over two hundred and fifty pages of selections from the writings, sermons, and personal correspondence of Abbot Dom Guéranger, Dom Paul Delatte, his saintly successor, and Abbess Cecile Bruyère, foundress of the abbey of Sainte Cecile. The latter two lights of the Church, with Guéranger, make a dynamic trinity of what was a unified effort of soul to revive the Benedictine life and spirit in 19th century France. These readings reveal a deep spirituality at work in these three reformers, a spirituality that, in effect, became a *tour de force* moving the generous hearts of men and women of the Catholic Church, and the nation called her "eldest daughter,"to champion their cause.

Sewn-softbound 266 pages $19.95

THE PAPAL MONARCHY

Dom Prosper Guéranger, O.S.B.

When nineteenth century Christendom shifted its allegiance from a divine authority to the revolutionary ideals of egalitarian democracy and false liberty, Dom Guéranger's writing contributed more than any other contemporary work to uphold the papal monarchy in all of its divinely ordained prerogatives. This work helped to restore the spiritual sword to Catholic Europe, and over all to the Vicar of Christ the King, simply by appealing to the simplicity and clarity of the gospels, the universal Christian tradition, and the common *consensus fidelis.*

Sewn-hardbound, 387 pages, $27.95

OUR GLORIOUS POPES

Sister Catherine Clarke M.I.C.M.

The author takes us on a journey through four hundred years of tempus ecclesiae, from the entrance of St. Peter into the fearsome capitol of Satan's doomed empire, to the triumph of the Council of Chalcedon, held under St. Leo I. Vividly brought to life is the maturation of the Church Militant from its infancy in Jerusalem. The remaining bulk of information dovetails into the major periods of religious crises and tells of those heroic popes who steered the Church through these gravest trials. This book restores hope and confidence in the might of the papacy.

Sewn-softbound 266 pages, $12.95

www.loretopubs.org

The Mystery of the Crown of Thorns
A Passionist

Contemplating the Holy Face on the Shroud of Turin, one sees above our Lord's right eye a large wound planted there by one of the seventy two thorns in His crown. From the many figures of that spiny diadem in the Old Testament to the reality of the instrument of torture beaten into the head of the Son of God amidst insults and spittle, this terrible book, unforgettable in its endearing pathos, will surely help us to understand something of the true ugliness of sin and the awesome price the Just One had to pay in conquering it.

Sewn Softcover — 302 pages — $17.95

Life of the Good Thief
Msgr. Gaumé

Monsignor Gaume opens his story with a description of the life of a highway brigand in the days of the Caesars. He presents the meeting of our thief and the Son of God in Egypt on the occasion of the flight of the Holy Family from the sword of Herod. The rest of the story is the story of the passion as seen through the eyes of Dismas, a man dying on a cross with Christ, whose only request from his "Lord" was but a "remembrance" in His Kingdom!

Softcover — 208 pages — $14.95

Why Must I Suffer?
Fr. F.J. Remler

Whether it be due to our own over-indulgences in abusing the goods of this earth, our transgressions against God's commandments, or the providentially paternal designs of our Creator, we will all have our lot of suffering in this life. The question is how to benefit from it unto everlasting happiness. Suffering and death are part of our debt due to original sin. Hence, they are necessary for our good; but, why such a debt as this? Fr. Remler provides fifteen reasons why we ought to embrace our trials. This is a practical book, for it has a foolproof game plan, that if followed well, will cut short dramatically our time in purgatory. However, it is much more than that. This magnificent analysis of suffering, as to its cause, its value, and its ultimate effect (i.e., conformity to Christ, the Man of Sorrows) will give us more strength to bear not only our own cross, but to willingly share in the suffering Jesus endured for all men.

Softcover — 96 pages — $9.95

THE GREAT COMMENTARY
on THE FOUR GOSPELS
by Cornelius aLapide, S.J.

QUOTES FROM THE REVIEW by SCOTT HAHN

Cornelius aLapide, S.J. (1568-1637) is a giant figure in the history of Catholic biblical interpretation. Born in a tiny Catholic enclave in the Calvinist Netherlands in the bloody generation after the Reformation, Lapide grew to be one of the Church's most gifted scholars and spiritual interpreters of the sacred page.

Between 1614 and 1645, Lapide wrote commentaries on every book of Scripture except Job and Psalms.

To read Lapide four hundred years later is to enter a nearly forgotten world of biblical interpretation ...more striking – the sheer breadth and density of Lapide's interpretative matrix or his audacity in summoning all these resources to the interpretation of the sacred text.

Lapide himself takes a breathtaking high view of Scripture's purpose: Lapide prefaces his commentary with thirty-eight "canons of interpretation," which reflect a wise and prayerful method. "

It is clear that the Fathers hold pride of place for Lapide in his interpretative work.

- *6"x 9" Book format*
- *2900+ Pages in four volumes*
- *First complete English translation*
- *Sewn Binding & Headbands*
- *Bonded Leather Covers &*
  Satin Ribbons
- *Greatest Catholic Bible*
  Commentary ever
- *Extensive discussion of Greek*
  and Hebrew words
- *$199. Per four volume set*

The Mystery of the Wizard Clip
Diabolical Activity, Priestly Intervention, and Conversions in Colonial America
Raphael Brown

This tale is almost too strange for belief. It features a Russian prince, a Lutheran family, an Irish priest, several Protestant ministers, diabolical activity, traveling salesmen, and Colonial farmers, as well as delicate and intricate family relationships. It has all of the elements of an exciting Catholic novel...AND IT IS ALL TRUE! Don't miss this wonderful story.

44 pages - Small Book - $5.95

Counsels to Confessors – St. Leonard of Port Maurice	$6.95
Treatise on the Spiritual Life – St. Vincent Ferrer	$5.95
The Storm Novena – St. Benedict the Moor Mission	$4.95
The Dogma of Faith – St. Benedict Center	$4.95
Boy Heroes – Dom Alban Fruth O.S.B.	$4.95
Breaking With the Past – Francis Aidan Gasquet, O.S.B.	$5.95
50 Meditations on the Passion – Alban Goodier, S.J.	$5.95
The Wisdom of St. Francis DeSales	$5.95
Meet Brother Martin – Norbert Georges, O.P.	$5.95
Explanation of the Veni Sancte Spiritus – Fr. Nicholas Gihr	$6.95
Our Lady of Perpetual Help – Francis J. O'Connell, C. SS. R.	$5.95
The Poetry of Joseph Mary Plunkett	$6.95
The Conversion of Marie-Aplhonse Ratisbonne	$6.95
The Wife Desired – Fr. Leo Kinsella	$7.95
The Poems of Virginia Techan	$6.95
The Gift of Self to God – Fr. Nicholas Grou, S.J.	$5.95
The Mystical Body and It's Head – Fr. Robert Hugh Benson	$6.95
The Woman of Genesis – Br. Thomas Mary Sennot, M.I.C.M.	$7.95